Re-Writing
Jesus

For Father Kevin Morris
On the 25th anniversary of his priesting

Re-Writing Jesus

Christ in 20th-Century Fiction and Film

Graham Holderness

B L O O M S B U R Y

LONDON • NEW DELHI • NEW YORK • SYDNEY

Bloomsbury Academic

An imprint of Bloomsbury Publishing Plc

50 Bedford Square   1385 Broadway
London   New York
WC1B 3DP   NY 10018
UK   USA

www.bloomsbury.com

Bloomsbury is a registered trade mark of Bloomsbury Publishing Plc

First published 2015

British Library Cataloguing-in-Publication Data
A catalogue record for this book is available from the British Library.

ISBN: HB: 978-1-4725-7332-2
PB: 978-1-4725-7331-5
ePDF: 978-1-4725-7334-6
ePub: 978-1-4725-7333-9

Library of Congress Cataloging-in-Publication Data
A catalog record for this book is available from the Library of Congress.

Typeset by Newgen Knowledge Works (P) Ltd., Chennai, India
Printed and bound in India

CONTENTS

P58.9
Quote?

ACKNOWLEDGEMENTS

Earlier and shorter versions of some chapters were published as: '"Half God, half man": Kazantzakis, Scorsese, and The Last Temptation', *Harvard Theological Review*, 100: 1 (2007), pp. 47–64; 'Word and Image: Burgess, Zefirelli and the Man of Nazareth', in *Reading Spiritualities: Constructing and Representing the Sacred*, eds D. Llewellyn and D. F. Sawyer (Ashgate, 2008), pp. 205–22; 'Jim Crace, *Quarantine* and the Dawkins Delusion', *Critical Survey*, 22: 3 (2010), pp. 69–91; and '"Animated Icons": Narrative and Liturgy in *The Passion of the Christ*', *Literature and Theology*, 19: 4 (Oxford University Press, December 2005), pp. 384–401. I am grateful to editors and publishers for permission to reproduce this material in revised form.

Introduction

I

Dan Brown's *The Da Vinci Code*, published in 2003, had by 2009 sold 80 million copies worldwide. This appears to mean, prima facie, that astonishing numbers of readers have revealed an interest in conspiracy theory, cryptography and appallingly bad writing. It also appears to indicate, however, that those millions of readers have taken the trouble to engage with fundamental issues of Christian theology and history: such as the Incarnation; Gnosticism and orthodoxy; canonicity and apocrypha; ecclesiology; the apostolic succession – none of which are headline topics in contemporary media or fiction. The film of the novel[1] was the second-highest grossing movie of 2006 (after *Pirates of the Caribbean: Dead Man's Chest*).

Since Dan Brown's attitude to what he represents as the church, and Christian orthodoxy, is systematically hostile, this mass readership and spectatorship can easily be interpreted as an endorsement of secularization, highlighting the decline of the church, or the relativizing of Christianity among other world faiths and varieties of humanism. Or it can be taken to demonstrate that there remains, all over the world, a huge interest in, and appetite for, information, knowledge, imagery and narrative about and around Christianity, its historical origins and foundational texts, its modes of organization and tradition, its literature and ideas.

Above all, there is a need for a reliable source of information and commentary on the *representations* of Christianity that constitute knowledge of Christianity for millions of people. If Christian church attendance and traditional religious education are currently in decline in the West, then people are deriving their perceptions of Christianity not from direct acquaintance with the Bible or from ecclesiastical dogma, but from the cultural representations of Christianity that surround them. Most people are more likely to derive impressions of Christianity from fiction, film and visual art than they are from scripture or church teaching. 'A great many adherents' of Christianity, claim Darren J. Middleton and S. Brent Plate, in a discussion of Jesus on film, 'garner their personal Christologies from what they have seen acted out on screen'.[2]

Writing, performance and visualization of Christianity have been going on now for over two thousand years, producing an immensely varied, diverse and complex tradition of representation and appropriation. Fictional and filmed version of the New Testament story still command audiences. It is possible that these traditions and interventions penetrate deeper into popular religious mentality than church teaching, or formal religious instruction. These versions of Christ and Christianity can be produced by Christians of various denominations, or exponents of other faiths, or agnostics or atheists. They are not controlled or limited by church authority, academic theology or systems of orthodoxy.

The Da Vinci Code debate is an instructive one. Brown's fiction simultaneously claims and disclaims pretensions to truth and fictionality. *The Da Vinci Code* purports to reflect historical fact, while operating in an absurdly surreal territory of manifest artifice. Churches have sought to reclaim Brown's territory as their own, correcting his false and distorted impressions. Religious scholars and educators have painstakingly pointed out the errors and absurdities in the fiction. In each case Dan Brown's fiction is challenged on the basis of a claim to theological or ecclesiastical truth. But ironically these truth-claims seem less powerful for many people than the persuasions of fiction.

There are a number of reasons for this. Different Christian denominations appeal to different theological truths that inevitably conflict with one another, and may for the curious bystander merely cancel one another out. The lure of conspiracy theory induces scepticism about all defensive truth-claims, which always already seem cover-ups masquerading as truth. Above all, there is a failure to grasp the extent to which all religion does consist very largely of artifice, representation and fiction. The pulp fiction novelist and the popular film-maker may be wiser in this respect than many much more learned and eloquent apologists.

II

When, in the last few years, successful and popular authors such as Anne Rice, Philip Pullman, Jeffry Archer, Colm Toibin,[3] have published novels on the life of Jesus, neither they nor their reviewers seemed to betray any awareness that they were working within a tradition, now almost exactly a century old, that can be identified as the 'Jesus-novel': a prose narrative constructing a biographical portrait of the person of Jesus, set in a distinct historical context; the story of Christ written as a human life.[4] When these works appear, they seem to be read in a vacuum. Toibin's novella *The Testament of Mary* (the Mary in question being the mother of Jesus), was a strong contender for the Man Booker Prize. Much emphasis was laid by reviewers on the originality of the novel's point-of-view, Mary's story having never, allegedly, been fictionalized before as first-person narrative. Yet anyone acquainted with the literature would be aware that a similar Marian testimony is one of the monologues of Canadian novelist Nino Ricci's book *Testament* (Toronto: Doubleday, 2002).

The 'Jesus-novel' tradition has attracted both major and minor writers in English, as well as authors writing in other languages. I have focused in this study mainly on a group of novels by major writers that exploit to the full the complex potentialities of the form: Nikos Kazantzakis's *The Last Temptation*, Anthony Burgess's *Man of Nazareth* and Jim Crace's *Quarantine*. I have subjected each of these texts to a full critical analysis and appraisal. The 'Introduction' sets the scene by providing briefer discussions of the tradition's foundational texts, Ernest Renan's *Vie de Jesus* (1863), and George Moore's *The Brook Kerith* (1916). I have then traced the evolution of the tradition via two other influential examples: D. H. Lawrence's *The Man who Died* (1929), and Robert Graves's *King Jesus* (1946).[5] There are many other novels of interest and literary quality that are not discussed here, since I have chosen to undertake comprehensive studies of a few major texts, rather than a broader survey.[6] My subject is, if you will, and according to a wide scholarly consensus, the 'great tradition' of Jesus-fiction.

The Jesus-novel form originally grew out of nineteenth-century biblical criticism and philosophical scepticism about the divinity of Christ. An important precursor of the tradition was French thinker

Ernest Renan, who in his enormously popular *Vie de Jesus* (1863) (*Life of Jesus*) reproduced the gospels in the form of a historical and biographical narrative.[7] Renan's wok was preceded by the monumental *Das Leben Jesu, kritisch bearbeitet* (1836) (*The Life of Jesus, Critically Examined*) by David Strauss, widely circulated in English in the form of the 1846 translation by Marian Evans (George Eliot).[8] Strauss's book applied the methods of biblical criticism to the life of Jesus, detaching the historical Jesus from the divine Christ, but did not actually make the breakthrough into modern biography. He provided the materials required for the construction of a historical biography, rather than a historical biography proper. *Leben Jesu* is much more a work of historical scholarship and theological argument than it is a narrative of the life of Christ.

Renan's *Vie de Jesus* retains the full panoply of textual scholarship and biblical criticism, but renders this material ancillary to the biographical narrative, placing much of it footnotes rather than in his discursive text. Moreover, he repositions the role of the historical element, by locating the narrative firmly in the concrete historicity of the actual places where the events of the gospels occurred, much in the manner of a nineteenth central realist writer like Flaubert. Renan made this explicit in his Preface:

> To the perusal of documentary evidences I have been able to add an important source of information – the sight of the places where the events occurred. The scientific mission, having for its object the exploration of ancient Phoenicia, which I directed in 1860 and 1861, led me to reside on the frontiers of Galilee and to travel there frequently. I have traversed, in all directions, the country of the Gospels; I have visited Jerusalem, Hebron, and Samaria; scarcely any important locality of the history of Jesus has escaped me. All this history, which at a distance seems to float in the clouds of an unreal world, thus took a form, a solidity, which astonished me. The striking agreement of the texts with the places, the marvellous harmony of the Gospel ideal with the country which served it as a framework, were like a revelation to me. (p. 17)

Renan's research thus included geography as well as history and textual scholarship, as he located the documentary sources in concrete historical place. Realizing that this project constituted something more than a critical interpretation of biblical materials, he boldly defined his work as a modern supplement to the sacred scriptures, a new gospel:

> I had before my eyes a fifth Gospel, torn, but still legible, and henceforward, through the recitals of Matthew and Mark, in place of an abstract being, whose existence might have been doubted, I saw living and moving an admirable human figure. (p. 17)

A human and historical Jesus takes the place of the 'abstract' biblical Christ. Renan goes on to apologize for the biographical form of his narrative, justifying it by reference to the theory that history is made by remarkable individuals:

> Many will regret, perhaps, the biographical form which my work has thus taken. When I first conceived the idea of a history of the origin of Christianity, what I wished to write was, in fact, a history of doctrines, in which men and their actions would have hardly had a place. Jesus would scarcely have been named; I should have endeavoured to show how the ideas which have grown under his name took root and covered the world. But I have learned since that history is not a simple game of abstractions; that men are more than doctrines. (p. 18)

The problem of integrating the life of Jesus, a documentary fact that had become inseparable from Christian 'ideas', and from the apparatus of organized religious belief and doctrine, into a historical narrative, had already been largely solved for Renan by the biblical criticism on which his work was based. Theologians and philosophers had already significantly downplayed the divinity of Christ, dismissing the miracles of the gospels as mere credulity, demonstrating the local historicity of Jesus's own messianic claims, and regarding the Resurrection as a historical mystery to be solved by rational means. Here, for example, is Renan's account of the Resurrection:

> On the Sunday morning, the women, Mary Magdalene the first, came very early to the tomb. The stone was displaced from the

opening, and the body was no longer in the place where they had laid it. At the same time, the strangest rumours were spread in the Christian community. The cry, 'He is risen!' quickly spread amongst the disciples. Love caused it to find ready credence everywhere. What had taken place? In treating of the history of the apostles we shall have to examine this point and to make inquiry into the origin of the legends relative to the resurrection. For the historian, the life of Jesus finishes with his last sigh. But such was the impression he had left in the heart of his disciples and of a few devoted women, that during some weeks more it was as if he were living and consoling them. Had his body been taken away, or did enthusiasm, always credulous, create afterward the group of narratives by which it was sought to establish faith in the resurrection? In the absence of opposing documents this can never be ascertained. Let us say, however, that the strong imagination of Mary Magdalene played an important part in this circumstance. Divine power of love! Sacred moments in which the passion of one possessed gave to the world a resuscitated God! (pp. 271–2)

'For the historian, the life of Jesus finishes with the last sigh.' Jesus, Renan assumes, was a remarkable man, who died on the cross. He was not the Son of God, and he did not rise again. Belief in the Resurrection of Jesus was generated by the 'enthusiasm' of the apostles, and by the power of their love for him. It is significant that Renan attributes the growth of Resurrection faith principally to the 'strong imagination' of Mary Magdalene. As we shall see, in the tradition of the Jesus-novel various other candidates come to be held responsible for the founding of Christianity. Renan was an early proponent of the popular modern idea that Christianity was, or ought to have been, established by a woman.

A biographical narrative cannot of course be constructed only from the materials of textual exegesis, historical scholarship and geographical survey. In order to fully realize a historical life in narrative form, the writer also needs to exercise a form of imaginative speculation, to reconstruct the experiential presence of a living subject in history, to get into his mind. 'In such an effort to make the great souls of the past live again, some share of divination and conjecture must be permitted.' Renan was well aware of how controversial this factor would become, once embedded in the medium of biographical narrative: since according to traditional Christian doctrine, which holds Jesus both human and divine, the writer would be purporting to get into the mind of God. Here for instance is Renan's reconstruction of the 'Agony in the Garden':

> During these last days a deep sadness appears to have filled the soul of Jesus, which was generally so joyous and serene. All the narratives agree in relating that, before his arrest, he underwent a brief phase of misgiving and trouble, a kind of agony in anticipation. A terrible anguish weighed him down; but resignation to the divine will sustained him . . . Terror and hesitation seized him and cast him into a state of exhaustion worse than death itself. (pp. 238–9)

At one level this is Renan simply expanding on what the gospels themselves provide, a description of Jesus enduring extreme anguish of spirit, 'sorrowful even unto death'. The human nature of Jesus faces up to the mortal agony of existential terror. The divine nature must therefore be in abeyance, since it is inconceivable that God could know a fear of death. But by describing the psychological trauma of a man facing his end, Renan emphasizes the human agony of Gethsemane to the exclusion of any category of divine knowledge. He goes further, and in a passage that anticipates the later development of the Jesus-novel in the hands of Nikos Kazantzakis, suggests that at this point Jesus might have experienced fundamental doubts about his entire mission. Perhaps in the Garden of Gethsemane Jesus began to fervently wish he had not undertaken his sacrificial vocation at all. Perhaps the abandoned possibility of an ordinary but contented human existence presented itself to him as a wished-for alternative.

> He who has sacrificed his repose and the legitimate rewards of life to a great idea ever experiences a feeling of revulsion when the image of death presents itself for the first time to him, and seeks to persuade him that all has been in vain. Perhaps some of those touching memories preserved by the strongest souls, at times sharp as a sword, came to him at this moment. Did he remember the clear fountains of Galilee where he might have found refreshment; the vine and the fig-tree under which he might have rested, the

young maidens who perhaps might have consented to love him? Did he curse the cruel destiny which had denied him the joys granted to all others? Did he regret his too lofty nature, and victim of his greatness, mourn that he had not remained a simple artisan of Nazareth? We know not. For all these internal troubles were evidently a sealed chapter to his disciples. They understood nothing of them, and by simple conjectures supplied what in their master's great soul was obscure to them. It is at least certain that his divine nature soon regained the supremacy. He might still have escaped death; but he would not. Love of his work sustained him. He was willing to drink the cup to its dregs. Henceforth we behold Jesus entirely himself, and his character unclouded. (p. 239)

Clearly the Jesus characterized here is a Jesus with a single, not a dual, nature. No such doubt or fear could assail the mind of a divine being. Renan portrays a human Jesus almost seduced by the lure of an average human life. This is the Jesus of 'the last temptation'.[9] It is the Jesus of nineteenth-century historical biography, and the Jesus of twentieth-century narrative fiction. It is the Jesus of history; it is the human Christ.

The twentieth-century Jesus-novel was fully established in English, however, by Irish writer George Moore, whose historical and biographical 'Life of Jesus' novel *The Brook Kerith*, published in 1916, departed much more radically than Renan's work from the gospels, and offered a highly critical and sceptical interpretation of Jesus's life. A naturalistic writer, and admirer of Emile Zola, Moore intended to prove that the Jesus of history was not the Jesus of the modern church, or the Christ of modern theology, but a mere man whose life could be fully expounded by the techniques of the realist novel.

For the novel's first half, the narrative viewpoint is that of Joseph of Arimathea, the gospel character who provides a sepulchre for Jesus's entombment. He is conflated with two other New Testament figures, the rich young man who is told by Jesus to sell all that he has and give to the poor; and the young man who hesitates to follow Jesus in order to bury his father. Jesus is a simple shepherd from Galilee who joins a community of Essenes, the ascetic and separatist Jewish sect described in detail by Josephus in his *Jewish Wars* (c. 75), of which John the Baptist is also a member. Joseph is filled with a powerful desire to follow Jesus, but never quite resolves to commit to his movement. Moore's Jesus resembles the Jesus of the New Testament in many respects: he is wise beyond his years, is rumoured to have turned water into wine, and in his preaching and proselytizing develops an apocalyptic message sustained by a fervent belief in his own Messiah-ship: 'The day is coming, I say unto you, when the Son of man shall return with his Father to remake this world afresh' (p. 144). Many of his sayings echo or replicate those of the biblical Jesus – 'God hath no need of temples in Paradise, nor has he need of any temple but the human heart wherein he dwells' (pp. 143–4) – and his gospel of universal salvation is equally innovative and radical, particularly to the Jews: 'Heaven is open to all men that love God'. (p. 145) Joseph himself appears to have witnessed some of Jesus's miracles of faith healing:

> He saw sight restored to the blind, hearing to the deaf, swiftness of foot to cripples, issues of blood that had endured for ten years stanched; the cleansing of the leper had become too common a miracle. (p. 160)

Half way through the novel, Joseph learns simultaneously that his own tomb, earlier contracted for construction, has been completed, and that Jesus has been crucified outside Jerusalem. He rushes to Golgotha, but Jesus appears to be already dead. He stops the Centurion from piercing the body with his lance, and has it taken down before the Romans have chance to break his legs (the common method of accelerating death). Joseph negotiates with Pilate to take possession of Jesus's corpse, which is laid in his garden in preparation for burial.

But Jesus is not dead. He revives, with no memory of his ordeal or his previous mission. Secretly Joseph protects Jesus from discovery and conceals his identity. He is aware that the disappearance of the body is likely to arouse a belief in his Resurrection. Joseph

> . . . had done well to refrain from closing the sepulchre with the stone, for the story of the resurrection would rise out of the empty tomb, and though there were many among the Jews who would not believe the story, few would have the courage to inquire into the truth of a miracle. (p. 252)

The Resurrection of Jesus is based on an illusion. The gospel story of the disciples meeting him on the road to Emmaus, in which Jesus professes ignorance of their recent experience, is cleverly adapted by Moore as a chance meeting with a man who genuinely does not remember what has come to pass. Shortly afterwards Jesus learns that Joseph has been killed by a Zealot in Jerusalem, and from this point the novel's narrative point of view becomes that of Jesus himself. Witnessing a crucifixion, he remembers his past:

> He was too tired to think of what he had seen and heard, and sat in peace watching the sunset till, as in a vision, a man in a garden, in an agony of doubt, appeared to him. He was betrayed by a disciple and taken before the priests and afterwards before Pilate, who ordered him to be scourged and crucified, and beneath his cross the multitude passed, wagging their heads, inviting him to descend if he could detach himself from the nails. A veil fell and when it was lifted Joseph was bending over him, and soon after was carrying him to his house . . . He had lived in the ever-fleeting present for many years – how many? The question awoke him from his reverie, and he sat wondering how it was he could think so quietly of things that he had put out of his mind instinctively, till he seemed to himself to be a man detached as much from hope as from regret. It was through such strict rule that I managed to live through the years behind me, he said; I felt that I must never look back, but in a moment of great physical fatigue the past returned, and it lies before me now, the sting taken out of it, like the evening sky in tranquil waters. Even the memory that I once believed myself to be the Messiah promised to the Jews ceases to hurt; what we deem mistakes are part and parcel of some great design. Nothing befalls but by the will of God. My mistakes! Why do I speak of them as mistakes, for like all else they were from the beginning of time, and still are and will be till the end of time, in the mind of God. (pp. 341–2)

Jesus recalls his belief in himself as Messiah as an illusion, though one that should not be regretted, since it forms part of 'some great design' intelligible only to God. Thus Moore's Jesus arrives at a very human renunciation of any pretensions to divine mission, and an acknowledgement that humanity can never aspire to a godlike status.

Jesus resolves to return to the life of a shepherd in the Essene community. He is more than ever confirmed in his religious faith, but he has abandoned all notions of a divine plan of salvation in which he had a major role to play. His faith evolves into a kind of pastoral pantheism, in which he becomes literally, not metaphorically, a 'good shepherd', and in which God and nature are indistinguishable:

> A good shepherd can think while watching his sheep, and as the flock was feeding in good order, he took up the thread of a thought to which he had become attached since his discovery that signs and sounds of God's presence are never lacking on earth. As God's constant companion and confidant he had come to comprehend that the world of nature was a manifestation of the God he knew in himself. I know myself, he said one day, but I do not know the God which is above, for he seems to be infinite; nor do I know nature, which is beyond me, for that, too, seems to run into infinite, but infinite that is not that of God. A few moments later it seemed to him he might look upon himself as an islet between two infinities. But to which was he nearer in eternity? Ah, if he knew that! (pp. 245–6)

Meanwhile, however, Christianity is developing independent of Jesus's new-found rural tranquillity and resignation. Paul appears, preaching the life and death of Jesus Christ, a new faith based on the Crucifixion and Resurrection of one who was manifestly the Son of God:

> I spoke of the Lord Jesus Christ, Paul answered, the one Mediator between God and man who was sent by his Father to redeem the world. Only by faith in him the world may be saved, and the Jews will not listen. A hard, bitter, cruel race they are, that God will turn from in the end, choosing another from the Gentiles, since they will not accept him whom God has chosen to redeem men by the death and resurrection from the dead of the Lord Jesus Christ, raised from the dead by his Father. (p. 382)

Paul asserts this Resurrection faith, in flagrant disregard of the evidence of Jesus's survival, in language that replicates the New Testament Epistles. He preaches:

> . . . faith in our Lord Jesus Christ that died to redeem us from the law, and was raised from the dead by his Father, and who appeared

to the twelve and to five hundred others, some of whom are dead, but many are still alive. But this Christ, who was he when he lived upon this earth? Manahem inquired. Son of the living God, Paul answered, that took on the beggarly raiment of human flesh at Nazareth, was baptized by John in Jordan, and preached in Galilee, went up to Jerusalem and was crucified by Pilate between two thieves; the third day he rose from the dead, that our sins . . . Didst say he was born in Nazareth? Hazael asked, the word Nazareth having roused him from his reveries, and was baptized by John in Jordan, preached afterwards in Galilee, and suffered under Pilate? Was crucified, Paul interjected; then you have heard, he said, of the resurrection? Not of the resurrection; but we know that our Brother Jesus was born in Nazareth, was baptized in Jordan by John, preached in Galilee and suffered under Pilate. (pp. 426–7)

Jesus dissociates himself from this teaching, declaring it to be based on a falsehood, and in words that anticipate D. H. Lawrence's *The Man who Died*, declares his preaching to have been an error:

In my teaching I wandered beyond our doctrines and taught that this world is but a mock, a shame, a disgrace, and that naught was of avail but repentance . . . I should have remained an Essene shepherd following my flocks in the hills . . . [The Baptist's] teaching was true when he was the teacher, but when I became his disciple his teaching became false; it turned me from my natural self and into such great harshness of mind that in Nazareth when my mother came with my brothers and sisters to the synagogue I said, woman, I have no need of thee . . . But my passion was so great in those days that I did not see that my teaching was not less than blasphemy against God, for God has created the world for us to live in it, and he has put love of parents into our hearts because he wishes us to love our parents, and if he has put into the heart of man love of woman, and into the heart of woman love of man, it is because he wishes both to enjoy that love. (pp. 433–4)

The Brook Kerith founded the modern Jesus-novel by converting the gospel affirmation of Christ as the Incarnated deity, to a historical and biographical narrative of a wholly human being living a rationally intelligible mortal life. Jesus survives the cross, resigns his ministry and stands by while Paul establishes Christianity through preaching the Resurrection. Thus the modern Jesus-novel begins in an environment of theological scepticism and anti-clericalism, and with a mission to promote a wholly human Jesus who could never be mistaken for God; and a religion fraudulently based on a sacrifice that never happened.

III

Just over a decade after Moore's novel appeared, an early admirer of his work, D. H. Lawrence, wrote the story initially published as 'The Escaped Cock', and later anthologized as *The Man who Died*.[10] Lawrence had a conflicted, but lifelong, relationship with Christianity, and continually returned in his writing to Christian themes and topics.[11] In the story a man (not named as, but clearly identified with, Christ) wakes from death, or near-death, by crucifixion:

> Strength came from somewhere, from revulsion; there was a crash and a wave of light, and the dead man was crouching in his lair, facing the animal onrush of light. Yet it was hardly dawn. And the strange, piercing keenness of daybreak's sharp breath was on him. It meant full awakening.
>
> Slowly, slowly he crept down from the cell of rock with the caution of the bitterly wounded. Bandages and linen and perfume fell away, and he crouched on the ground against the wall of rock, to recover oblivion. But he saw his hurt feet touching the earth again, with unspeakable pain, the earth they had meant to touch no more, and he saw his thin legs that had died, and pain unknowable, pain like utter bodily disillusion, filled him so full that he stood up, with one torn hand on the ledge of the tomb.
>
> To be back! To be back again, after all that! He saw the linen swathing-bands fallen round his dead feet, and stooping, he picked them up, folded them, and laid them back in the rocky cavity from which he had emerged. Then he took the perfumed linen sheet, wrapped it round him as a mantle, and turned away, to the wanness of the chill dawn.
>
> He was alone; and having died, was even beyond loneliness. (pp. 6–9)

Like Moore's Jesus, Lawrence's Christ – 'the man who died' – resolves to renounce his mission of salvation, and to re-enter 'the phenomenal world' in search of personal healing and fulfilment. Also like Moore, Lawrence used fiction to attack Christianity for promoting a false ideal, a distortion of human nature through the denial or demonization of sexuality, and an ascetic revulsion from the natural world. Jesus had offered his body for violation, and thus transgressed the Lawrentian ethic: the resurrected Jesus has to learn to see the body as a phenomenon inscribed within the great Hericlatean flux of nature itself, and to understand that vivid and sensuous living is a higher destiny than sacrificial dying.

> The man who had died looked nakedly on life, and saw a vast resoluteness everywhere flinging itself up in stormy or subtle wave-crests, foam-tips emerging out of the blue invisible, a black and orange cock or the green flame-tongues out of the extremes of the fig tree. They came forth, these things and creatures of spring, glowing with desire and with assertion. They came like crests of foam, out of the blue flood of the invisible desire, out of the vast invisible sea of strength, and they came coloured and tangible, evanescent, yet deathless in their coming. The man who had died looked on the great swing into existence of things that had not died, but he saw no longer their tremulous desire to exist and to be. He heard instead their ringing, ringing, defiant challenge to all other things existing. (p. 17)

When Jesus returns to the empty tomb and meets Mary Magdalene, he comes to the realization that it is not only by the surrender to a violating death that he has separated himself from the natural world; his mission of salvation is also redefined as an attempt at 'interference' in the natural processes of birth and growth, death and rebirth. In the tale, both the life and death of Jesus are shown to be modes of alienation from the world of life and growth, the continually self-renewing and 'undying' world of nature.

Resurrected, and determined to seek a new direction, Lawrence's Jesus wanders off into an existential quest into the world, initially simply in search of a healing 'aloneness'. Some months later he encounters an Egyptian priestess, who has established a temple to Isis, and devoted her life to worship of the goddess, and to the search for the lost Osiris. Thus the story fuses a connection between the risen Jesus and the priestess within larger vision of the synthesis between two belief-systems, pagan and Christian. Within the framework of a narrative of existential quest and sexual fulfilment, Lawrence proposes what he sees as a completion of the Christian resurrection by its merger with the myth of Osiris. The specifically female powers of goddess and priestess are harnessed to heal the broken and fragmented body of the god, to restore it through ritual initiation and rebirth to a genuinely new form of 'risen' existence. Sexual union brings both physical recuperation and healing, and a re-connection of the body to the living powers of the universe, so the man–god becomes 'risen' in a synthesis of Christian resurrection, pagan initiation and sexual awakening.

> Now all his consciousness was there in the crouching, hidden woman. He stooped beside her and caressed her softly, blindly, murmuring inarticulate things. And his death and his passion of sacrifice were all as nothing to him now, he knew only the crouching fullness of the woman there, the soft white rock of life . . . 'On this rock I built my life'. The deep-folded, penetrable rock of the living woman! The woman, hiding her face. Himself bending over, powerful and new like dawn.
>
> He crouched to her, and he felt the blaze of his manhood and his power rise up in his loins, magnificent.
>
> 'I am risen!'

Lawrence's version of the Jesus-novel takes the form in a new direction, away from the sceptical, secular and materialistic humanization of George Moore, and towards the later efforts of Nikos Kazantzakis to recreate Jesus by merging the physical with the spiritual. Lawrence naturally placed much more emphasis on the sex life of Jesus, a concern that remains central to the Jesus-novel tradition; and brought his own vivid poetic sensibility to describing the experiences of resurrection and re-initiation.[12] The risen body in Lawrence is not the material body of science, but a sensuous living entity, spiritualized by the refreshment of pre-Christian pagan belief. As Bibhu Padhi puts it, 'the tale does not undermine or subvert orthodox Christian belief, but rather redefines the Christian idea of resurrection and renovation in a neo-Christian framework with the support of Lawrence's personal religious vision'.[13]

If Lawrence was a neo-Christian, Robert Graves, author of *King Jesus*, was a neo-pagan.[14] Graves believed, as Lawrence also partly believed, that all religions derived from a substratum of primitive mythology that formed the bedrock of human belief. Judaic and Christian monotheisms reproduced older pagan archetypes: Jehovah was another form of the Greek Zeus; Christ was another version of the dying and rising God of ancient fertility cults. Graves was particularly attached to the notion of a pagan femininity, suppressed by the phallocentric masculinity of Christianity.[15]

Graves claimed that *King Jesus* was historical,[16] but it is much more a romance of secret marriages, hidden identities, royal blood concealed and revealed, not unlike *The Da Vinci Code*. In *King Jesus* Graves makes Jesus into a 'sacred king' of pagan mythology. He really is descended from a royal house (Mary is secretly married to Herod the Great's son Antipater) and he really is the rightful heir to the throne of Israel. He sees himself, and others see him, as the Messiah prophesied in the Old Testament, the Messiah born to restore Israel to its former political and military power. Pontius Pilate even offers to make him King of Israel under Roman supremacy.

But Jesus refuses, since he believes in another kind of kingship, the primitive sacred kingship in which the ruler is sacrificed by his subjects – a human sacrifice – and then rises again. This plan goes wrong – the disciples misunderstand his command that *they* should sacrifice *him* – and Pilate reluctantly has Jesus crucified. The *titulus*, the sign fixed to the cross proclaiming Jesus as 'King of the Jews', is an accurate identification: this is who he really was, the true King of Israel, the last King of the Jews. But his passion is a mere accident, and has no soteriological value in any theological scheme of redemption.

With his interests in mythology, pagan religion and Gnosticism, Graves brought the Jesus-novel into the territory later so ably exploited by Dan Brown. In *King Jesus* the alternative explanations of the life and death of Jesus that had become commonplace in both theology and fiction are proposed as a kind of fundamental 'bedrock' truth, obscured by centuries of falsehood and manipulation. Thus the novel becomes an unmasking of the conspiracy by which Christianity replaced the freedom of pagan goddess-worship with the tyranny of a paternalistic church. Later, feminist author Michele Roberts in *The Wild Girl* was to deploy the same conspiracy theory, making Mary Magdalene the founder of an alternative Christian church that was suppressed and deformed by St Peter and the power of the Roman church. These and other neglected Jesus-novels are stations on the route to *The Da Vinci Code*.

IV

From a traditional Christological point of view, the Jesus novel may be considered to have its origins in a theological error. Studies in Christian theology frequently begin with an assertion that the Gospels are not a 'biography of Jesus Christ'. Clearly there are sound historical, literary and theological reasons for this emphasis. The earliest Christian writings were probably records of 'the sayings of Jesus', the emphasis falling on the gospel rather than the man, on the Word rather than the flesh it had become.[17] Christian theology is posited on the doctrine of the Incarnation, and must recognize in Christ both divinity and humanity: but the 'life' that was in Jesus was, as St John affirms, the light of men, the effluence of the eternal Word. There can be no biography of God. Lastly there is the fact that the gospels are only part, though a central part, of the whole body of Christian writings we know as the Bible, which charts the relations between God and his people, through from the earliest times, to time's imagined end. It can be argued that the 'life' of Jesus should not therefore be disjoined, on the one hand from Old Testament history and prophecy, and on the other from the narrative of the church's foundation, and the theological explications of St Paul in Acts and the Epistles.

Paul frequently employed the words and actions of Jesus in interpretative ways that trespass on the territory of what we now recognize as narrative fiction. In his writings however, and in those of the Church fathers of the early centuries who followed him, theological explication was paramount, and the life of Jesus largely the historical fact (the Incarnation and Redemption) that underpinned the doctrines. To abstract from those doctrines the human life of Jesus, and to reproduce it as a historical biography, would appear to be a departure from the mainstream of Christian theology, and to play naturally into the hands of a rationalistic secular ideology that inevitably ends up denying the divinity of Christ.

The novel, a secular form originating in the rationalist eighteenth-century middle-class culture of Samuel Richardson and Daniel Defoe, was designed to portray the human world, and is not a natural vehicle for representing the divine. Hence it is hardly surprising that when the novel began to approach the person of Jesus, it did so in the form of an anticlerical, secular and humanizing project. The Jesus of the novel tends to be what he is in *The Brook Kerith*, a historical human being prised away from theological doctrine and ecclesiastical dogma. He may be prophet, poet, teacher, Carlylean hero, Nietzschean superman, moral exemplar and martyr, but he is not the crucified and risen Christ.[18] He is rather what he becomes in the title of Kahlil Gibran's powerful poetic fiction, *Jesus the Son of Man*.[19] It is this Jesus, man rather than God, who appears as the prototype of all the wretched and oppressed, the archetype of rebels and hippies, in Dostoevsky's novels, in *Godspel*, in *Jesus Christ Superstar*. In general, twentieth-century writers, including some of those discussed in this book, have set out to take the person of Jesus and secularize it into a wholly human, though certainly admirable, personality. But this is invariably man without God: Jesus of Nazareth, not Jesus the Christ.[20]

But at the heart of Christianity, what distinguishes it from other religions, is the dual nature, the doctrine of the Incarnation, the combination in Christ of both divinity and humanity. As Rowan Greer puts it with admirable simplicity:

> First, since Christ is the Savior and since only God can save, Christ must somehow be God. Second, since the only way God can save us is by touching us and our human condition directly and fully, Christ must somehow be identified with our humanity. Third, these two aspects of Christ's identity must be kept distinct but must not compromise his unity.[21]

The Word that became flesh was the Word that was from the beginning, the one and only true God. Because the Word became flesh and dwelt among us, Jesus became *bios*, a living being, a candidate for biography, and an appropriate object of representation in fiction and film. But unless novel and film can in some way express the dual nature of Christ, it is hard to see how they could be anything other than secular rebuttals of Christianity.

V

By contrast with these authors who have sought to portray Jesus as
wholly human, there are novelists who have attempted to represent
the dual nature of Christ, human and divine. Most of them have
however imaginatively shied away from the implications. Often
writers of prose fiction have felt inhibited from representing Jesus
at all, and instead, in Hans Küng's words, 'edge towards the figure
of Jesus, speaking of him only indirectly and almost timidly . . .
he is observed in the effects he produces on other people . . . he is
approached as we pass by the place where he is standing'.[22] Here
novelists, wishing to depict Jesus in God's world, have tried to place
God within it: but have shrunk from such depiction on the grounds
that human consciousness cannot aspire to a perception of divinity.
So we get images of Jesus such as that in the Hollywood Biblical
epic film of Lew Wallace's *Ben Hur*, where his face, being the
unrepresentable face of God, is never seen.[23] As Küng points out,
this technique symptomatizes a profound 'respect' for the person
of Jesus, an admiration that survives loss of faith and transcends
religious and ethical controversy. But equally it betrays a lack of
conviction about that most fundamental Christian doctrine, that
which differentiates Christianity from the other great world-faiths:
the Incarnation. The church holds that Jesus was at all times fully
God, and fully man. If God as man is not representable in the way
that human beings are, then the Incarnation has not truly taken
effect. Fiction bifurcates along the division the Incarnation exists
to elide, between the divine and the human. Scepticism about the
Christological possibilities of imaginative prose has encouraged
scholars to assume that the Christ of the novel is invariably the
human Jesus, since Christ as incarnate God is not representable
in modern fiction. As Hans Küng puts it, in a discussion of novels
on Jesus, 'It is . . . doubtful whether the stylistic aids and methods
of literature are really adequate to give expression in words to the
life of Jesus, his person and cause, the divine and human elements
brought together in a historically concrete person' (p. 139).

Kung's assertion is certainly exemplified in some novels written
by authors from within the church, or at least within the faith, which
attempt to translate the incarnational faith of the gospels into prose
narrative, and to realize the dual nature in fiction. In such works

Jesus is both human and divine. But the works themselves have no literary merit. They come across as novelized piety, rather than a successful synthesis of theology and fiction.[24] Ann Rice's *Christ the Lord: Out of Egypt* and *Christ the Lord: The Road to Cana* belong to this variant of the Jesus-novel tradition. Such failed novels seem to indicate that in dealing with the person of Jesus, the novel and Christian theology remain obdurately incompatible bedfellows.

The brief summary provided earlier of the Jesus-novel tradition suggests that, as a literary form with any chance of artistic success, it lies outside any denomination of the Christian church, and even beyond the horizons of the Christian faith. Novels written to recuperate the dual nature in fiction fail to achieve literary distinction. Successful Jesus-novels in general have been written by authors hostile to the church – Moore, Lawrence, Graves – and written with a mission to discredit, or at least revalue, Christianity's incarnational beliefs. At least some of these books, however, as this study aims to demonstrate, stand out from this norm, and engage with the dual nature of Christ in ways that seem to surpass and even contradict the author's express intentions. Some Jesus-novels generate far more complex images of Jesus than the merely humanizing and secularizing effects of historical biography.

VI

Jesus-novels and Jesus-films originate and take their shape from specific contexts of Christian theology. Both *Vie de Jesus* and *The Brook Kerith* were clearly predicated on the 'Life of Jesus' movement in nineteenth-century liberal thinking. Hence the Jesus-novel began, indeed grew out of, a crisis in Christian theology. Even before Moore's novel was published, Martin Kahler decreed that the 'Life of Jesus' movement in theology was at a dead end, since its practitioners were merely exercising their creative imaginations on the person of Jesus, not locating the true Jesus of history. Simultaneously Albert Schweitzer showed conclusively that the nineteenth-century 'quest for the historical Jesus' had constructed a biography of Jesus conforming to the norms of modern liberal theology.[25] Thus the twentieth-century Jesus novel begins at exactly the point where theologians were beginning to dispense with the liberal 'biography' as a useful

Christological form. The nineteenth century was the high point of theological interest in the life of Jesus, and by the early twentieth century attacks on liberal theology were targeting such 'sacred biographies'[26] as fanciful and subjective. 'I regard the entire "Life of Jesus" movement as a blind alley,' wrote Kähler, who restored the crucifixion and resurrection to their Pauline centrality, and reduced the rest of the gospels to 'extended introductions' to the 'passion narratives'.[27] *The Brook Kerith* exemplifies the humanist liberal theology Kahler and Schweitzer were attacking, in that Moore's Jesus is clearly 'a figure designed by rationalism, endowed with life by liberalism, and clothed by modern theology in a historical garb'.[28]

The Jesus of both liberal theology and secular fiction, in the late nineteenth and early twentieth centuries, is naturally man more than God. Theodor Kiolkowski suggested that historical novels about Jesus, 'fictionalizing biographies,' differed little from nineteenth-century liberal biographies such as Ernest Renan's *Vie de Jésus*, 'a literary biography of a humanized Jesus'.[29] Both types present the human or the historical Jesus; their common territory is Christology 'from below'. This is the Jesus of history, not the Jesus of faith: Jesus of Nazareth, not Jesus the Christ. As John Macquarrie says, this 'will not do' for an incarnational faith: 'If we assimilate him too closely to the common human condition, then he is in the same boat with the rest of us, and cannot be the Redeemer.'[30]

VII

For most twentieth-century writers, embarking on a Jesus-novel has entailed a direct confrontation with the church, and with orthodox Christian doctrine. Yet in many cases, as my analysis will show, some novelists ultimately find themselves working very close to the cutting edge of advanced theological speculation. This is despite the fact that, in general, theologians have not shown much respect for the Jesus-novel, or for its contribution to theological debate. With the demise of liberal theology, the 'first historical Jesus quest' and the biographical–historical form deployed by writers like Renan and Moore, the novel seemed to have no further purchase on theology. Instead critics have turned their attention to works of fiction containing 'transfigurative' versions of Christianity, Christ-figures rather than figurations of Christ, where the Christian gospel can be found at work in contemporary society, not in a remote history, and in an increasingly dubious historical character.

Hence the Jesus-novel is a neglected literature, stranded somewhere between a literary history that sees it as an eccentric curiosity, and a theology that often treats it as irrelevant. This project will attempt to reconstitute the form, and explain why it is that the Jesus-novel is continually consigned to the dustbin of history, and yet continually displays a capacity for survival. In addition the book attempts to explore and explain the relationship between these texts and twentieth-century Christology. It is my argument that although these novels were usually written against the church, and even against Christianity, they can nonetheless be seen as making a contribution, if only indirectly, to the development of Christian religious belief.

The great themes of twentieth-century Christology are those arising from the classical Christology of Nicaea and Chalcedon, but presented to a secular age: from Jesus's own question, 'Who do you say that I am?' to Dietrich Bonhoeffer's 'Who is Jesus Christ for us today?' The questions posed by Christology and the Jesus-novel are the same questions: was Jesus God on earth? Or a man chosen by God to represent Him? Was he a man who exemplified godliness? Or was he, after all, 'just a man'? Did he believe himself to be the Son of God, or the Messiah, or the Saviour of humanity? Did he know himself as God in a man's body? Often these questions focus on the self-consciousness of Jesus, conceived as a subject, immanent and incarnate, divine and human. 'What would it be like for someone to exist who would be both divinely infinite and humanly finite?' If Jesus mediated/mediates between God and man, 'how must we think of someone who can sustain these relations'? These are novelistic questions, but here they are posed by theologians writing Christology.[31]

VIII

The Jesus-novel is not of course the only aesthetic form that can readily be adapted to convey humanized and historical images of Jesus. The art of film, which overlaps in countless ways with the novel, has also taken up the challenge of representing Jesus as God and man.[32] Embodied initially in the Hollywood Biblical epic, Jesus has appeared in a number of thoughtful and respectful film treatments by directors such as George Stevens, Pier Paolo Pasolini and Roberto Rosselini. I have made reference to some general surveys of this history, as well as more detailed studies of its earlier stages. I have elected here to offer detailed analyses of a small number of Jesus-films made between 1977 and 2005: Franco Zefirelli's *Jesus of Nazareth*, Martin Scorsese's *The Last Temptation of Christ* and Mel Gibson's *The Passion of the Christ*. The final chapter addresses, by way of a coda to the book, an extraordinary Jesus-film from South Africa that promises to revolutionize the entire form: Mark Dornford-May's *Son of Man*.

Although all these films are equally based on the original gospel narratives of the life of Jesus, each also draws on an intermediary literary text. The films of Zefirelli and Scorsese have their grounding in the novels by Kazantzakis and Burgess; while the other two films are based respectively in a nineteenth-century work of devotional mysticism, and a cycle of mediaeval mystery plays. In the cases of the two films based in novels, I have undertaken a comprehensive analysis of the relations between novel and film. In the case of the other two films, the relation between film and literary source assumes less significance, but is given due attention. Ultimately, the medium of film has its own methods of representing the life of Jesus, and its own ways of interacting with contemporary currents in Christology. Jesus movies may, in the words of Jeffery L. Staley, be read as 'gospel interpreters and supplements', while the gospels may be read as 'interpreters and supplements to Jesus movies'.[33]

Relations between film criticism and theology are less developed than those between theology and literary criticism. As Martin and Ostwalt put it,

Scholars engaged in prevailing modes of film criticism have almost nothing to say about religion. And scholars who study religion have almost nothing to say about Hollywood film.[34]

In an essay called *Imaging Jesus in Film*, Lloyd Baugh exemplifies the confrontation of disciplines that occurs when academic theology and film studies attempt to converge.

The *genre* of film is radically different from the Gospel *genre*. The latter, as well we know, is the medium of the written word, clear,

elementary, the word of faith, born and transmitted through the
oral tradition, a holy word which for Christians is inspired and
guaranteed by God . . .

En outré, la parole filmique n'est jamais d'inspiration divine,
quelle soit approuvée et louangée par les autorités ecclésiastiques
ou non.[35]

This seems to me a simplistic understanding of the Gospels,
traditional in religious studies, but highly controversial anywhere
else; and a reductive definition of film, derived uncritically from
the secular discipline of film criticism and theory. It is possible
not only to accept the Gospels as the word of faith, but also to
regard them, even in the process of their original composition,
as sophisticated literary texts, and as writings that certainly
cannot be accessed independently of the vast project of literary
interpretation, adaptation and appropriation that has been going
on around them for over two millennia. Conversely the medium
of film is no more immune than any other art form to divine
inspiration. Notwithstanding its technological dimensions and
context of popular entertainment, film also has 'the potential'
as David Jasper says of literature 'to reconfigure theological
discourse'.[36]

The relationship between any Jesus-film and the literary
and other texts on which it is predicated is always much more
complex than film-makers are likely to acknowledge. Directors
will claim that their primary source is the gospels.[37] But even
these foundational sources exist of course in multiple and
contested versions, and in a tangled relationship with non-
canonical apocryphal narratives.[38] The gospels are silent on many
aspects of Jesus's human existence in which the agent of historical
or biographical reconstruction is bound to be interested.[39]
Centuries of narrative interpolation and redaction, commencing
as early as the second- or even the first-century AD, overlay the
texts of the gospels; and centuries of traditional appropriation
have elaborated on the gospel narratives, producing stories and
images that in popular culture have become inseparable from
the gospels themselves.[40] Two millennia of scriptural exegesis
and interpretation, produced by innumerable different Christian
sects, interpose between the contemporary artist and the texts on
which his or her art is based.[41]

IX

I have described and analysed the twentieth-century representation of Jesus through extensive case studies of three novels and four films. In each case I have analysed the presentation of Jesus in terms of the theology of the dual nature, and suggested ways in which the work can be seen as contributing, whether intentionally or not, to key debates in modern Christology. To some degree this entails a consideration of cultural and theological context. Just as Kazantzakis's work has to be read in the context of the Greek Orthodoxy, so the films of Zefirelli and Scorsese must be seen in the light of their respective forms of Roman Catholicism. I have mined these texts for their Christological content, and analysed their potential impact on contemporary assumptions and perceptions about the fundamentals of Christian theology. In the case of my final example, *Son of Man*, context can be seen to overwhelm content, without ever losing the integrity of the biblical–biographical narrative.

In the rest of this 'Introduction' I will provide brief introductions to the three Jesus-novels and three Jesus-films that lie at the heart of this study.

Charlotte Allen called *The Last Temptation* 'Renan's *Life of Jesus* for the twentieth century',[42] and the work can certainly be read as a representative twentieth-century demythologizing Jesus novel. In many ways *The Last Temptation* seems to operate in the medium to which the 'fictionalizing biography' seems best adapted, to deprive Jesus of divinity, to humanize and secularize him into a form acceptable to a modern, generally non-Christian, even non-religious readership. In one of his letters Kazantzakis declared similar aims:[43]

> I wanted to renew and supplement the sacred Myth that underlies the great Christian civilization of the West. It isn't a simple 'life of Christ'. It's a laborious, sacred, creative endeavour to reincarnate the essence of Christ, setting aside the dross – falsehoods and pettinesses which all the churches and all the cassocked representatives of Christianity have heaped upon his figure, thereby distorting it . . .
>
> Parables which Christ could not possibly have left as the Gospels relate them I have supplemented, and I have given them the noble

and compassionate ending befitting Christ's heart. Words which we do not know that He said I have put into his mouth, because He would have said them if His disciples had had His spiritual force and purity. And everywhere poetry, love of animals and plant life and men, confidence in the soul, certainty that light will prevail.

The objectives Kazantzakis set himself sound very similar to those of Renan, Moore, and indeed the whole nineteenth-century critical movement: to liberate Jesus from the church, and to bypass both the Christian doctrine devised by Paul and the 'falsifications' of the gospel writers, in order to get at the historical truth about Jesus of Nazareth. Much of this language recalls Renan, seemingly endorsing Peter Bien's assertion that 'aside from the Gospels, Renan seems to have been Kazantzakis's major source'.[44] But Kazantzakis clearly read widely and voraciously in biblical history and criticism while writing the novel, as he writes, 'For a year now I've been taking out of the library at Cannes all the books written about Christ and Judea, the Chronicles of that time, the Talmud and so on. So all the details are historically correct, even though I recognize the right of the poet not to follow history in a slavish way'.[45] Kazantzakis seems to have absorbed late-nineteenth-century biblical criticism, together with something of the 'historical Jesus' quest; and it was clearly as a disciple of Nietzsche that he found the courage to offer to 'renew' the Christian 'Myth'. As Colin Wilson commented:

Kazantzakis was not intent on creating a sinless god-man. He wanted to create Christ in his own image – tormented by everlasting temptation; a Promethean Jesus, learning, step-by-step, to cast off the fetters of the family, the body, the ego.[46]

All this is consistent with the way in which the novel was received and read as a blasphemous and sacrilegious assault on traditional Christianity and even the faith itself. It explains why it was placed by the Vatican on the index of forbidden books and condemned as 'indecent, atheistic, and treasonable' by the Orthodox Church of America. It illustrates why in 1960, fundamentalist American Protestants tried to have it removed from public libraries. There seems almost sufficient justification here to agree with Peter Bien that Kazantzakis effectively 'did not believe in God and was not a Christian'.[47] And yet as my analysis will show, this is not the end of the story. Kazantzakis's novel has much more to offer to Christological thinking than a simple recuperation of the historical and biographical 'Life of Jesus'.

In the 'Prologue' to his novel, Nikos Kazantzakis identified his central and abiding theme as 'The dual substance of Christ':[48]

> The yearning, so human, so superhuman, of man to attain to God, or more exactly, to return to God and identify himself with him – has always been a deep inscrutable mystery to me . . . My principal anguish, and the wellspring of all my joys and sorrows from my youth onward has been the incessant, merciless battle between the spirit and the flesh.

Speaking of his film version of the novel, *The Last Temptation of Christ* (1988), Martin Scorsese echoed this formulation:[49]

> Kazantzakis took the two natures of Jesus . . . this was Christologically correct: the debate goes back to the Council of Chalcedon in 451, when they discussed how much of Jesus was divine, how much human.

Both novelist and film director explicitly took their bearings from that ancient theological language, 'dual substance' and 'dual nature' of the early church councils. The Council of Nicaea (325) declared that Christ was consubstantial with the Father ('ὁμοούσιυ τῶ πατρί') and yet 'became human' and 'incarnate'; the Council of Chalcedon (451) affirmed the dual nature of the Son: 'our Lord Jesus Christ . . . truly God and truly man . . . consubstantial with the Father as regards his divinity, and the same consubstantial with us as regards his humanity'.[50] This remained the orthodox formulation, as embodied in the Athanasian Creed: 'our Lord Jesus Christ, the Son of God, is equally both God and Man'.[51]

Both Kazantzakis and Scorsese thus located their work at the heart of Christianity's most complex internal controversy, the relation between divinity and humanity in the person of Christ. Implicit in the gospels ('the Word became flesh,' John 1.14) and explicit in the Pauline epistles ('God was revealed in the flesh,' 1 Tim. 3.16), the dual nature, or dual substance, of Christ has always been, and still remains, an intellectually challenging, doctrinally controversial but nonetheless unavoidable cornerstone of Christian belief and worship.

Although both novelist and director were brought up in religious communities and had good religious educations, neither was a professional or academic theologian. They both tended to think, for example, in a dualistic rather than a Trinitarian way and neither had anything to say in this context about the origin or operation of the Holy Spirit. Both engaged creatively with the central problem of the dual nature of Christ and produced fictional works pervaded by complex and profound explorations of Christology. In Chapter 1, I will explore the theological underpinnings of both versions of *The Last Temptation*, and attempt to demonstrate the value of their contributions to theological discussion and debate.

X

My second chapter also deals with the interrelationship of a novel and a film, and seeks to clarify their respective contributions to theological debates on the dual nature. The film is Franco Zeffirelli's TV film *Jesus of Nazareth* (1977), and I have studied its tortuous relationship with Anthony Burgess's novel *Man of Nazareth* (1979). Burgess was commissioned by Zeffirelli to write for his planned TV film a screenplay, which was later developed by Zeffirelli himself with Italian screenwriter Suso Cecchi d'Amico. Burgess's script was preceded by a draft of the novel that was later published as *Man of Nazareth*.[52] The novel and the film are so radically different that most people assume little of Burgess's script survived the process of development and the making of the film, and certainly Burgess in his autobiography implied that this was the case. To complicate the issue further, the film's producer Vincenzo Labella commissioned a 'novelization', 'based on the film' and 'from the script', written by the prolific Scots academic theologian and popular communicator William Barclay, and published in 1977. Barclay claimed that:

> The book is based on Anthony Burgess's script of the television film of *Jesus of Nazareth*. The script of the film was in my hands when I wrote it, and there are large areas of the book where I did no more than change the script into narrative form.[53]

This was done however without the knowledge or approval of Burgess, who recalled waking up one Sunday in May 1977 to find Barclay's book topping the best-seller lists. 'It was made out of my own script for the Zeffirelli series, the script being a commodity bought by the production company, its novelisation assigned to a novelising hand not mine'.[54] And the result was quite strikingly different from either Burgess's novel or Zeffirelli's film.

I initially describe the process by which Burgess and Zeffirelli together and separately approached their respective tasks of novelist and director. Then I explore, through comparative examples, the parallels and dissimilarities between novel, film, and to a lesser extent, novelization. The primary aim of this study is to describe the relationship between film and novel as an illuminating model of how in practice the 'life' of Jesus is reproduced as fiction and as film. In addition to mapping this complex process of textual production I will seek to disentangle some of the theological ideas implicit in, and disseminated by, the fertile matrix of these linguistic and audio-visual artefacts.

XI

My third case-study is the novel *Quarantine*, by Jim Crace. Crace wrote a preface to the novel in which he describes his fictional undertaking as an act of religious iconoclasm:

> When I began my novel *Quarantine* (which retells the story of Christ's forty days of temptation in the wilderness) I expected – indeed, intended – to inflict some bruises on religious dogma. An easy target, I thought. Christendom has never been in such an undernourished and diminished state. Every week the godless mechanics of the universe, from Big Bang to the tiny chemical percussions of the brain, are revealed in finer detail . . .

> It would be a simple matter. Take a venerated Bible story (Christ's Judean fast), add a pinch of hard-nosed fact (nobody going without food and drink could survive for anything like forty days) and watch the scripture take a beating. *Quarantine* with Science as its sword would kill Christ after only thirty days

in the wilderness. There'd be no Ministry or Crucifixion. The
novel would erase two thousand years of Christianity.[55]

Crace describes himself as embracing, with all the excitement of
assumed novelty, the task of demythologizing Christianity. In
fact he was of course embarking on a very well-trodden path,
the enlightenment project of disproving the Christian gospel by
revealing the historical truth underlying its claims: the project that
has been a common feature of Christology since the eighteenth
century, and is the basic agenda of the naturalistic Jesus-novel from
George Moore onwards.

There are, however, substantial differences between the traditional
demythologizing project and Crace's fiction, and the differences
are at once strange and instructive. As early as the seventeenth
century the sceptic Reimarius argued that Christianity was founded
not by Jesus, but by apostles who falsified his doctrines and
exaggerated his claims for their own advantage. As we have seen,
the separation between the Jesus of history and the Christ of faith,
and the subsequent attempt to locate the former (the 'first historical
Jesus quest') dominated nineteenth-century Christology and the
Jesus-novel it produced. Crace converged, wittingly or not, on a
well-established fictional form, which specializes in a naturalistic
biographical representation of Jesus in a fully realized historical
setting, and aims to challenge the gospels, the faith and the church
by revealing the true history of Jesus's life and death. He did so on
the basis of a professed adherence to modern scientific paradigms
such as those of evolutionary biology; and he clearly sees his fiction
as in some sense constituting a 'scientific' representation of the
world. The Messianic claims of Jesus are assumed to evaporate
under this scrutiny, and the truth-claims of religion itself to crumble
beneath the application of scientific observation and the invocation
of scientific laws.

But he differs from his predecessors and peers (whose works
he does not appear to have read) in certain key points. Novelists
such as George Moore, Ivan Naschiwin, Nikos Kazantkzakis and
Norman Mailer also explore the gap between the Jesus of history
and the Christ of faith. But they pin their narratives to those
historical facts that do provide independent confirmation that Jesus
lived, preached and died on the cross: the facts of condemnation by
Pilate, the crucifixion, the impact and dissemination of the Christian

gospel, all recorded by Tacitus, Suetonius and Josephus as well as by the authors of the gospels. They also predicate their fictions on the existence (if not necessarily the truth or accuracy) of the New Testament writings, composed by Paul and by others from the mid-first century onwards, and incorporating older apostolic traditions. These novelists certainly undertake a critical and challenging exploration of how the Christian narrative emerged from its historical context, and seek to exploit the discrepancies between the two. But they base their fictional reconstructions on known historical facts, and on those persons (Paul, Matthew, Thomas) whose names appear as authorial signatures on the scriptures themselves.

The most unusual feature of *Quarantine*, this novel by a professed scientific atheist, is that it avoids the attested historical facts altogether. Crace's Jesus never gets as far as the historical events that independently ascertain his existence – preaching in Jerusalem, arrest and trial before Pilate, death on the cross. This Jesus never enters history, but dies during that sojourn in the wilderness that the gospels designate as the very beginning of Jesus's sotereological career, an event for which there is no contingent historical evidence. Indeed since the 40 days in the wilderness are the scene of Jesus's temptation by the devil, the incident represents one of the very few in the gospels where Jesus is represented as occupying a supernatural plane, as distinct from bringing the miraculous into ordinary life (other examples are the Baptism, the Transfiguration, the Ascension). Crace thus locates his historical Jesus in a space outside history, in a hinterland beyond the reach of documentary evidence. *Quarantine* lies somewhere between myth and history, or as Philip Tew puts it 'operates on the very margins of both myth and reality'.[56]

Equally fictional is Crace's narrative hypothesis as to the origin of the Christian gospel. It clearly does not originate from Jesus himself. But nor is it developed and disseminated by the New Testament authors or their apostolic predecessors. Instead it is to be circulated as a new commodity, 'merchandise', by the corrupt and unscrupulous merchant, Musa: 'He'd travel to the markets of the world. He'd preach the good news.'[57] The Christian gospel is not only a baseless illusion or a distorted fable, as it is in *The Brook Kerith* and in Naschiwin's *A Certain Jesus*. It is to be promulgated by a professional liar, a man whose vocation is to exchange untruth for profit. Thus Christianity is seen from the outset as a hoax peddled by a dishonest merchant; a means by which a tradesman can sell lies and grow fat on the proceeds; indissolubly bound up with mercantile exchange and financial markets. Musa 'merchandises the storytelling possibilities of a belief system'.[58] Other novelists certainly attribute corrupt motives to those who write and preach the gospel; and even the imputation of shady dealing is not unfamiliar in post-enlightenment Christology (Reimarius asserted that the apostles preferred skimming the collection plate to working for a living). But Crace is quite distinctive in his direct equation of Christian evangelism with the basest of characters, and with the most extreme manifestation of the capitalist profit-motive.

XII

There can be little doubt that the currency of the Jesus-film has been hugely enhanced by the success of Mel Gibson's film *The Passion of the Christ*. In March 2004 author Philip Pullman and the Archbishop of Canterbury staged a conversation at the National Theatre, chaired by Robert Butler, around the dramatization of Pullman's epic trilogy *His Dark Materials*. The subject of film and religion comes up, and it is suggested by Robert Butler that film represents religious stories in 'a very realistic way' – 'you're encouraged to think you're there' – whereas the theatre works in a more mediated manner, through metaphor. Rowan Williams argues to the contrary that film in fact is 'deeply metaphorical', a 'highly patterned and stylized visual sequence'. The film medium is inhabited by 'animated icons rather than representation'.[59]

The speakers then turned to discuss Mel Gibson's *The Passion of the Christ*, though neither had seen it. The film is described as selling itself on the basis that it is supremely realistic, enabling viewers to get close, 'to see what happened'. The atheist Pullman and the Archbishop both agree that this is undesirable: the former because moral reformation is not achieved by 'seeing someone tortured to death', the latter because 'the pivotal event in the history of the universe' cannot be represented naturalistically. Pullman asks which was the pivotal event, the Crucifixion or the Resurrection, since the latter 'doesn't come into the film' at all (in fact it does, but only as a brief concluding coda). Williams then defines the 'pivotal event' as neither the one nor the other, but rather the redemptive totality of the story, 'the whole Easter complex'. From the entry into Jerusalem to the post-Resurrection appearances that conclude three of the gospels, this 'complex' is certainly a sequence of events that can be found narrated in the gospels; but more importantly it represents a series of kerygmatic ritual moments which forms the basis, in the Catholic (or here of course Anglo-Catholic) church's traditional practice, for the liturgies of Holy Week:

> You walk through the experience of Holy Week in a . . . ritual way . . . watching through the night; participating in a very curious and distinctive liturgy for Good Friday, with the bare cross being brought in and unveiled. All that attempting to say what a mere recitation of the story, or a mere photograph, couldn't say.

Using Karen Armstrong's distinction between 'myth' and 'logos',[60] Pullman then suggests that cinematic representation must inevitably be 'rational', and must thereby eliminate the 'mythical' from its horizon.

If this were true, then film and religion would be incompatible. Film would be able to show only the observable psychological and social effects of religious experience, not spirituality itself; only the human nature of Jesus, not the divine. Indeed Joseph Cuneen[61] has argued that film's 'inevitable bias towards realism' explains the lack of interaction between film criticism and religious studies – 'serious study of religion in narrative film has been extremely limited'. In addition, argues Cuneen, the Hollywood system, oriented towards popularity and profit, does not allow directors 'to make personal movies that suggest the depth of religious mystery' (p. 93).

This chapter seeks to interpret the controversy surrounding Mel Gibson's *The Passion of the Christ* by situating the film into debates about film narrative, Catholic liturgy and ritual, and the sacrament of the Eucharist. Although the film is based on the gospel narratives, it is argued that its handling of time and space has more in common with the liturgical structure of the Tridentine mass. As such it is both more and less than a film, requiring of the spectator not a cinematic 'gaze', but rather a corporeal participation akin to the experiential quality of Catholic sacramental ritual. There is no questioning here of the dual nature of Christ. But the film goes beyond theological debate to situate the Incarnation into everyday ritual and worship as well as into history. *The Passion of the Christ* is, as Timothy K. Beal and Tod Linafelt put it, 'a significant moment in the cultural afterlife of the biblical passion stories of Christian scripture'.[62]

XIII

The last film discussed here, Mark Dornford-May's *Son of Man*, could not be more different, in many ways, from Mel Gibson's *Passion of the Christ*. While Gibson's film, marginal and controversial as it may be, is still a Hollywood studio product featuring experienced screen actors, Dornford-May's is an independent South African film that uses only black actors from theatrical backgrounds. For all its idiosyncracy, *The Passion of the Christ* operates in the tradition of the Western Jesus-film; while *Son of Man* radically challenges, from a post-colonial perspective, the very basis of that tradition. Gibson mediates the gospel to the present by a reverential reconstruction of the past, using an intermediary literary source, as well as the gospels and Christological tradition; Dornford-May, like Dostoevsky, drags the historical Jesus into the harsh light of modernity, goes straight back to the gospels and reconstructs them in the light of modern political and racial oppression, violence and struggle. *The Passion* visually alludes to Renaissance painting, *Son of Man* to contemporary newsreel footage. The one preaches a gospel of non-resistance to evil, and celebrates the capacity of the individual to endure suffering; the other is a manifesto for non-violent resistance, and welcomes the emergence of a new political community.

Of course there are also similarities. But as Reinhold Zwick observes, the two films exhibit certain resemblances that are subsumed within a larger and more fundamental difference:[63]

> The dramaturgy of *Son of Man* shows some similarities to Mel Gibson's *The Passion of the Christ* and to numerous other Jesus movies from the silent era onwards in depicting a close relationship between Mary, the mother of Jesus, and Mary Magdalene . . . Another similarity to Gibson's film is the repeated visible presence of Satan, who is shown as the secret force behind the intrigues against Jesus and as the personification of evil. Whereas Gibson opens his movie with the *last* temptation of Jesus

by Satan in the garden of Gethsemane, Dornford-May opens
with the *first* temptation, the temptation in the desert. Despite
these parallels, *Son of Man* is antithetical to Mel Gibson's movie
both theologically and aesthetically.

Son of Man presents us with an unusual, and astonishingly creative,
variant on the Jesus-film. As indicated right at the beginning of this
study, scholars generally accept a fundamental distinction between
historical Jesus films, and films that deploy transfigurative Christ-
figures. As Lloyd Baugh puts it in an essay on *Son of Man*, 'More
than 125 films represent the Gospel story literally: these are best
described as the Jesus films. Many more relate the Gospel story
metaphorically: these may be termed Christ-figure films.'[64] All three
of the major films discussed here are historical Jesus-films, setting
the stories of the Gospels into a reconstructed first-century Judaea.
'Christ-figure films' films typically mediate the Gospel stories to
a contemporary, or near-contemporary world, and dramatize
the effects of the Gospel on modern characters. A representative
example would be *Jesus of Montreal*, which pursues the stories of
Jesus via parallels and interactions between the Gospels as scripture
and drama, and the lives of people in the contemporary world.[65]

As I will argue later, *Son of Man* puts the distinction between
biographical Jesus-film and transfigurative Christ-film into question.
The film's setting is the modern word, but there is nothing in the lines
of the narrative that is not also in the gospels. Contemporary reality
functions here not as an enclosing and defining context, but rather
as a theatrical backdrop for a religious drama; one that is posited on
the problem posed by Dostoevsky in his 'Grand Inquisitor' fantasy
in *The Brothers Karamazov*: what happens when Jesus is suddenly
revealed in the context of modern life? Or in the evangelical slogan:
if Jesus returned, would you recognize him?

1

'Half-god, half-man': Nikos Kazantzakis's *The Last Temptation* and Martin Scorsese's *The Last Temptation of Christ*

You may have heard of the Blessed Mountain.
It is the highest mountain in our world.
Should you reach the summit you would have only one
desire,
and that to descend and be with those who dwell in the
deepest valley.
That is why it is called the Blessed Mountain.

KAHLIL GIBRAN[1]

I

For Nikos Kazantzakis, Jesus was both truly man and truly God, and the novelist set himself the task of finding some means of representing this unique being within the boundaries of prose fiction:

> Great things happen when God mixes with man. Without man, God would have no mind on this Earth to reflect upon his

creatures intelligibly and to examine, fearfully yet impudently, his wise omnipotence. He would have on this Earth no heart to pity the concerns of others and to struggle to beget virtues and cares which God either did not want, or forgot, or was afraid to fashion. He breathed upon man, however, giving him the power and audacity to continue creation.[2]

Although apparently denying divine omniscience (and indeed attributing to God indifference, amnesia and fear), Kazantzakis here fleshes out a persuasive model for understanding the purpose of incarnation. Mortal consciousness provides a perspective on existence that must be epistemologically different from divine knowledge. To know earthly intelligence, feel human pity, encounter 'the struggle to beget virtue and cares' – these are forms of experiential awareness accessible only to man or to an incarnate God. When Kazantzakis's work was published, this image of a passible God provoked outrage, particularly in his own Greek Orthodox Church,[3] while today it has become much more familiar. Indeed Alister E. McGrath goes so far as to suggest that it has become a 'new orthodoxy' for modern Christians to speak of a God who suffers within our world.[4] Rowan Williams finds this emphasis as far back as the post-Apostolic writings of Ignatius of Antioch:

God was active to save in Jesus of Nazareth; but this activity extends to the suffering and death of Jesus. Is this suffering (so to speak) purely 'instrumental' to God? Or is it *his* suffering?[5]

In the twentieth century Dietrich Bonhoeffer, Jürgen Moltmann, Kazoh Kitamori[6] and many others have written eloquently of the pain and suffering of God, of 'the love of the Son and the grief of the Father'.[7] If Jesus lived fully as a man of his own time, in Brian Hebblethwaite's words, 'subjecting himself to the limitations of real humanity in order to achieve his purposes of revelation and reconciliation',[8] then he suffered as a man; if God was truly revealing himself in Jesus, then as Hebblethwaite says, the incarnation must also have left its mark on God:

It lies at the heart of Christianity to suppose that God's omnipotence was both exercised and revealed in his becoming man, subjecting himself to cruel limitations and dying a cruel death. Moreover, that humanity and that human experience are believed to have been permanently taken into the being of God.[9]

The suffering of Jesus, says Rowan Williams, is in some way 'taken into God'.[10] 'God's "pain"', affirms Kitamori, 'is at once his "love"'.[11] 'I felt', wrote Kazantzakis in his notebook, 'the "suffering god" deeply within me'.[12]

God, affirms Kazantzakis, is incomplete without man. But the contrary is also true:

> But man, without God, born as he is unarmed, would have been obliterated by hunger, fear and cold; and if he survived these, he would have crawled like a slug midway between the lions and lice; and if with incessant struggle he managed to stand on his hind legs, he would never have been able to escape the tight, warm, tender embrace of his mother the monkey.[13]

By divine *afflatus* alone man becomes capable of intellectual and emotional creativity. As recipient of that godly breath, he acquires 'the power and audacity to continue creation' and to do God's work in the world.[14] 'Man without God' is a mere animal, haunted by his anthropoid ancestry, and struggling to extricate himself from the coils of evolution. But conversely God without man could have no direct physical knowledge of the human existence that he himself had created.

In this remarkable meditation, Kazantzakis links the dual substance of Christ with the dual nature of man as the product of both nature and God. Creationism and evolution are juxtaposed as respectively theocentric and anthropocentric explanations of the universe. Evolution gets man up onto his hind legs. But the breath of God makes him want to stand. In his autobiographical work *Report to Greco*, Kazantzakis recalled the two great lightning bolts of scientific knowledge that shook his faith as a young man: the solar system and the theory of evolution.[15] The latter destroyed for him the creation story of Genesis:

> The Lord God did not breathe into his nostrils the breath of life, did not give him an immortal soul. Like all other creatures, he is a rung in the infinite chain of animals, a grandson or great-grandson

of the ape. If you scratch our hide a little, if you scratch our soul a little, beneath it you will find our grandmother the monkey![16]

Obsessively the young Kazantzakis used to watch the behaviour of a neighbour's pet monkey, now seen as 'a caricature of man'. He writes, 'Was this my grandmother? . . . was I not a son of God, but of the monkey?'[17] He gives the monkey wine to drink and finds himself in its quasi-sexual embrace; as he writes, 'Its whole body pressed against mine, it kept sighing like a human'.[18] He views the encounter as a 'black Annunciation' and the monkey as some 'dark angel departing from my window'.[19] This attempt to bond with a simian is seen in the autobiographical narrative as both a liberation from dogma and a temptation to embark on a downward course of rediscovering the animal life of the flesh to search for the dark human roots that Darwin had uncovered.

Kazantzakis's view of the 'dual substance' of Christ assumed then that the two natures were utterly distinct, absolutely different and violently inimical one to another. In taking on human flesh, Jesus inherited and inhabited the contaminated body of human evolution, which Kazantzakis considered a dark material vulnerable to the influence of chthonic powers. Human beings, made equally in the image of God, share this ontological conflict:

> Within me are the dark immemorial forces of the Evil One, human and pre-human; within me too are the luminous forces, human and pre-human, of God – and my soul is the arena where these two armies have clashed and met.[20]

Christian theologians throughout the centuries have struggled to define this 'absolute paradox' as Kierkegaard called the incarnation, to keep the two natures distinct, yet to explain their mysterious concurrence, and to understand how the two natures could have interacted in the one person, Jesus Christ. Kazantzakis's talk of God 'mixing' with humanity seems to fall into the 'heresy' the confusion of the natures, against which those early credal statements sought so carefully to guard:

> Now this is the catholic faith, that we worship one God in Trinity, and Trinity in Unity, without either confusing the persons or dividing the substance.[21]

More than any other foundational doctrine of Christianity, this supposedly symmetrical and stable relationship between the persons of the Trinity has proved in practice a site of controversy. Kazantzakis was a novelist rather than a theologian, but his imaginative attempts to revalue the two natures, to think and feel across what St Thomas Aquinas called that great 'impassible' boundary,[22] deserve to be read alongside the more fully developed philosophical arguments of contemporary Christology.

II

Kazantzakis's Jesus is predominantly human, 'full of weakness, self-doubt, and ambivalence'.[23] He is not at first consciously aware of his own divine status, his mission of salvation or his destiny of crucifixion. He encounters his divinity as something hostile and alien: a possession, a persecution, a haunting. Although messianic hope is second nature to him, as he is physically and emotionally joined to the suffering body of the Israelite people,[24] he does not initially associate the coming with his own destiny. God comes to him as a dementia, a seizure or the sensation of claws dug into his skull. This seems less like a perfect hypostatic union than an uneasy affiliation between a weak and fearful human consciousness and a slumbering, latent divinity. Throughout the novel Jesus retains a love of life and of the earth, which seems to conflict with his divine destiny. This attachment is focused in his love for Mary Magdalene, his soul mate.[25] In interior dialogue with a divine voice (a conversation dramatized as Jesus talking to himself), he affirms this conflict and this loyalty:

> I don't care about the kingdom of heaven. I like the earth. I want to marry, I tell you; I want Magdalene.[26]

In the anachronistically named desert 'monastery' (a version of an Essene community that also recalls Kazantzakis's own experiences of monastic communities as described in the 'Mt. Athos' and 'Sinai' chapters of *Report to Greco*), Jesus confesses and is absolved,[27] although in orthodox teaching he was of course incapable of sin: 'His subjection to human weaknesses in common with us did not mean that he shared our sins.'[28] Kazantzakis relates a number of Christ's parables but then supplements them with alternative endings. Lazarus, for instance, persuades God to refresh the rich man for all eternity,[29] and the foolish virgins are invited into the wedding.[30] Kazantzakis writes, 'Man forgives . . . is it possible then that God does not?'[31] He even conceives the possibility that ultimately God's mercy might prove infinite, and the devil be welcomed back into heaven like the prodigal son.[32] He gives Judas a special place in the working-out of his destiny, flirts closely with pagan symbolism and contemplates abdicating the responsibility of the cross. During the final 'temptation' 'dream' he lives as a family man with a number of sexual partners. In the same vision he rejects the formation of his own doctrinal legacy both in the gospel according to Matthew and in the teaching of Paul.

This predominantly monophysist account however provides only a partial reading of the novel. Kazantzakis's Jesus may not be conscious of his identity and destiny, but is certainly subconsciously aware of them at the level of dream and vision, where much of the novel's narrative operates. Judas sees the cross foreshadowed in Jesus's eyes,[33] and Jesus sees in Judas the vision of his own crucifixion. Jesus speaks in a kind of instinctive prophecy of a messiah much like himself:

> He will die, die wearing his rags . . . He will die all alone at the top of a barren mountain, wearing on his head a crown of thorns.[34]

However resistant and reluctant a messiah he may be, Jesus leaves home to find God, to turn flesh into spirit, and to seek paradise;[35] thus he spends the entire novel pursuing a spiritual journey that will eventually lead him to Golgotha. The structure of his journey, which corresponds loosely to the four phases mapped out in Kazantzakis's sketchbook (son of the carpenter, son of man, son of David, son of God),[36] shows a Jesus growing through successive stages of evolution into consciousness of his mission in a way perhaps suggested by Luke: 'Jesus grew in wisdom and stature, and in favour with God and men' (Luke 2.52).

Each stage begins with a significant experience and a life-changing development in consciousness. In the monastery Jesus realizes through the vision of the coupling serpents that 'everything has two meanings',[37] and that the snakes represent human desires. As Kazantzakis writes, 'he was able for the first time to look into the darkness of his heart and distinguish, one by one, the serpents, which were hissing within him'.[38] As the gospel relates, 'He did not need man's testimony about man, for he knew what was in a man' (John 2.25). Immediately after this Jesus admits that he has a prompting to 'speak to men'[39] and, though unsure of what he will say, has confidence in God to inspire him: 'I'll open my mouth, and God will do the talking.'[40] In this first phase, the 'son of man' phase, Jesus preaches a gospel of love,[41] partly through an adaptation of the Sermon on the Mount, and partly through the 'supplemented' parables.[42] In this phase he saves Mary Magdalene from stoning.[43] This is Jesus the prophet of love, who moves through Galilee like a bridegroom welcoming the people to a wedding in heaven. Forgiveness is infinite;[44] love replaces law ('The law goes contrary to my heart.')[45] This phase draws to a close with Jesus attempting to open a dialogue with God and initially meeting 'an abrupt silence'.[46] But like Christ in Gethsemane, Kazantzakis's Jesus finds the answer to his questions in submission to God's will:

'Lord, O Lord', he murmured, 'I cannot fight with you. Tonight I surrender my arms. Your will be done!'[47]

The second phase begins with baptism in the Jordan, where Jesus is inspired by John to assume the mantle of Israel's zealotry and prophetic rage. This Jesus is the 'Son of David', who now preaches a Nietzschean gospel of destruction. 'The tree is rotten',[48] and Jesus has inherited the Baptist's axe. To this phase belongs the temptation in the wilderness, where Jesus is initially visited in spirit by John. The three temptations of the snake, the lion and the burning archangel are the core temptations of humanity. The snake is desire, love of the earth, the yearning to have a wife and children and the hunger for Mary Magdalene. The lion is the fierce and violent passions of animal instinct: the visionary beast proclaims that he is 'the deepest voice of your deepest self'.[49] The archangel tempts Jesus to think of himself as God. As temptations of desire, power and authority, these correspond closely enough to the accounts of Matthew and Luke. In the gospels Jesus is not tempted to sin or crime and not offered the violent delights of human depravity. He is tempted by the most natural promptings of human instinct: hunger, evolutionary aspiration and the will to power.

This is where Kazantzakis parts company with the natural logic of the genre in which he is working. He admits that these promptings are constitutive temptations for human nature and should therefore be accepted as normative rather than as 'evil'. He does not however, as one might expect from his attachment to both pagan religions and modern philosophy, and from his affection for Dionysus,[50] Freidrich Nietzsche and Karl Marx, assert that these natural instincts have been perverted and demonized into 'temptations' merely by Christian ecclesiastical dogma. Kazantzakis was not, as William Blake described John Milton, unconsciously of the devil's party; he only thought that the devil should be given his due. His characterization of Judas – a figure he aimed to 'sanctify' against the dominant tradition that had demonized him[51] – gives a powerful and compelling voice to these instincts: the need for bread ('the foundation is the body')[52] and the search for justice through power ('the deliverance of Israel').[53]

But Jesus is explicitly counterpoised as Judas's opposite in every respect. In the temptation in the wilderness, in the continual ideological struggle with Judas, and in the 'Last Temptation' itself, Jesus shows himself fully a man with a man's weakness and desire but a man determined to wrestle with them and to transcend human limitations in a search for godliness. The temptations experienced in the wilderness bring knowledge of the human heart, belly and mind; this knowledge modifies and enriches Jesus's divine consciousness.

> For surely it is not with angels that he is concerned but with the descendants of Abraham. Therefore he had to be made like his brethren in every respect . . . For because he himself has suffered and been tempted . . . we have not a high priest who is unable to sympathize with our weaknesses, but one who in every respect has been tempted as we are, yet without sinning. (Heb 2.16–18; 4.15)

Kazantzakis's Jesus resists the temptations in the wilderness, survives the ordeal and goes on to master the final temptation from the cross. During this third phase, 'the Son of David' phase, Jesus seems at times indistinguishable from John the Baptist;[54] he wields the axe against the rotten tree and wages war against the old law. He is the Son of David, a messiah who will cleanse the world. The raising

of Lazarus[55] heralds the opening of the fourth phase, when Jesus
fully recognizes himself as Son of God. The awareness is terrifying
but also inevitable: God and humanity are one; Jesus the man must
submit himself to a divine weight of responsibility. This is the full
meaning of incarnation:

> If the strength of the soul was so all-powerful, then all the weight
> of perdition or salvation fell upon the shoulders of mankind; the
> borders of God and man are joined.[56]

Jesus reveals to Judas that he is the Messiah. In a prophetic vision
of Golgotha he reaffirms the prophecies of Isaiah: 'I am the one who
is going to die.'[57] He explains, 'For the world to be saved, I, of my
own will, must die.'[58] The shadow of the cross is seen to fall from
Jesus's own body.[59] Mary Magdalene anoints him for burial, and
Jesus declares his mission of salvation at the Last Supper. When he
bids Judas to go and to do what he has to do,[60] the passion play is
complete. He dies on the cross, crying, 'It is accomplished'.

It was as though he had said: Everything has begun.[61]

III

'Every man is half God, half man,' wrote Kazantzakis.[62] The duty
of a human being is to imitate the model provided by the divine and
human incarnated Christ:

> This book was written because I wanted to offer a supreme model
> to the man who struggles . . . In order to mount to the Cross, the
> summit of sacrifice, and to God, the summit of immateriality,
> Christ passed through all the stages which the man who struggles
> passes through. That is why his suffering is so familiar to us; that
> is why we share it, and why his final victory seems to us so much
> our own future victory. That part of Christ's nature which was
> profoundly human helps us to understand him and love him and
> to pursue his Passion as though it were our own. If he had not
> within him this warm human element, he would never be able to
> touch our hearts with such assurance and tenderness; he would

not be able to become a model for our lives. We struggle, we see
him struggle also, and we find strength. We see that we are not
all alone in the world; he is fighting at our side.
Every moment of Christ's life is a conflict and a victory. He
conquered the invincible enchantment of simple human pleasures;
he conquered temptations, continually transubstantiated flesh
into spirit, and ascended. Reaching the summit of Golgotha, he
mounted the Cross.[63]

However deeply coloured by his intimacy with Nietzsche, Lenin
and the Buddha, ultimately Kazantzakis was writing in *The Last
Temptation* a Christian affirmation. The book was written, he states,
'in a state of deep religious exaltation, with fervent love for Christ
. . . in Christian love'.[64] Kazantzakis believed that his imaginative
identification with Christ provided him with a specialized knowledge
inaccessible to theologians: 'while I was writing this book, I felt what
Christ felt. I became Christ. And I knew that great temptations,
extremely enchanting and often legitimate ones, came to hinder him
on his road to Golgotha. But how could the theologians know all
this?'[65]

Kazantzakis saw his work not as a repudiation of Christian
truth but rather as a revaluation of Christian spirituality for
a modern age. But this is not generally how the novel has been
read. Kiolkowski argued that Kazantzakis merely coloured in the
outlines of the biblical narrative and contrasted his raw 'imaginative
power' unfavourably with Robert Graves's meticulous biblical
scholarship.[66] Yet Kazantzakis was clearly attempting a theological
as well as an imaginative reworking of the life of Jesus. In trying, as
he explicitly affirmed, to 'supplement' both scripture and tradition,
he was undertaking a theological revision of key doctrinal matters
such as the incarnation and the atonement. Morton P. Levitt[67] drew
a parallel between Kazantzakis's revisionism and the 'flexible and
evolving canon' of Christian scripture in the first-century AD, in
particular the shift of contextual focus from Jewish prophecy to
Eastern mystery religions. '*The Last Temptation*', he argues, 'is
well within this religious tradition'. Kazantzakis's Jesus may not
be exactly the Jesus of the Athanasian creed and the definition of
Chalcedon. But he is a Jesus for the twentieth century. As Levitt
puts it, 'What at first seems heresy is in fact an act of devotion.'[68]

IV

In *The Last Temptation*, Kazantzakis confronted the theological and fictional problems of the incarnation head on, with results that have obviously remained controversial. When Martin Scorsese conceived the idea of adapting the novel into film (with even more controversial repercussions), he followed Kazantzakis into this doctrinal minefield with reckless enthusiasm.

> I found the representation of Christ, stressing the human side of His nature without denying that he is God, the most accessible to me. His divine side doesn't fully comprehend what the human side has to do; how He has to transform Himself and eventually become the sacrifice on the cross – Christ the man only learns about this a little at a time. In the whole first section of the book, He is acting purely on human emotions and human psychology, so he becomes confused and troubled. I thought this neurotic – even psychotic – Jesus was not very different from the shifts of mood and psychology that you find glimpses of in the Gospels.[69]

Despite the disclaimer with which the film opens, 'This film is not based on the Gospels but upon this fictional exploration of the eternal spiritual conflict', Scorsese clearly thought of the film as involving scriptural exegesis as well as imaginative dramatization. He suggests that the 'confused and troubled' consciousness of Jesus could be inferred from the gospel narratives.[70] Like Kazantzakis, Scorsese had no doubts about Jesus's divinity and dual nature but felt that a representation of Jesus in film should be more humanized in order to engage a modern audience:

> I believe that Jesus is fully divine, but the teaching at Catholic schools placed such an emphasis on the divine side that if Jesus walked into a room, you'd know He was God because He glowed in the dark, instead of being just another person. But if He was like that, we always thought, then when the temptations came to Him, surely it was easy to resist them because He was God.[71]

'Since the earliest times', says Macquarrie, 'a kind of unconscious docetism has been at work'[72] in Christian tradition. Scorsese needed to emphasize the human nature, not simply because it was

Christologically correct, but because it was necessary in order to create character and drama in film. The film was designed not as an epic but as 'an intimate character study',[73] and its key psychological and moral drama was to be, as in Kazantzakis, the struggle between the human and divine natures:

> I found this an interesting idea, that the human nature of Jesus was fighting him all the way down the line, because it can't conceive of Him being God. I thought this would be great drama and force people to take Jesus seriously – at least to re-evaluate his teachings.[74]

Scorsese's scriptwriter and collaborator Paul Schrader, a former Calvinist divinity student, was also fully alive to these issues and spoke of them with learned scholarship:[75]

> The two major heresies which emerged in the early Christian Church were the Arian heresy, from Arius, which essentially said that Jesus was a man who pretended to be God,[76] and the other was the Docetan heresy, which said Jesus was really a God who, like a very clever actor, pretended to be a man. . . . *The Last Temptation of Christ* may err on the side of Arianism, but it does little to counteract the 2,000 years of erring on the other side, and it was pleasant to see this debate from the early Church splashed all over the front pages.

The most fundamental distinction between fictions that evade, and those which, like *The Last Temptation*, seek to engage imaginatively with the incarnate Christ, is the difference between objective and subjective representation. In fictions that show only the reflection of light or shadow cast by Christ over the people around him or 'the effects he produces on other people'[77] or in works that approach Jesus via the point of view of other biblical or invented characters, Jesus is an object, but not a subject, in the fictional narrative. He is there, and the effects of his being there can be represented, but he is not accessible to the novelist's psychological curiosity. His being is set apart, off limits, and 'hidden with Christ in God' (Col 3.4). Kazantzakis broke this taboo and treated Jesus's dual nature as open to subjective representation, partly as Robin Riley puts it by 'introducing psychological instability and doubt into the

Jesus character's experience',[78] and partly by treating the divine as a domain accessible to the human imagination. Riley goes on to suggest that Martin Scorsese also saw the possibility of 'placing viewers within Jesus's existential condition of doubt through point-of-view camera work and voice-over narration'.[79] Scorsese himself described this technique in detail. He admitted to using:

> a lot of moving camera . . . a very fluid and almost nervous way of moving the camera. Because [Jesus] was unsure of himself, the camera would be hiding and creeping around Him, caught between following him, and, at the same time, trying to pull back.[80]

In Franco Zeffirelli's *Jesus of Nazareth*, Riley goes on, Jesus's 'consciousness' is 'a sacred space inaccessible to viewers'.[81] Scorsese's approach is to get 'inside Jesus' mind', and to attempt to 'gain access to an area inaccessible to the church itself, Jesus' conscience'.[82] Again Riley acknowledges this process as a theological activity and a work of scriptural exegesis (though of a kind he finds repellent). As he writes, 'Scorsese has taken a position that his film provides new information about the Christian saviour.'[83] Although clearly many saw this effort as blasphemous, Scorsese himself called it 'an affirmation of faith'.[84] 'I made it', he writes, 'as a prayer, an act of worship. I wanted to be a priest. My whole life has been movies and religion. That's it. Nothing else.'[85]

'Whenever filmmakers approach the character of Jesus Christ, as many have done in the short history of cinema', writes Lloyd Baugh, 'inevitably there is a Christology discernible in the image they create.'[86] Just as Kazantzakis sought to 'supplement' the gospels, so Scorsese hoped, according to Riley, to extend and to elaborate on traditions of Jesus representation and to add something new and different to human knowledge of Christ and therefore of God. Certainly Schrader saw this in Kazantzakis: 'the greatness of the book is its metaphorical leap into this imagined temptation; that's what separates it from the Bible and makes it a commentary upon it'.[87]

V

Both novel and film approach the Promethean task of representing Jesus as God and man in a complete and complex Christology combining the human and the divine. Both novel and film break the taboo of religious fiction by treating the mind of God as accessible to the human imagination, and the taboo of the secular Jesus-novel by insisting on the historical and psychological veracity of the dual nature. Both novel and film present a Jesus scandalous or offensive to Christians of many creeds, yet do so while affirming a deeply Christian devotional commitment of faith and love.

Ultimately there is a distinction to be made. Kazantzakis, it seems to me, remains uncomfortably trapped within a fundamental dualism that sees human life as constructed from irreconcilable antinomies: flesh and spirit, evolution and creation, the body struggling to differentiate itself from its animal roots, and the divine spark donated from above.

> Struggle between the flesh and the spirit, rebellion and resistance, reconciliation and submission, and finally – the supreme purpose of the struggle – union with God: this was the ascent taken by Christ, the ascent which he invites us to take as well.[88]

Although Kazantzakis began with the Christological language of 'dual substance', the two natures of Christ seem ultimately in his novel anything but hypostatically united. Flesh and spirit, body and soul, are always seen as irreconcilable opposites. The path that his Jesus follows towards greater understanding is a way of *askesis*, of spiritual struggle, that entails divesting the spirit of its encumbrance of flesh. To get nearer to God, you have to get further away from the human condition. Kazantzakis writes, 'In order to mount to the Cross, the summit of sacrifice, and to God, the summit of immateriality, Christ passed through all the stages, which the man who struggles passes through.' This path of spiritual ascent is always from the material to the immaterial[89] and from the flesh to the spirit. The 'Last Temptation' is the culmination of this process and the final and ultimate rejection of the domain of the senses, the realm of the flesh and the world of common human destiny. But this seems to be a betrayal of the principle of incarnation, since it shows Jesus unable to reconcile godliness and life in the body. As Macqarrie says, 'to save the whole of man Christ must have taken on the whole of man'.[90] 'What has not been assumed', said

Gregory of Nazianzus, 'has not been healed; it is what is united to His divinity that is saved.'[91]

Scorsese by contrast views the temptation through a 'sacramental' view of life, which admits no absolute separation between body and spirit or between flesh and Word. As Michael Bliss puts it,

> through the film, it is the reward of God's plan that one can usually only realise the spiritual through the material realm. What the Last Temptation posits is that once one realises the essential divinity in all material things – . . . one transcends the material aspect of objects and sees deep into their true nature, which is divine.[92]

As a number of critics have recently argued, Scorsese's films reveal a world in which religion and reality continually interpenetrate. Richard A. Blake has written of the sacramental universe of Scorsese's films, where material objects reveal the absence of the holy as well as its presence.[93] In Scorsese the spiritual is always immanent in the material, and the material always ready to split open to disclose its spiritual content. This 'sacramentalizing of the real', as Leo Braudy[94] calls it, provides a different conception of the relationship between materiality and the divine from Kazantzakis's tortured dualism.

Christine Hoff Kraemer has argued that Scorsese shared Kazantzakis's dualism but with a fundamental difference:

> The common . . . assumption has long been that where there is a dichotomy, one side must triumph over the other; one side must be associated with good while the other is associated with evil. Yet Scorsese's delicate handling of the life of Jesus demonstrates that this is not so . . . Spirit and flesh may be at war, but as the Christ, Jesus affirms both to be good. Though his destiny is to take a path of nearly pure spirit, he is tempted by the beauty of material creation because it too is of God.[95]

'Both sides of the paradox', as John Macquarrie said of the incarnation, 'must find adequate expression.'[96] Here in Scorsese's film, flesh and spirit can find a possible, though never easy or painless, reconciliation. This truly is, as far as the world of art is concerned, incarnation or the Word become flesh.

VI

The distinction I am making here between Kazantzakis and Scorsese is a distinction between dualistic and holistic Christian theologies: one docetic, the other incarnational; one in search (to use Rowan Williams's dichotomy) of 'enlightenment', the other of 'wholeness'.[97] But this assumes that Kazantzakis was working, as he claimed to be, within a framework of Christian ideas. Was this actually the case? Or would it be truer to concur with the view summarized by Darren J. N. Middleton, that 'his religious vision falls outside the traditional bounds of Christian speculation'?[98] A voraciously eclectic thinker, Kazantzakis absorbed and adopted philosophical ideas from a number of sources and authorities. He was particularly influenced for instance by Buddhism, which seems to be strongly reflected in his notion of spiritual ascent. In *Zorba the Greek*, Buddha is the 'last man', the 'pure soul' which has 'emptied itself'.[99] In *Report to Greco*, Kazantzakis described a glimpse of the possibility of enlightenment that is expressed in this same language of an upward spiritual climb:

> An ascent flashed before me, a rocky ascent with a red track upon it and a man who was climbing . . . I suddenly discerned the supreme peak above me – the Silence, Buddha. Finally I saw the yearning which began to rage inside me, the yearning to extricate myself forever from all deceptions.[100]

'The message of the Buddha', says Carnegie Samuel Calians, 'is to free oneself from fear and hope by giving up desire. Kazantzakis, a man of desires, had an undying struggle with the Buddha, which left its imprint as indicated on his tombstone epitaph.'[101] Many other critics have identified naturally in Kazantzakis's notion of spiritual ascent the Buddhist search for enlightenment. As Lewis Owens writes:

> Kazantzakis . . . considered humanity's greatest duty to be the transubstantiation of all matter into spirit, an idea drawn predominantly from Buddha and from Bergson's immanent life force, the *élan vital*, which seeks freedom from material obstruction and imprisonment.[102]

Charalampos-Dēmētrēs Gounelas defined Kazantzakis's philosophy as 'a conjunction between Christian asceticism and Buddhism'.[103] But it is not necessary to seek explanation in other faiths and philosophies for Kazantzakis's ascetic dualism. The notion of the 'spiritual ascent' lies at the heart of the Greek Orthodox spirituality in which he was raised, especially of its monastic culture. It was articulated in *The Ladder of Divine Ascent* by St John Climacos, a seventh-century writer whose memory is celebrated twice a year in the Orthodox Church. The book describes how the spiritual struggler must pass through 30 stages of spiritual development upwards towards the ultimate goal of *askesis* – *theosis*, divinization and salvation from mortality. Paintings and mosaics of the ladder are to be found prominently in the narthex of some of the churches of the holy mountain of Athos.[104]

Throughout his life Kazantzakis was fascinated by the monastic ideal of withdrawal from the world and by the ascetic *vita contemplative* of the desert fathers. As a young man he undertook pilgrimages, as described in *Report to Greco*, to the monastic communities of Mt Athos and to St Catherine's monastery in Sinai. From the hermit Father Makarios on Mt Athos, he receives the uncompromising message that there is only one way to salvation.

> Ascent. To climb a series of steps. From the full stomach to hunger, from the slaked throat to thirst, from joy to suffering. God sits at the summit of hunger, thirst and suffering; the devil sits at the summit of the comfortable life. Choose.[105]

One would expect to find such views promulgated by ascetics of whatever creed, but the 'high Christology' implied by such asceticism runs deep in Orthodox theology. Indeed some of its leading authorities concur that there is a particularly distinct continuity between monastic culture and lay belief. 'There is a great richness of forms of spiritual life to be found within the bounds of Orthodoxy', writes Vladimir Lossky, 'but monasticism remains the most classical of all.'[106] 'The best way to penetrate 'Orthodox spirituality' said Paul Evdokimov, 'is to enter it through monasticism'.[107]

The Orthodox Church of course owed its separate identity to those same disputes over the 'dual substance' of Christ with which we began. The schism of 1054 was triggered by the addition of the *filioque* clause to the Creed, a doctrinal difference that still separates the Western and Eastern churches.

> Western theology confesses that in the immanent Trinity the Holy Spirit proceeds from the Father and the Son, and Eastern theology confesses that the Holy Spirit proceeds from the Father only.[108]

In Orthodox theology 'God is the wholly Other',[109] 'absolutely transcendent',[110] and the 'divine incomprehensibility'.[111] Proximity to God consists in a 'spirituality of the surpassing of all created being'.[112] God is immaterial and unknowable, so to approach him is to effect a 'transition from the created to the uncreated'.[113] Reconciliation with God can be achieved only through a 'way of ascension',[114] which entails detachment from all created things and ends only in a transformation of the human into the divine or a 'union with God or deification'.[115] Orthodox belief deploys the distinctions, devised by Pseudo-Dionysius the Areopagite (late fifth/early sixth centuries), between cataphatic and apophatic, and between affirmative and negative theologies:

> The first leads us to some knowledge of God, but is an imperfect way. The perfect way, the only way that is fitting in regard to God, who is of His very nature unknowable, is the second, which leads us finally to total ignorance. All knowledge has as its object that which is. Now God is beyond all that exists. In order to approach Him it is necessary to deny all that is inferior to Him, that is to say, all that which is.[116]

Lossky then defines the path towards God in terms of an 'ascent' that chimes exactly with Kazantzakis's language of spiritual struggle:

> It is by unknowing that one may know Him who is above every possible object of knowledge. Proceeding by negations one ascends from the inferior degrees of being to the highest, by progressively setting aside all that can be known, in order to draw near to the unknown in the darkness of absolute ignorance.[117]

It has been suggested that Orthodoxy has always been instinctively more docetist than the Western church, and that the contrast can be illustrated by comparing the Eastern Orthodox icon, with its hieratic elevated figures of spiritual authority, with the suffering body on the cross. As Allen writes, 'The focus of Eastern Christianity was on Jesus' incarnation, the process by which the divine being descended from heaven to become a man.'[118] In Christ, Lossky states, 'transcendence is made immanent'.[119] Icons are 'expressions of the inexpressible, and have become possible thanks to the revelation of God, which was accomplished in the incarnation of the Son'.[120] Here contingency is virtually an accident of the incarnation, where the perfect almost reluctantly reveals itself through imperfection. As Rowan Williams said of Gnosticism, this theology entails 'a flight from the particular':

> If this is so, there can be no sense of human experience in its entirety and its individual variety as the theatre of God's saving work, a work of art to be completed. What is 'authentic' in human life is solely what is radically free from the conditioned and the historical.[121]

These tensions are certainly present in East–West Christian dialogue, as they have been present ever since writing about the incarnation of Jesus first began; and one can certainly link Eastern spirituality with high Christologies, and vice versa. Process theology and the suffering God are scarcely compatible with the 'absolutely transcendent' God of Orthodox theologians, who insist that no created thing has any communion with the supreme nature.[122] Even the *filioque* dispute itself, which Ware admits is 'technical and obscure'[123] but by no means 'trivial', remains to characterize God the Father in Eastern spirituality as sole begetter and to clear the Holy Spirit of any possible contamination from the human nature adopted by the Son.[124]

VII

I shall now proceed to compare the 'Last Temptation' sequences in novel and film in order to test the hypothesis that Kazantzakis and Scorsese represent widely different points on the spectrum of Christological doctrine.

> Temptation – the Last Temptation – was waiting for him upon the Cross. Before the fainted eyes of the Crucified the spirit of the

Evil One, in an instantaneous flash, unfolded the deceptive vision of a calm and happy life.[125]

Should the 'Last Temptation' sequence of the novel (chapters 30–33) be read as a 'deceptive vision' or as a confrontation with what Kazantzakis called 'the invincible enchantment of simple human pleasures',[126] which refers to temptations that are as natural to human life as spirituality? If the former, then the entire sequence narrated in these chapters is a dream or a hallucination constructed by the 'Evil One', and the Last Temptation is a mere momentary distraction from the stern duty of salvation. Renunciation of this world and its pleasures is the price that has to be paid for spiritual transcendence. If the latter, then it scarcely needs the mediation of the 'Evil One' to reveal that love, sex, the pleasures of family and children and affinity with the earth, are natural human affections and that, as Alfred North Whitehead put it, 'appetitive vision and physical enjoyment have equal claim to priority in creation'.[127] On this reading the temptations are both 'enchanting' and 'legitimate', and the death of the cross should subsume and enfold the temptations into a vision of ultimate reconciliation between God and humanity, humanity and the earth and spirit and body. The world is not the stony wilderness where Mary Magdalene meets her death, but a place of beauty in which humanity can meet God without surrendering physical nature. It is a world re-enchanted by God's return and humanity's spiritual struggle to realize God. In terms of atonement, the former view is consistent with ideas of satisfaction and penalty, since Christ is paying the price of renunciation as well as the penalty of sin. Humanity is so utterly and originally corrupt that only the supreme penalty of death can redeem us from the doom of divine displeasure. But the latter is more consistent with significant currents of modern Christology, since it shows Christ as a God who 'so loved the world' and humanity that his attachment to it constituted a true sharing of humanity in all its joys and sorrows, pains and pleasures.

God in Christ takes upon *himself* responsibility for all the world's ills. God bears the brunt of suffering and evil by subjecting *himself* to their cruelty and horror. By so doing, he reveals, as he could in no other way, the reality and depth and costly nature of his forgiving love. And by this identification of himself with us and our predicament he draws us to himself in an utterly moral and personal way.[128]

This of course has profound implications for the 'imitation of Christ', one of Kazantzakis's key themes ('I became Christ'),[129] and for our whole view of the material world:

> The belief that God's love is enacted and made manifest in the Incarnation and the Cross . . . shows that the material is not alien to the spiritual, but that the body is to be seen as the vehicle of the spirit. This is spelled out further in Christian sacramental theology, and is often generalised as a sacramental view of the universe.[130]

I shall argue in conclusion that Kazantzakis's novel is closer to the 'deception' reading of the 'Last Temptation', in which the world of the flesh is thoroughly contaminated by sinful desire and the presence of evil, and only a fierce asceticism can achieve the renunciation and purification required for redemption. Martin Scorsese's film, on the other hand, seems to me to bring about the reconciliation of spirit and flesh in a sacramental vision of a re-enchanted world, fulfilling Kazantzakis's stated intention

> to reconcile those two primordial forces which are so contrary to one another, to make them realise that they are not enemies but rather fellow-workers, so that they might rejoice in their harmony.[131]

VIII

In the novel, the 'Last Temptation' itself begins as an experience of resurrection. In keeping with mediaeval symbolism and iconography, the cross has transformed into a flowering tree,[132] Golgotha into paradise, and pain into healing: 'the compassionate tree shed its flowers, one by one, into his thorn-entangled hair'.[133] The first suggestion that this resurrection is illusory appears in the figure of the 'guardian angel', who accompanies Jesus throughout the vision. The angel is suspiciously humanoid and sensuous with eyes 'full of passion',[134] hairy legs and sweaty armpits. 'You lived your entire Passion in a dream'[135] he tells Jesus. Reality and dream are inverted; Jesus mistakes reality for dream and dream for reality. The dream offers the simple pleasures of the earth: 'Wine, laughter, the lips of a woman.'[136] The earth seems transfigured into paradise, where 'the earth is good'[137] but only because Jesus's perception of it has changed; previously he was alienated from the earth but now reconciled with it. 'Harmony', Kazantzakis writes, 'between the earth and the heart, Jesus of Nazareth: that is the Kingdom of heaven.'[138] The angel shows Jesus a young black bull tethered in a thicket and offers to release him. Here Jesus is initiated into pagan mystery, since the bull is bull-horned Dionysos himself, 'a dark and wounded God'[139] who represents the physical being 'full of virility'.[140] As the bull is released and begins to mount a field full of heifers, Jesus is rejoined by Mary Magdalene. But this Mary seems of a piece with the dream and an instrument of delusion: 'he saw her eye frolic seductively, cunningly, like the eye of the angel'.[141] Mary inducts Jesus into a new faith in the world and the body: 'I never knew the world was so beautiful or the flesh so holy.'[142] For Kazantzakis this is a new incarnation: 'The road by which the mortal becomes immortal, the road by which God descends to earth in human shape.'[143]

What happens to Mary Magdalene however confirms the status of this 'deceptive vision'. Immediately following their reunion, she finds herself outside the dream paradise and in a barren landscape – 'Rocks, flints, a few brambles' – and there meets the death by stoning (now at the hands of Saul of Tarsus) that she would have received had Jesus not saved her. This is more than a 'deceptive vision'; it is a reordering of reality, the emergence of an alternative history in which the saving power of the Messiah has never been exercised; it is an alternative reality in which Mary pays the full penalty of the Mosaic Law. Jesus's mind leaves his body and follows Mary in the form of a hawk. By this clumsy device, Jesus is able to observe what happens outside his own dream. But the episode makes clear the implications of the 'Last Temptation': the world really does lie unredeemed, sins unforgiven, the old law still in place and mankind unsaved.

Still inside his dream, the death of Mary hardly touches Jesus. Awakening as if in the tomb on 'rich mortuary soil'[144] Jesus has only an impression of Mary's death, 'stones, a woman, and blood',[145] but is further seduced by the song of another woman: 'a weaver sitting before her machine and singing. Her voice was exceedingly sweet and full of complaint'.[146] The angel guides Jesus towards another mate, Mary the sister of Lazarus, since all women are one woman or anonymous representatives of the archetypal feminine. Mary the weaver recalls Athena the master weaver as well as Odysseus's faithful Penelope. Earlier Mary Magdalene, unconsciously preparing for his death, had been shown weaving a woollen cloak to protect her lover against the cold.[147] In that earlier passage, she is also guardian of a pomegranate tree; so she is Persephone as well as Penelope. Jesus met her there as the bridegroom from the Song of Songs and raised her from the ground as both a bride and as the human soul.[148] Mary, the sister of Lazarus, is also described as 'seeking' Jesus; so she also, like the priestess in D. H. Lawrence's story *The Man Who Died*, is Isis in search.

The angel however gives Jesus a false account of Mary Magdalene's death; pierced by the divine arrow, 'at the peak of her happiness . . . can there be a greater joy for a woman'?[149] The discrepancy between his description and the earlier narrative makes clear again the distinction between reality and 'deceptive vision'.[150] Jesus drifts into polygamy, taking both Mary and Martha as wives, under the seductive advice of the angel: 'That is the way the Saviour comes: gradually, from embrace to embrace, from son to son. That is the road.'[151] The first realization of the true status of the vision comes through Mary, who has a dream, a dream of reality, within the dream. Instinctively she realizes that their dream life is a tissue of 'Lies created by the Tempter to deceive us'.[152]

But Jesus's meeting with Paul again confirms that the vision is not just illusion but rather the imaginative realization of a world in which Christ has not died. Paul has no choice but to construct the fiction of Jesus's death and resurrection: 'The Crucified and Resurrected Jesus has been the one precious consolation for the honest man.'[153] This belief survives the realization that it has no historical foundation: 'I create the truth, create it out of obstinacy and longing and faith.'[154] Jesus repudiates Paul's theology but does not shake his faith. 'Who asked you?' responds Paul, 'I have no need of your permission. Why do you stick your nose in my affairs?' It is the Grand Inquisitor's question from *The Brothers Karamazov*: 'Why hast thou come now to hinder us?'[155] Paul has become the Paul of *The Brook Kerith*, because Jesus has not died on the Cross.

But this is not of course where Kazantzakis comes to rest. The arrival of the apostles signals the breaking of the spell, the enchantment dissolved and the illusion revealed. The guardian angel was Satan. Jesus completes his final cry, and empties himself into the death of the cross. Both the passion, and the novel, are 'accomplished'.

Scorsese's film treatment seems to have shared the same objectives as the novel. The 'Last Temptation' was to be in his words represented as a 'fantasy', a 'hallucination' and a 'diabolical temptation'.[156] In an early draft of the script, there were to be two figures of Jesus; one remained unchanged on the cross, while the other lived through this hallucination of ordinary life. This technique would have secured a visible gap between unredeemed reality and deceptive vision. But when the angel shows Jesus the world, saying 'we really envy you', where Kazantzakis could fabricate in prose a poetic paradise that also seems fully dreamlike, both enchanting and deceptive, Scorsese's camera shows only a real landscape of breath-taking beauty with Jesus and the angel poised at the edge like figures in a mediaeval or renaissance painting. The viewer is provided with no aesthetic or moral space in which such beauty could be identified as an illusion.

Scorsese's treatment, though often taken word for word and image for image from the novel, is radically different from Kazantzakis's in its dramatic and poetic effects. His choice of a beautiful young girl dressed in peasant costume but with the face and hair of a renaissance angel is a decisive departure. He considered using a young Arab boy or an old man[157] but settled on the young girl partly (and surely ironically) as an echo of Pasolini's angel Gabriel.[158] The angel remains throughout her performance sensitive and sympathetic; gone are Kazantzakis's transformations from angel to Ethiopian slave or the clear signals in the novel of demonic deceitfulness and dissimulation. In the draft script the angel is identified as Satan by Judas and assumes a suitably diabolical form:

As they watch he transforms himself into a death figure in a black monk's habit.

Jesus is left alone with the 'death figure', who speaks to him:

'I told you would meet again . . . There's nothing you can do. You lived this life. You accepted it. It's over now. Just finish it and die like a man.'[159]

Jesus has to crawl past the 'death figure' to make his way outside, where he begs the Father to restore him to the Cross.

In the final film version, the angel is certainly intended as Satan, explicitly identified by Kazantzakis as the 'Evil One'. Judas unmasks her, and we glimpse again the burning archangel of the temptation in the wilderness. The child's face, however, shows only hurt and disappointment. This is either a Satan of supremely compelling persuasiveness or a Satan who presides innocuously over the simple pleasures of everyday life, 'the invincible enchantment of simple human pleasures' and the 'harmless attachment to places and things'[160] like some minor pagan domestic god. The effect is utterly different from what it would have been, if the 'death figure' from Schrader's draft script had been retained.

It is also what Scorsese adds to Kazantzakis's narrative that complicates the representation. The angel's first action, in an interpolated sequence that has no place in the novel, is to take Jesus down from the cross, and to gently remove the nails and to kiss the wounded, bloodstained hands and feet.[161] The poetic impact of this moment is extraordinary. It has all the beauty of a renaissance deposition together with the highly charged eroticism of mediaeval Catholic martyrology (Scorsese admits that as a child such images made him go 'weak at the knees'). Many viewers have flinched at this moment in the film. Either Satan is duping everyone – character, actor, director, viewer – or the spectator is compelled to accept these images – images of healing, liberation from suffering, manumission from pain, images, in short, of redemption – at face value.

The complexity deepens when the angel draws a comparison with the story of Abraham and Isaac:

> Remember when he told Abraham to sacrifice his son? Just as Abraham lifted his knife, God saved Isaac. If he saved Abraham's son, don't you think he'd want to save his own? He tested you, and he's pleased. He doesn't want your blood.[162]

But it was not the devil in disguise, who called to Abraham, but the angel of the Lord; it was not the suggestion of Satan, but the command of God, that made Abraham stay his hand. Just as Kazantzakis supplemented Christ's parables with redemptive conclusions, so Scorsese retrospectively completed the parallel between the sacrifices of Isaac and of Jesus by arresting the process of crucifixion. Again this is entirely consistent with some modern Christologies. If the purpose of the passion is to enact and manifest God's love, then the supreme sacrifice has already been made, through suffering and subjection, and does not need to fulfil itself in death. Isaac was just as surely restored to Abraham, as Kierkegaard made clear, though he did not pay the penalty of death.[163] Hebblethwaite adds, 'God's forgiving love does not depend on the death of Christ, but rather is manifested and enacted in it.'[164] '*He doesn't want your blood.*'[165] The affection with which the angel kisses Christ's wounds echoes the love practised for centuries by Catholic Christians in the adoration of Christ's wounds or in the veneration of the cross. Here we see both human and divine love, enacted, manifested and mutually reciprocated. The identity of the liberator as Satan simply evaporates from the visual poetry of the film.

In the controversial scene where Jesus and Mary Magdalene make love, many viewers again seem to have had their vision obstructed by moral outrage. Jesus and Mary spend 50 seconds having sexual intercourse. But almost two minutes of screen time are devoted to Mary dressing the dead Jesus's wounds, which she washes and anoints with some kind of healing ointment. His body lies across her knees as in a *Pieta*. Here Mary is not anointing the body for burial but healing the body for a physical resurrection. Like the priestess of Isis in Lawrence's story, she heals the wounds of the cross with love and brings her Osiris back together with feminine power and sexual healing.

Scorsese faithfully follows the logic of Kazantzakis's 'deceptive vision': the invented gospel of Paul, the embittered disciples and Jerusalem in flames. But there is a substantial difference as exemplified in the description of Mary Magdalene's death. Kazantzakis shows the world deprived of salvation and Mary dying as she should have without Jesus's salvific intervention. Scorsese shows Mary Magdalene smiling beatifically in rapture as God takes her into the light. In the draft script Mary even says: 'Death is kind' (scene 77).[166] In Kazantzakis this is how the angel *pretends* she died.[167] In Kazantzakis this discrepancy is an element of satanic 'deception'. But for Scorsese this is how it should happen: Mary should be taken peacefully to God's mercy in a world of enchantment without any shadow of disillusion.

IX

The glamour of asceticism both drew and repelled Kazantzakis and to some degree persuaded him to see corporeal existence as a degradation and contamination of spirituality. He always wanted to ascend the holy mountain, the 'Blessed Mountain' of spiritual transcendence, but in keeping with the aphorism of Kahlil Gibran that prefaces this chapter, once at the summit, he always wanted to come down again. Nonetheless he left something of himself up there. Ultimately it is this passion for transcendence that explains why Kazantzakis's vision finally belongs, perhaps surprisingly, to 'Christology from above' rather than 'from below'.

> Kazantzakis relates materialism to Everyman, making Jesus resist the universal temptation to place comfort, security, reputation and progeny above the pain, loneliness and martyrdom of a life devoted to the spirit.[168]

He insisted so forcefully on Christ's humanity precisely because he was reacting so strongly against the relative abstractedness of a high Christology. But this docetism was within him as well as without. Even as a child, as he claims in *Report to Greco*, he wanted to be both hero and saint.[169] He clearly drew the aspiration from his immediate religious context, but his performance of it, if truly delineated, rendered him a strange and idiosyncratic figure within his culture. He was, in the end, a loyal son of his church, a heretic perhaps, but very much a Greek Orthodox heretic, and no other kind.[170]

Although Martin Scorsese was also drawn to the sacerdotal life, glimpses of the blessed mountain only confirmed him in his commitment to 'those who dwell in the deepest valley'.

> I've read about many aspects of Kazantzakis' life . . . I find it fascinating how he followed different routes to find God or his spirituality, going up to Mount Athos and staying in a monastery, and finally writing these books in the last ten years of his life . . . I go more towards *Mean Streets* where you try to find yourself, because I'm dealing with this urban existence. I'm not like Thoreau, I don't go to Walden.[171]

Scorsese's imagination as an artist has always occupied the 'Mean
Streets' of the modern city, and the quest for spiritual understanding,
whether of the self or of God, has to take place in that 'deepest
valley'. Again, though a lapsed Catholic, it was the urban Latin
Catholicism of New York's Little Italy from which his lapsing took
place and which paradoxically provided him with the language
and iconography of his apostasy. Capable of seeing the ordinary
transfigured by grace, Scorsese sees no fundamental or absolute
distinction between mountain and valley or between the spirit and
the world. 'The supernatural should exist alongside the natural', he
said of his film; 'I wanted to take the risk and keep the supernatural
on the same level as the natural.'[172]

Both Kazantzakis and Scorsese were consciously and explicitly
working outside the church and outside the framework of what
they knew as official Christian doctrine. Kazantzakis embraced the
identity of the heretic as hero, and Scorsese spoke rather sadly of his
reluctant separation from the church. Neither speaks for the church
or for a denominational creed.

What we do find in their work is vivid, imaginative and
intellectually strenuous engagements with fundamental issues
of Christian theology in each case distinctively marked by the
character of the particular mother church. Both show themselves,
in their work, to be genuine lovers of Christ; both seriously accept
a vocation of Christian loyalty and devotion. Both are artists
speaking to a wide community of readers and spectators composed
of Christians, agnostics, atheists and members of other faiths. They
both attempted to reinterpret Jesus and his salvific destiny for
themselves in exercises of devotional meditation and for others in
narrative and poetic extrapolations of the Holy Scriptures. Both
operated in creative media that have been saturated (not naturally,
but by tradition and convention) with the material world and with
the physical body including the discursive and visual languages of
landscape, the city and the human voice and face; yet both insistently
pursued, in their chosen creative language, the difficult and elusive
matrix of incarnation.

By courting controversy, both artists ensured that their work
would be challenged and condemned by many as irreligious and
anti-Christian. Some interpreters have endorsed this perspective and
claimed *The Last Temptation* for humanism: 'I do not wish to claim
that Kazantzakis was an orthodox Christian,' wrote Peter Bien. 'He

lost his faith while still a teenager because he could not reconcile Darwin's teachings with Christianity's promise of an afterlife.'[173] Calians presents a finely balanced reading of Kazantzakis that leaves the writer poised between Christian orthodoxy and heresy:

> Kazantzakis' understating of God is both an affirmation and a denial of traditional Christian theology. His radical affirmation of the incarnation (God coming into human flesh) is at the same time a denial of the incarnation (transforming *all* matter into spirit). Christian theology insists on the organic oneness of flesh and spirit as witnessed in the incarnation of Jesus Christ.[174]

Others however have acknowledged the contribution made by both Kazantzakis and Scorsese to Christian ways of seeing, thinking and feeling. Darren J. N. Middleton hoped to 'rehabilitate' Kazantzakis and 'to rescue him from those who have disowned him as an unbeliever'. Middleton shows that in his views on the mutability of God, the humanity of Christ and the participation of mankind in salvation, Kazantzakis was closer to modern Christology than to the traditional teaching of the church in his own time.

> His soteriological beliefs were so radical at his time that there were few bridges to link him to the Christian past or present. Therefore, we cannot entirely blame the Church of the 1950s for labelling Kazantzakis's soteriology 'scandalous'. Nevertheless . . . leading Christian writers in the modern period are reinterpreting the soteriological aspects of the faith in ways more conducive to Kazantzakis's own soteriology and to the spirit of our age.[175]

Martin Scorsese has also been recognized as one whose imaginative recreation of the gospels constituted a genuine theological exploration of areas often deemed taboo to the faithful. As Les Keyser puts it:

> In *The Last Temptation of Christ* Scorsese echoes traditional Christian dogma as he develops the themes of incarnation, atonement, and redemption. Scorsese, however, explores the concept of Christ's humanity more fully than most Christians, trying to fathom the essence of incarnation and to explore the

psychological and theological implications of a deity made flesh, of a God in a man's body.[176]

Some of the shifts in Christian doctrine reflected here may even be attributed, partially and indirectly, to the influence of people such as Kazantzakis and Scorsese: lay believers and unbelievers, who in their faith and in their doubts challenged Christianity from the inside. Both may be considered, perhaps, as Middleton describes Kazantzakis, to be among 'the many makers and remakers of Christian doctrine'.[177]

2

Human and sacred: Anthony Burgess's *Man of Nazareth* and Franco Zefirelli's *Jesus of Nazareth*

I

Commenting on his experience of writing the film script for Franco Zefirelli's TV production *Jesus of Nazareth*, Anthony Burgess explained that his customary method was to draft a novel before producing a scenario. The draft *Man of Nazareth* was written in the summer of 1975. In an 'Author's Note' to *The Kingdom of the Wicked* he describes having done this, 'composing literary works first' for three television series, *Moses the Lawgiver, Jesus of Nazareth* and *A.D.*[1] In his autobiography *You've Had Your Time*, speaking of *Man of Nazareth* Burgess again referred to 'the preliminary novel' which had to be composed before he could venture on dialogue and camera directions.[2]

In this memoir Burgess, a self-confessed unbeliever[3] committed to collaborating with orthodox Catholics, appears acutely conscious of his own sceptical and independent viewpoint on matters of faith and doctrine. He distinguishes between the synoptic gospels and the 'highly romantic novella written by St John', the gospel of choice for orthodox Roman Catholicism, and therefore naturally Zeffirelli's own 'romantic preference'.[4] Burgess also consulted Josephus's *History of the Jews*, and books on the technique of crucifixion, where he found discrepancies between history and tradition. He considered that it would be 'dangerous' to deny traditional iconography, as for instance by having Jesus carry the crosspiece, not the whole cross.[5] He initially thinks of the synoptics as more historically reliable than John, but gradually becomes more and more 'dissatisfied with their telling of the sacred story': 'They remain fine propagandists but mediocre novelists.'[6] The Evangelists were for example content with 'inadequate motivation', such as the explanation of Judas's betrayal in terms of demonic possession: 'The devil entered Judas.' As Burgess was looking for something more credible in psychological terms, he had to remake Judas, and describes the process by means of which Judas becomes the 'palimpsest' of duped innocence, uncertain zealotry and frustrated idealism we see in the film.[7]

Burgess felt that he needed to expand and elaborate on the gospels in order to produce a narrative with sufficient psychological depth to form the basis of a film treatment. He states that the 12 apostles are not well characterized in the gospels, so he set about giving them 'individual traits'.[8] In seeking a convincing image for Jesus himself Burgess decided, fairly arbitrarily it seems, that he should be physically a very big man, massive and muscular, 'a gigantic Christ'. The stated pretext for this assumption is that Jesus must have had enormous lungs in order to deliver an audible sermon on a mount![9]

Out of this novel came a script which Zeffirelli considered 'ludicrous'.[10] Burgess was not at all surprised. In addition he encountered opposition from the committee of theologians appointed by the production company Radiotelevisione Italia to advise on the project. Burgess saw them as too small-minded and parochial to take the true measure of 'a great international production'.[11] On the other hand Burgess could hardly have been surprised at Catholic reaction to some of his heretical ideas. He thought it providential that the members of the ecclesiastical advisory panel had not read the draft novel, which even at that stage contained a married Christ. Burgess admits that he never delivered a 'satisfactory script', and that Suso Cecchi d'Amico also failed to produce what Zeffirelli required. Burgess implies that Zeffirelli then simply re-wrote the script himself. Burgess proposed publishing *Man of Nazareth* in tandem with the broadcasting of the film, but Labella had already pre-empted this by facilitating Barclay's novelization. Zeffirelli also established literary ownership of the project by publishing in 1977 his own 'spiritual diary' of the making of the film, *Il Mio Gesu*.[12]

With some sourness Burgess comments that his book had to be published in French and Italian before being published in English, and then not in Britain but America.[13] His thunder had been stolen by Barclay and by Zeffirelli himself. He makes very little comment in these reminiscences on the film itself, but the overall impression created here is that in his perception, very little of his contribution survived into the making of *Jesus of Nazareth*.

II

Zeffirelli's recollections, in both *Il Mio Gesu* and his own autobiography, are quite different in content and tone. He refers to Burgess with respect, even reverence (his generous tributes contrasting with Burgess's acidic portrait of Zeffirelli),[14] praising his writing skills and his encyclopaedic memory.[15] Incorrectly Zeffirelli states that Burgess was an agnostic convert to Catholicism, an impression Burgess may have given him. Zeffirelli's description of the process by which Burgess produced the script is interestingly different from that of Burgess. 'In only sixteen days he sketched a skeletal story of six acts.'[16] This was produced spontaneously, without reference to other work, and elicited a draft script 'profoundly permeated with the tone and meaning of the Gospel narrative', but with dialogue that 'did not fit the Gospel records'. Hence 'a conflict arose between my aim and the historical, theological and mystical reworking of the Gospels that Burgess had prepared'.[17] In this contretemps Zeffirelli found himself siding with the ecclesiastical advisory team. Burgess wanted to give Jesus 'mere human words'; while Zeffirelli felt that the words attributed to Jesus in the Gospels were definitive and 'irreplaceable'.[18] Jesus must display a 'sacred quality' in every word and action. Burgess's construction of a 'humanly believable' Jesus was destructive of Zeffirelli's own higher Christology: 'Burgess ultimately destroyed the charismatic, mystical stature that for me sustained the character of Christ.' However Burgess in Zeffirelli's recollection had given him enough to be going on with:

> In those sixteen days of work, carried almost to the limits of human endurance, Burgess dashed off the story of Christ as he remembered it. And so he put an outline at our disposal, a

framework that . . . embodied all the story lines I as director needed for the film.[19]

Burgess then, according to Zeffirelli 'took leave of us' and was not heard from for two years. Zeffirelli claims that Burgess saw the first print of the film and, 'profoundly moved', approved it.[20]

Zeffirelli clearly did not object to the structure of Burgess's draft script, or for the most part with the gospel episodes and incidents he chose to include and exclude. The six-part narrative structure ('a skeletal story of six acts'), is visible in the novel, evident in the film and closely copied by Barclay in the novelization.[21] Gospel materials common to novel and film include the betrothal of Joseph and Mary, the Annunciation, the birth of Jesus in Bethlehem, Jesus and the Elders, the Baptism and the calling of the disciples. Also present are various miracle cures (of a possessed man, a paralytic, a man born blind, the Centurion's servant, Jairus's daughter and Lazarus) and miraculous interventions (the draught of fishes, the miracle of the loaves and fishes). We hear the Sermon on the Mount, the Paternoster, several of the parables; and we see Peter's confession of faith, the woman taken in adultery and Jesus chasing the money-changers from the Temple. Novel and film both conclude with a full repertory of Passion events, the Last Supper, Gethsemane, the Trial, the Crucifixion and the Resurrection.

Significant gospel episodes missing from the film, but present in the novel, are represented only by the Temptation in the wilderness, and the wedding at Cana; while missing from both are the Transfiguration, and the story of Jesus walking on the waves. The film also preserves some material invented by Burgess that has no precedent in the scriptures, such as Jesus meeting Barabbas, the Rabbi from Nazareth accompanying Mary to Golgotha, and in particular the invented character of Zerah, who plays a major role in the events leading to the crucifixion, and serves to completely reorientate the role of Judas.[22] Thus in terms of content and structure, and in terms of their incorporation of biblical and invented material, novel and film remain very close to one another.

Zeffirelli focused his reservations over Burgess's script not on structure and content but on dialogue, specifically the 'mere human words' Burgess attributed to Jesus. But the way in which Burgess has Jesus speak is not simply a choice of conversational style, or even a linguistic choice like that between the use of ancient or modern English in a church liturgy. The idiomatic and colloquial English Jesus speaks in *Man of Nazareth* flows naturally from Burgess's distinctive conception of how a modern Jesus-novel could be written.

III

It is here that the most striking contrast between novel and film appears. Burgess frames his novel with opening and closing reflections from a narrator, 'Azor the son of Sadoc'. Like the narrator in Robert Graves's *King Jesus*, Azor is an invented character not tied to historical evidence, who narrates retrospectively, and professes independence of the matters of belief and doctrine implicit in his narrative. The narrator is characterized in some detail, and given some degree of obtrusive presence within the text (though for most of the narrative he recedes into invisibility). Azor is a writer and a linguist fluent in many tongues; he has many nicknames; he is learned and of a philosophical inclination; and he takes a sceptical and independent view of the material he is presenting to the reader. In other words he is a semi-transparent proxy for the polyglot, polymathic, pseudonymous, sceptical author Anthony Burgess himself.

The device of a narrator enables Burgess to avoid that 'absolute directness of presentation'[23] characteristic of the gospels, replicated by the Hollywood Jesus-film, and which Zeffirelli clearly wanted to emulate. Instead the text becomes pervaded by modernist irony and detachment, distance and indirection. Azor begins by explaining to the reader the practice of crucifixion. The evidence of such inhumanity seems to bespeak not the presence of justice but rather 'a great principle of wrong in the world'.[24] As in Foucault's *Discipline and Punish*, this method of execution seems to not only demonstrate the arbitrariness of power,[25] but also to compel from the spectator a contrary response of pity for the victim, which then calls into question the justice of the punishment.[26] This principle of wrong is then extrapolated to a description of the universe as dualistic in nature: 'the world is a twofold creation', a Manichean balance of good and evil, light and darkness.[27] From this we can infer that the narrator is neither a Jew nor a Christian, since his

Manichean philosophy insists that the conflict between good and evil remains eternally 'unresolved'.[28] The power of goodness is always limited and relative to its opposite. At the end of the novel Azor makes his free-thinking perspective explicit: 'I am no Christian'. He anticipates that 'official' accounts of Jesus will be written, and will acquire the status of enforced orthodoxy.[29] His version makes no claim to be a sacred text, but is rather the kind of 'disinterested' account that could be produced only by a 'non-believer'.[30] Azor then tries to locate the significance of Jesus into this Manichean universe, in which goodness will not triumph and humanity will never be free from evil: and concludes that the Christian gospel can only be understood in 'ludic' terms, as a game. To love one's enemy is an impossibility, but conceived as a game the doctrine is perfectly playable and makes life 'uncommonly interesting'.[31] Playing the game of 'Love Thy Neighbour' develops necessary 'skills of tolerance, forbearance and affection' which are predicated on the possibility of loving both oneself and one's enemy. The alternative, conflict and violence, is 'destructive of self as well as of enemy'.[32]

It is hard to see how a portrait of Jesus and his apostles as men who 'did not take life seriously' could be regarded as compatible with orthodox Roman Catholicism. Burgess was much more concerned here with promoting his own post-modern point of view on the universe, than with attempting a historical reconstruction of early Christianity. Burgess styled himself a 'Manichean', asserting that 'duality is the ultimate reality'.[33] 'His overtly religious narratives', said Harold Bloom, '(the book-length poem *Moses* and such excursions as *Man of Nazareth*) are interesting primarily as instances of the writer's Manichean dualism'.[34]

Zeffirelli stated that one of his objectives was to recreate in film 'the historical Jewish Jesus'.[35] Burgess also conceived of the project very much in historical terms, reading by way of preparation Josephus and other documentary sources. He did not exactly go in quest of the 'historical Jesus' in the manner of nineteenth-century liberal theology (though his method displays some similarities), but rather pursued Zeffirelli's objective of realizing Jesus as a character 'who grew out of the cultural, social and historical background of the Israel of his time' (Zeffirelli's words):

I was to produce a series of films for television which would convey the life and words of Christ taken quite literally from the commonly agreed texts of the New Testament without recourse to legend or tricky cinematic mysticism. The reality which film can create was to be used to show the humanity of Christ.[36]

To this extent Burgess was working within the parameters of the Jesus-novel as defined in Theodore Kiolkowski's term 'fictionalizing biography'.[37] In fact Burgess used an almost identical phrase when he affirmed that the historical novel 'is at its best when it is a fictionalized biography'. In the same context he admitted however that in the case of Jesus, the usual matrix of history, character and fiction is harder to map: 'one has to be a very bold novelist indeed to attempt to recreate Jesus Christ'.[38] As Martina Ghosh-Schellhorn says, however, *Man of Nazareth* is not a fictionalized biography at all, but rather a 'parody of the mode of fictionalizing biography through the character of Azor the narrator'. The novel does not take you closer into a more intimate understanding of Jesus in his history, but rather displaces and diverts the object of its representation via scepticism, irony and grotesque comedy. All this stylistic modernism, this 'overtly emphasized artificiality', is consistent with Burgess's 'grotesque vision',[39] and also with Azor/Burgess's post-modern view of life as a game. The problem noted by some reviewers is that of the apparent incompatibility between these techniques and a positive and affirmative Christian spirituality. What is left of history, biography and faith in a novel which, to quote a negative review, 'behaves throughout as though the secret of revitalization lay solely in lightness or off-handedness – in empty urbanity, breezy colloquialism and the rhetoric of scepticism and comical play'?[40] Has Burgess produced, in short, a modern version of the liberal–theological Jesus-novel in the tradition of George Moore, as one reviewer read it: 'the portrait of Jesus as a good and brilliant man for whom the kingdom of heaven could be on earth'?[41] Or has he rather produced, as Gerald Twomey put it, 'a "fifth" gospel': 'Burgess's novel succeeds admirably in depicting Jesus as both true God and true man?'[42]

IV

In order to explore this problem I propose to examine a number of episodes in novel and film where the events derived from the gospels initially involved, entailed or implied some form of supernatural agency; where we find, in the gospels, demonstrated, described or adumbrated some miraculous transgression of the ordinary laws of space and time. As we have seen, both novel and film omit two such incidents, the Transfiguration and Jesus walking on the waves. But both novel and film include key kerygmatic events from the life of Jesus: the Annunciation to Mary; the Baptism; the raising of Lazarus; the Last Supper with the Institution of the Eucharist; and the Crucifixion and Resurrection of Christ.

In the novel both the Annunciation, and its precursor the vision of Zacharias in the Temple, are given a full-dress supernatural treatment. The Archangel Gabriel appears in the concrete solidity of a tangible apparition to both Zacharias and Mary. Zacharias encounters him in the Holy of Holies, and as the priest will not accept his message he is struck dumb. Burgess does not suspend his ironic and humorous tone for a heavenly revelation: Gabriel is busy curiously cleaning his fingernails, 'as if he had only recently been issued with them';[43] and when he dissolves into air, his fingernails are the last things to disappear.[44] In the Annunciation to Mary, the angel disturbs the family pets, a cat and a dog. Gabriel speaks words very close to those of Luke's, though cast into a more idiomatic style. He enchants the cat who leans against his ankles, and falls over when the angel disappears.[45]

In these passages Burgess finds a playful and facetious way of bringing the supernatural onto the same level as the natural, and thereby transmitting the full miraculous content of the scriptures in the medium of fictional prose. The formal language characteristic of these exchanges in the Bible is cleverly adapted so that colloquial observations lead easily into the great familiar scriptural utterances. Occasionally the sceptical narrator obtrudes, but never sufficiently to undermine the assumed truth of the revelations. The visions come to only one person at a time, so there are no witnesses: but the reader is presented with these events directly as things that objectively happened. There is humour and irony, but no satire or historical criticism. The comedy does not undermine the spiritual realism: after all, as Elizabeth says, it is possible that God Himself take an amused view of the world: 'May one say that God is a laughing God and dearly loves a jest?'[46]

Burgess's dramatization of the Baptism in the Jordan is, by contrast, entirely dismissive of mystery and supernatural revelation. In the gospels the Baptism represents a moment of epiphany, in which Jesus is recognized as the Lamb of God, acknowledged as the Son of God by a voice from heaven and marked by the appearance of the Holy Spirit in the form of a dove. In *Man of Nazareth* John recognizes Jesus, but only because he is already well-known to him: 'He saw his cousin Jesus.' Azor the narrator rejects the 'superstitious tales' that have 'obscured' this event, stories involving birds and sudden accessions of light.[47] John is baptizing a garrulous old man, who seems to speak the gospel words: 'This is my beloved son . . .' John asks him what he said, and it was only 'it didn't take long'.[48] The confrontation of John and Jesus is in itself wholly scriptural: John defers to him, and Jesus insists on the performance of the ritual. But Burgess has removed any basis for perceiving this event as miraculous, as an extraordinary moment of epiphany through recognition, or as a manifest revelation of divine favour.

The raising of Lazarus is by contrast confronted directly as a genuine miracle. In remarks quoted above Burgess singled out this event as typical of St John's romantic and mystical narrative, and therefore appealing to Zeffirelli: 'I foresaw that we would have a full-dress resurrection of Lazarus.'[49] But in the novel there is no doubt whatsoever that Lazarus is dead and decomposing, and that Jesus brings him back to life. Even doubting Thomas differentiates this revival from the earlier awakening of Jairus's daughter: 'I don't think this one here was asleep.'[50] Jesus uses the Johannine words 'I am the Resurrection and the Life', and the incident is the immediate precursor of his entry into Jerusalem. Burgess hedges the miracle about with critical and sceptical suggestions. He notes that Lazarus's life was not worth saving, since the rest of it was 'wholly vicious'.[51] Thomas questions Lazarus about what it's like to be dead, but he remembers nothing. 'God . . . give nothing away', comments Thomas, 'He keeps the riddle going.'[52] And Judas is inspired by the miracle to rush to Jerusalem to carry the 'good news' to his contact in the Sanhedrin, and thus to begin the process of Jesus's betrayal. But all this is in keeping with the gospel of John, so the miracle is left to stand in the record.

Also at least open to the supernatural is the manner in which Burgess narrates the Last Supper, with the Institution of the Eucharist. Although the event itself does not entail any miraculous incident, in representing the very historical foundation of Christian worship, it is predicated on, and expressive of, an unmistakably divine power preparing to enact a sacrifice of redemption.

Burgess shirks nothing of the Catholic meaning of the Eucharist, depending heavily on John's gospel, and giving Jesus speeches that draw directly on the definitions of faith made by the early church councils. He speaks of his own immolation as 'the last of the sacrifices of flesh and blood' and of its salvific nature: 'it will be made to redeem mankind of all its sins'.[53] The sacrifice must not only be remembered but repeated, re-enacted daily in the ritual of the Mass. Jesus insists that the Eucharistic sacrifice will involve the real presence of the divine: 'when the words are spoken, it is also my body, my presence'. When the disciples perform the ritual Jesus will be with them, not just in spirit but in flesh and blood, 'under these two blessed forms' of bread and wine.[54] Jesus even anticipates the Reformation critique of the Eucharistic real presence, saying that the bread and wine will in the future be interpreted merely as symbols. But they do not constitute 'mere remembrance', but actual presence: 'I must be truly with mankind in these forms.'[55] Frank Kermode comments 'the Last Supper . . . insists a little more than it had to on the doctrine of the Real Presence'.[56] It is true that in the novel's Last Supper scene, nothing supernatural actually occurs: a man breaks bread, pours wine and speaks words. The elements are realized in detail as ordinary bread and wine, and the disciples react to Jesus's discourse with some scepticism and some bewilderment. But by using the Johannine version as the master-text here, and by invoking the language of Nicaea and Chalcedon, Burgess has welded his fiction so closely to Catholic tradition that the reader has little choice but to accept (or reject) an affirmation of the Eucharistic mystery.

These examples seem to reveal that Burgess was apt to strain at a gnat and swallow a camel. He demystifies the Baptism in the Jordan into a mere brief encounter; and yet narrates as miraculous the Annunciation and the Raising of Lazarus, and uncompromisingly promotes an orthodox Roman Catholic view of the Eucharist. Finally Burgess treats the Crucifixion and Resurrection with the same apparently random mixture of scepticism and faith. The scriptural details of the Crucifixion are narrated, with no particular theological meaning attributed to them. Azor discusses 'the legends that have accumulated about this moment' and disposes of them as mere superstitions. The storm was coming anyway; there was no earthquake; the veil of the Temple was rent only by an old priest falling and tearing it. Finally Azor accounts 'in the light of probability' for the story of Jesus's body transfixed by a spear producing water and blood, by suggesting that these details arose from the corpse's spontaneous phallic erection and involuntary emission of semen.[57]

Yet, despite all this, in the following chapters, the tomb is empty, and Jesus appears as a resurrected man. Claiming to be happy back in the flesh again, and with his mission at an end, he resembles D. H. Lawrence's 'Man who Died'. But unlike Lawrence's Christ, Burgess's Jesus affirms that he has achieved a conquest of death ('there is no death'), and reassures the disciples that he will be with them always, 'even unto the end of the world'.[58]

V

Burgess claimed that he accepted the *Jesus of Nazareth* commission to pay the bills, because he considered he could bring something unique to the project, and because if he didn't do it someone else would.[59] Zeffirelli's motivations in making the film were by contrast primarily religious and evangelical. A committed Catholic, he saw himself as literally called to a missionary vocation, to take the good news of Christ to the world through film and television. Although anxious to secure Catholic approval of his work, he conceived of his audience as universal, believers and unbelievers alike. Hence his Jesus had to be an ecumenical figure who would appeal to everyone, 'acceptable to all denominations'.[60] Aware of some currents in modern biblical scholarship, he wanted to relocate Jesus back into the social and cultural context of first-century Palestine, considering it 'essential to put into words the historical and social context of his times'.[61]

Zeffirelli mentions more than once how moved he was by the Vatican's promulgation in 1965 of reconciliation between the Catholic Church and other faiths, particularly Judaism. *Nostra Aetate* was, in Zeffirelli's words 'a plea for racial tolerance and human brotherhood'. 'The point I wanted to make most evident was that Christ was a Jew.' Jesus should be recreated in an appropriately Jewish historical background, and the Christian gospel seen as 'a continuation and fulfilment of centuries of Jewish religious teaching'.[62]

Zeffirelli evidently felt under some pressure from his Catholic affiliates to produce a 'low Christology' Jesus who would be virtually indistinguishable from any other common man of his time. To 'show the humanity of Christ'[63] might seem to entail showing him as ordinary. Zeffirelli quotes some recommendations made by Fr Lorenzo Milani to director Maurice Cloche on how to film Jesus, which included making him indistinguishable from his fellows at school, or among those coming to the Jordan for baptism, or those waiting to be arrested in the garden of Gethsemane. Zeffirelli must have shared these notes with Burgess, since he suggests in *Il Mio Gesu* that Burgess followed Milani's advice.[64] In his *Autobiography* Zeffirelli describes difficulties caused during filming by the fact that the rushes were being sent to Rome to be seen by the producers of Radiotelevisione Italia, who held a different view of the project from the director:

> There were still those who wanted an interpretation other than mine: Christ as the common man, Christ as someone indistinguishable from those around him.

Evidently the producers objected to the way in which Zeffirelli ensured his Jesus would be highly visible and distinctive: 'Those that held this view sniped away at my film for turning Christ into a star and for surrounding him with the famous faces of Hollywood.'[65]

Zeffirelli stuck to his guns and was rescued from this particular pressure by Lew Grade.[66] The criticism voiced here became however the basis of a routine castigation of *Jesus of Nazareth* in reviews and academic criticism. Here, for example, is Lloyd Baugh reiterating common observations:

> Zeffirelli's unfortunate decision to use 'name' actors is one of the major flaws of the film, and one of the major reasons for the perceived weakness of his Jesus. The character of Jesus ought to stand out morally and dramatically. Zeffirelli's Jesus gets lost 'in the shuffle' of 'guest stars'.[67]

The general critical argument here, which Baugh is largely reflecting, is that although Zeffirelli wanted to depart from the norms of Hollywood cinema, he failed to avoid being trapped by some of its insidious pressures to conform: 'Zeffirelli wanted at all costs to avoid the errors and excesses of the Hollywood Jesus-films. And yet he falls right into the trap.' The virtues of *Jesus of Nazareth* are those of 'fiction, not of biblical fact'.[68] Baugh criticizes the film for its overtly 'self-aware theatricality' and 'virtuoso composition', which 'draw attention to themselves as fiction rather than to the very real mystery of the life, death and Resurrection of Jesus the Christ they are meant to represent'.[69] Baugh speaks condescendingly of Zeffirelli's experience in theatrical design and his skills of visual composition (he 'began his career in show business') which though appropriate for grand opera are damaging to this film.[70]

Underlying all this negative description, much of it repeated from previous commentaries, is a particular and highly questionable view of the literary character of the gospels, and of what a Jesus-film ought to be like. Baugh speaks of the 'lean elliptical, challenging, tough text and style of the gospels' and argues that Zeffirelli consistently departs from and misrepresents them. 'There remain none of the crucial ellipses of the biblical text, none of its mystery, none of its radical questions to, and demands on the reader.'[71] Not surprisingly in the light of this view of the gospels, Baugh's films of preference are those of Roberto Rossellini and Pier Petro Pasolini.[72]

Zeffirelli was of course trying to do something quite different. He did not read the gospels in this way, nor did he make any attempt to drill down to some pure gospel bedrock by clearing away accrued layers of Catholic tradition. It is true that he brought to the film his own characteristic skills of design and visual composition, influenced by pictorial theatre and renaissance painting. He also however engaged with some of the fundamental problems of realizing Jesus on film as they were explored in Burgess's novelistic treatment. I will now compare Zeffirelli's presentation in the film of the same kerygmatic episodes discussed in the novel: the Annunciation, the Baptism, the raising of Lazarus, the Last Supper and the Resurrection. These analyses will show that the filmic text of *Jesus of Nazareth*, often dismissed as if it were a piece of crude televangelism, was in fact produced from a complex matrix of determinants, all present in the Burgess text, including both high and low Christologies, an interest in historical context, a strong commitment to a Jewish Christ and a willingness to use the medium of film to incorporate the language and gesture of Christian worship.

VI

Zefferelli said that when approaching the Annunciation scene, he could not conceive it literally. He 'obviously rejected the idea of having an angel with wings and a halo', which is not far off Burgess's version in the novel.

> Instead, God's message comes in the form of a silent beam of light that passes through a high aperture in the little mud-brick room to fall on the face of the young Madonna.[73]

Baugh comments on this scene that Zeffirelli tries 'rather artificially' to create 'a sense of mystery', 'with light and the sound of wind and almost baroque camera angles and movements'.[74] In fact the artifice of the film here could scarcely be more naturalistic. Zeffirelli gives no physical presence whatever to the heavenly messenger, showing only Mary's reaction to what she alone hears and sees. The wind is just wind sighing through a window. A dog barks in the street, perhaps an echo of Burgess's Archangel Gabriel disturbing the household pets. The light is technically adjusted to suggest an enhanced natural light rather than a divine illumination. Yet the scene creates an extraordinary atmosphere of spiritual wonder. Mary at first kneels quite naturally, in rapt attention; then clings to the wall in fear; and finally sinks to her knees in a formal and iconographic posture of prayer. You hear no message, only her reply; you see no angel, only the light on her face. With all the immense panorama of Renaissance Annunciations cramming his Italian head, the director chose to pare this scene right down to bare essentials: a young girl against a bare plaster wall, an open window, an invisible messenger, a vocation accepted. The scene is beautiful in its purity of design; Zeffirelli himself rightly described it as 'heart-stopping'.[75] Film, Baugh complains elsewhere, 'transforme l'invisible en visible, le spiritual en physique, et ne se retient pas devant le Mystère, préférant une matérialisation qui envahit, révèle et même explique de dernier'.[76] One could hardly imagine a more thorough controversion of this assertion than Zeffirelli's Annunciation.

Perhaps the most compelling aspect of this scene is the way in which Zeffirelli has solved the Christological problem of linking human and divine into a single medium, managing to secure both simplicity and transcendence. This is how God comes into the world; this is how the divine irrupts into the everyday. This is Incarnation.

Zeffirelli's Baptism scene[77] again operates in completely the opposite way from its equivalent in the novel. The Baptism in the novel is demystified, rationalized, just a historical event. Zeffirelli renders the Baptism as a supremely transcendent moment of recognition and acknowledgement, but he does this without a voice from heaven or a descending dove. He achieves the effect initially by concentrating the act of recognition on John, played by Michael York. We do not see Jesus approach the Jordan, though it is apparent that no one pays him any particular attention. After the Baptism he walks away looking as unobtrusive as anyone else, except in the gaze of John and his disciples.

What the viewer sees first of all is the compelling expression on John's face of wonder and fear as he recognizes Jesus. The two faces in extreme close-up exchange expressions; but all the charge of meaning is on the face of Michael York, as his expression registers the impact Jesus has on him. This moment exactly captures the spirit of St John's Gospel: 'The same came for a witness, to bear witness of the Light, that all men through him might believe. He was not that Light, but was sent to bear witness of that Light.' We see the light reflected onto John's face rather than glowing from the face of Jesus himself. The words that in the scripture come from heaven, here come through John 'I heard a voice saying . . .'[78] The words are displaced as they are in the novel, but here are not dispersed but returned to their true scriptural and sacramental meaning. John looks upwards, and we see a dove drifting and circling in the air. The iconography of the gospel is as it were cited, quoted, rather than represented. As Jesus walks away, John beckons Andrew and Simon to watch Jesus and to follow him. The formal liturgical words, 'Behold the lamb of God . . .' are spoken not just as dialogue or narrative, but also in a choric space of worship opened up within the film by the imagery and drama. They are the words attributed to John the Baptist in the gospels; they carry all the weight of Old Testament prophecy; and they are employed economically as an 'indexical sign' to denote John's concession of authority to Jesus: 'You must follow him now, not me.' They are also the words of the Mass, and they connect the text of the film directly into the language and context of daily Catholic worship.

A similar dimension of extra-contextual scriptural commentary appears in Zeffirelli's scene of the Raising of Lazarus.[79] The episode is set firmly within the structure of the Passion story, and serves in the film, as it functions in the gospel, as an illustrative example of the possibility of resurrection. As Jesus and the disciples are heading for Jerusalem, John and James talk of Jesus's mission: 'He said he was to be put to death . . . and will rise again.' Immediately a messenger tells Jesus about the sickness of Lazarus. He agrees to come. The film omits all the details from John's gospel that show Jesus delaying and promising to use Lazarus's death as an opportunity for glorification, but shows Mary the sister of Lazarus expressing absolute faith in Jesus as the Christ, the Son of God, the bringer of eternal life.

As Jesus approaches the tomb through the bleached white landscape of the cemetery, camera positions alternate between long shots towards the tomb, and medium shots from inside it. From behind we see Jesus kneeling in prayer; from within the tomb, the Lazarus view, we see him preparing to exercise his power. The disciples stand behind in medium shot, with John positioned centrally. We hear Jesus pray the words of John 11.41. Then from behind him, John the Evangelist is seen in close-up to quote from the *Book of Jonah* in the Hebrew Bible:

I went down into the countries underneath the earth,
to the peoples of the past.
But you lifted my life from the pit.[80]

Jesus raises his arms, outstretched in power but with an echo of the posture of crucifixion, and Lazarus emerges. Jesus quotes John 11.25: 'he that believes in me though he were dead yet shall he live', a familiar echo from Christian services for the burial of the dead.

Thus Zeffirelli has woven his materials together so as to emphasize the theological and dogmatic significance of the raising of Lazarus. The awakening of the dead man is both a demonstration of divine power, and a dress rehearsal for Jesus's own resurrection. Lazarus is not identified as someone Jesus knew well, or as a person we could come to know. The episode is positioned where it belongs in the denouement of the Passion narrative as a whole. The film uses the words of John's gospel to render the theology explicit, and also incorporates a passage from the Hebrew Bible in order to link Jesus back to Old Testament prophecy. The filmic image is thus both historical and future-oriented, as befits an episode of apocalyptic awakening ('Take away the stone!'). Lazarus stands at the mouth of the grave enfolded from head to foot in his white, anonymizing shroud, as a type of humanity. We do not see him divested of his cerements, or restored to individuality again. Linguistically the dialogue points back towards the Old Testament and forward to the New Covenant of Christianity. The familiar echo of the burial service links the spectator's own knowledge of loss with historical bereavement, both mediated through the saving power of Christ.[81]

Zeffirelli's portrayal of the Last Supper, although beautifully composed and lit, with the company seated on the floor in the low-ceilinged upper room, is not presented primarily as spectacle at all.[82] The shots that establish the visual design of the scene are few and short. Most of the drama is concentrated on the faces of Jesus and his disciples. The scene is dramatized more as a sacred ritual or liturgy than as a reconstructed historical event, though it is that too, with its detailed rendering of the traditional Passover feast. But the long expository passages of John 13–17, paralleled by Anthony Burgess's lengthy theological excursions on the meaning of the Eucharist, are here cut down to a text that aligns closely with the Ordinary of the Mass. Jesus speaks and acts as much like a priest celebrating Mass as a redeemer instituting that same custom of celebration. The apostles sit facing him, not alongside him as in many Da Vinci-inspired Last Suppers, in the position of a congregation. Thus the scene is anachronistic, in that it shows a group of believers performing a liturgy that has yet to be established, and presupposes a sacrifice that has not yet taken place. When Jesus directs them to take the bread, they simultaneously lift bread to their mouths with the absorption of communicants raising the host to their lips. The partaking of bread and wine is already a Christian sacrament. Jesus makes clear that the Passover feast they are historically celebrating is now superseded, and that from now on a new covenant will unite God and humanity.[83] Matthew holds the chalice and the bread together, as in the elevation of the Mass. The emotions of the scene are those of wonder, rapture and distress. The traditional remembrance of exile embodied in the Passover merges with mourning for the loss that all know is imminent, but has not yet come to pass. The luminous eyes of Jesus are by the end filled with tears; and the scene cuts straight to the Agony in the Garden.

The Crucifixion[84] scene is presented, as it is in *Man of Nazareth*, very much in terms of the human drama. Zeffirelli allows in a muted thunderstorm and some heavy rain, but otherwise no overtly supernatural events. The emotional pitch is of course at its most extreme, but the significance of the event is not to be read in the language of heavenly signs, but on the faces of the participants: the Centurion, Nicodemus, Mary and Mary Magdalene, John. A most powerful contribution is made by showing Nicodemus (Laurence Olivier) speaking the words of Isaiah on the Suffering Servant. Like John's quoting of Jonah at the Raising of Lazarus, this choric note links the Christian sacrifice back to the Old Testament and forward to the Redemption of mankind.[85]

Zeffirelli's handling of the Resurrection presents the most striking contrast between his Jesus and that of Burgess. In *Il Mio Gesu* he describes an unsuccessful attempt to film a resurrection scene that did not seem to work, as it was veering towards the sentimentality of the Hollywood epic. Filming was suspended to give him time to reflect. He prepared to film another scene, which was disrupted by the onset of a huge desert storm. Filming was abandoned. 'From that moment on, the Resurrection scene remained an unkept appointment' (95–6).

> For me it was an admission of defeat, or a secret lesson, a reminder of the limits of my professional powers of inspiration. It was a surrender . . . (p. 97)

Burgess suggested that Zeffirelli planned to end with the *Pietà* and forgo the Resurrection altogether.[86] This may have been an interim justification. Zeffirelli records how he realized that the film could not be completed without the Resurrection, and had to search through hours of tape to find a test passage that would serve, a scene of the resurrected Jesus talking to the disciples. Clearly this whole episode caused Zeffirelli much anguish: he tried to alter the account of his 'surrender' when the book was already in press, as noted by his editor Tiziano Barbieri, who added a brief postscript to set the record straight.[87]

VII

The similarities and differences between novel and film are not therefore what one would expect from the explicit credentials of novelist and director. The most extreme contrasts do exist, and accord with their respective 'house styles' of unbelief and orthodoxy: we could not imagine Burgess staging a Pieta in a thunderstorm, or Zeffirelli speculating about post-mortal erection. But as my examples show, Burgess was perfectly willing to narrate wholly supernatural events; while Zeffirelli preserves a remarkable restraint in avoiding any such overt and explicit supernatural reference. Burgess's Annunciation and Baptism are kerygmatic and divinely staged; Zeffirelli's equivalents are modest and naturalistic. Both novelist and director show the Raising of Lazarus and the Resurrection of Jesus as historical events. The unbeliever Burgess confronted the Resurrection with the imperturbable confidence of his own Jesus; while the orthodox Catholic Zeffirelli almost missed it out altogether.

In terms of high and low Christologies, Zeffirelli resisted external pressure on him to lower the theological horizon, but in the event delivered a Jesus who is both credibly human, and capable of a divine impact on those around him. Burgess played with both high and low Christologies, but again pays due tribute to the necessity of both in a fully incarnational Christian fiction.

The most compelling evidence for a certain imaginative sympathy between novelist and director, co-existing with the more obvious intellectual and artistic antipathies, is the way in which both novel and film incorporate into their language elements of liturgy and ritual which tie their fictions to gospel intertextuality and traditional Catholic worship. I have shown how this feature connects their respective versions of the Last Supper. Zeffirelli was much criticized for the 'utter theatricality' of those moments in the film where characters quote scripture as choric commentary on the action. Here in fact both novel and film are adhering closely to the gospels, not as lean spare simple narratives, but as the dense palimpsests of quotation and re-quotation they really are. In the film, after the Massacre of the Innocents, Zeffirelli inserted a wholly unscriptural appearance for Simeon, who emerges on to the steps of the Temple and quotes words of lamentation from the prophet

Jeremiah (31.15). Or at least the historical Simeon is quoting from Jeremiah. The filmic Simeon is quoting from the New Testament that has not yet been written:

> In Rama was there a voice heard, lamentation, and weeping, and great mourning, Rachel weeping for her children, and would not be comforted, because they were not . . . . (Matt. 2.17–18)

Or rather, to become completely post-modern, both are quoting from Antony Burgess's *Man of Nazareth*, where the narrator Azor pre-empts the composition of Matthew's gospel:

> This, they say, was foretold by Jeremiah the prophet. Something about a voice heard in Rama, weeping and great mourning, Rachael weeping for her children. And she would not be comforted, for her children were no more.[88]

3

Science and religion:
Jim Crace's *Quarantine*

I

Quarantine is a work of fiction that formally engages with both theology and science. Jim Crace is certainly a novelist, and a very accomplished one: but he is neither a theologian nor a scientist. What then is the value and effectivity of this novel's representation of a character who is supposed to be Jesus, within a fictional world that purports to be a historically reconstructed and scientifically valid first-century Judaea? Is it simply a belated rationalist demythologizing of the Christian gospel? Or does it have something meaningful to say to theology?

Crace described the genesis of the novel as inspired by observation of a group of social outsiders, psychiatric patients decanted from an institution into the 'community'.

> I was interested by people living on the edge, and impressed by the fact that otherwise they had nothing in common. It struck me as interesting to imagine another situation where everyone was living on the edge, with nothing in common save that their lives were teetering, either to fall into the abyss, or to be saved at the last moment.[1]

This marginalized group of outcasts formed the prototype for *Quarantine*'s pilgrims. In addition Crace wanted to transpose these people to a desert setting, fully realized within a 'sense of the landscape' he derived from experience of deserts in Africa and Israel (p. 116).

He did not, by his own account, begin with the objective of writing a novel about Jesus. 'There was originally no intention that Christ was going to be a major figure' (p. 115). Jesus came into the novel as an afterthought, an extra to the story of desert outcasts, only 'to illustrate that initial concept' (p. 116). There seems, then, initially to have been no particularly strong motivation on Crace's part to write a Jesus-novel, or to set about revising and demythologizing the Christian narrative. The novel seems to have originated in entirely secular and naturalistic preoccupations with people, landscape and social marginality.

Nonetheless, once Jesus entered the frame of the fiction, the secondary motivation of writing a Jesus-novel soon aroused Crace's interest. Crace defines himself as a 'post-Dawkins scientific atheist', and shares with that nominated mentor a strident ideological antipathy towards Christianity: 'I'm an atheist, impatient with the simple-mindedness of orthodox religion, its lack of imagination, its bafflegab.'[2]

The Christian explanations for the scientific world are babyish, simplistic . . . the simple-mindedness of those narratives undermines the wonders of the universe. If you were to stand on top of a hill in the 14th century – next to a religious practitioner and heard thunder and seen lightning, that religious practitioner might say, 'That is God expressing his anger at the sins of the universe'. It would have been the best available narrative. Indeed the best available narrative of the time would have been that the world was flat.[3]

Interviewing Crace for *The Guardian*, Sally Vincent elaborates further on his views of Christianity and science:

As a post-Dawkins scientific atheist and modern Darwinist, he doesn't believe there are any outside explanations for the world, only internal ones. They're the same shape, he knows, but one is the truth and one is a lie. To insist that the world was created in six days with one day off is a lie.

But there is another narrative, the narrative of evolution, of how the world has unfolded and spread itself out, which is a finer story, the truth narrative. Behind it is the view that nothing is unexplainable, there are simply some things that are still unexplained.[4]

The science–religion debate here is unscrupulously rigged. Fourteenth-century people did not think that the earth was flat: indeed the ancient Greeks had measured its circumference with some accuracy. Modern educated Christians do not believe that the world was created in six days with one day off. Crace is here adopting Richard Dawkins's polemical technique of setting up straw men as easy targets (though even Dawkins rarely resorts to such extreme caricature); and the tactic of pitting ancient beliefs against modern scientific theories, with the implication that this is an equal contest, is a ruse worthy of Dan Brown himself.

It is also clear, however, that the imaginative writer in Crace is at odds with the adherent of rationalism and positivistic science. He is actually attracted to the old grand narratives of religion such as creationism, for their value as stories: 'such grand stories are very simplistic and straightforward, like the Icelandic sagas, Beowulf or all the Greek myths'.[5] Even where he is advancing claims for the truth of science over religion, there is a sense in which he is weighing the relative value of narratives, rather than comparing the truthfulness of explanations. Evolution is simultaneously invoked as an irrefutable scientific truism, but then also as a more convincing fable than religion: 'a finer story, the truth narrative'.[6]

II

Crace may not have intended at the outset to write a Jesus-novel, or to make a contribution to Christological debate. But once the figure of Jesus wandered into his fictional desert, he committed himself to that enterprise with some enthusiasm. The trigger here was his professed militant atheism: 'His atheism is his driving force.'[7] He has also been described as 'the secular grand inquisitor of the big metaphysical questions'.[8] He wanted the novel to be (in Philip Tew's words) 'interrogative of its contexts', but also (in his own) 'to some extent didactic' (p. 115). The moral of that didacticism is that the supernatural does not exist:

> There is no Holy Ghost, there is no God, there is no Son of God, and there are no ghosts. There is nothing of the universe which is not contained entirely within it, which does not – or will not – have a thorough scientific explanation. (p. 123)

This paraphrases Richard Dawkins exactly:

. . . there is nothing beyond the natural, physical world, no supernatural creative intelligence lurking behind the observable universe, no soul that outlasts the body and no miracles – except in the sense of natural phenomena that we don't yet understand.[9]

There is no 'supernatural': there is only 'nature'. The term 'naturalism' readily attaches itself to Crace's work, for three reasons. His field is clearly the 'natural' as distinct from the 'supernatural', in which he does not believe. Second, his style is a form of intensified realism, with a close-up focus on concrete detail more usually associated with poetry, or akin to the microscopic vision of pre-Raphaelite painting, and thus echoing the 'naturalism' of the late nineteenth-century novel. Third, he evidently thinks of his way of representing the world as a kind of naturalism, a science of nature. Hence his interest in landscape and climate, earth and sky, animal and plant life; and hence his ability to create extraordinarily evocative representations of actual locations. 'The wilderness setting of this story is rendered in obsessive detail: the geography and geology of the area, its birds and animals, insects and plants . . .'[10] He shows, in John Updike's phrase, an 'archaeological command of the texture of life in Herod's Palestine'.[11] His prose is 'clear, hard, resonant' in its rendering of solid objects, resistant forces, palpable presences. He is expert in rendering 'the quotidian, the observable, the prosaic and relentless mechanisms of nature'.[12]

This applies particularly to his representations of the human body. Just as the physical environment of the novel in which people are located consists of an irreducible materiality, so the characters live wholly in the flesh, incarnate, locked into the intense sensuousness of the feeling body. Musa's obesity, Miri's pregnancy, Asaph's illness, Marta's barrenness, are all concrete experiential environments rendering the active consciousness of the character a site of perpetual sensation. Communication happens as much through the physical senses as through verbal intercourse: people know themselves, their surroundings and one another through smell and hearing and touch and taste. Bodies know themselves, and other bodies, through the medium of the body. People know that Musa is ill from the smell of his breath; Miri touches his chest to find it as damp and hot as newly baked bread (p. 1). She is intensely aware of the other person primarily through the sensations of her own body. Miri and Marta also encounter one another through the texture of skin, the one 'as full and oily as an olive', the other 'parchmenty' (p. 64). Jesus explores the landscape through his sense of smell: 'tasting the atmosphere for smells' (p. 21). Crace realizes the body in both living sensuousness and incipient decay. In the violent scene in which Musa kills his donkey, Crace's concrete and sinuous prose dwells obsessively on the physical detail of illness, decay, the strengths and fragilities of animal anatomy and almost sadistically on the aesthetics of injury : 'Her face was fruit. It bruised and split and wept' (p. 37).

At one level this is simply the way the 'naturalist' Crace sees the world. However since this is a Jesus-novel, its way of defining physical existence inevitably takes on theological dimensions. Here the body of Jesus is like every other body, subject to the common laws of biological survival. If there is no God, no Son of God, no Holy Ghost, then the Temptation in the wilderness can boil down only to a physical ordeal, an instance of the tenacity of the body tested against the limits of extreme endurance. There can be no miraculous delivery, no supernatural aid, no marvellous survival. The body that is denied sustenance will die, and the body of Jesus is no exception. By the end of his 30 days of total abstinence the body of Jesus is a dry husk, ready to crumble to dust, 'all surface, no inside . . . He was a dry, discarded page of scripture now' (pp. 191, 193).

In one sense this is the common fate of mortality, the dying body reducing down to its elemental constituents, evacuated of the fluids that maintain it. But this is a special body, and its decay represents also an evacuation of meaning. If Jesus becomes an ordinary corpse, there is no resurrection, and the gospel is false, then his status as the Messiah and Saviour of the New Testament is also eclipsed. He is not only a drying corpse, but a 'dry, discarded page of scripture'. This metaphor is crucial to Crace's secular ethic, though it is rich in ambiguity, and can be read with relish or regret, as pity or satisfaction at the surrendering of a grand and ancient narrative of consolation.

As indicated above, this unpacking of the Temptation as a real event was Crace's basic challenge to the gospel narrative: 'Take a venerated Bible story (Christ's Judean fast), add a pinch of hard-nosed fact (nobody going without food and drink could survive for anything like forty days) and watch the scripture take a beating'.[13] To reinforce this scientific critique of sacred legend, Crace places at the novel's opening an epigraph from what appears to be a scientific treatise on the limits of the human body, and which attests that nobody, no body, can survive without food and water for more than 30 days.

At first sight this appears to be a straightforward piece of enlightenment demythologizing, using methods practised since the eighteenth century to strip the gospels of legend, miracle, supernatural agency. But there are problems. To start with Crace is basing his scriptural presuppositions on a misreading of the New Testament. If we look at the various accounts of the temptation in the wilderness, Mark's (foundational) gospel does not even mention fasting. Matthew speaks of fasting for 40 days and nights, after which Jesus is 'famished'. Luke elaborates by saying that Jesus ate 'nothing at all during those days'. These accounts are entirely compatible with a credible story of a man fasting – abstaining from food but not from water – for the specified length of time.

Now for a bible student the narrative medium here is in any case mythical rather than realistic. The 40 days of the Temptation derive from the wilderness experiences of Moses and Elijah, and the 40 years in which the children of Israel wandered in the desert, rather than from specified dates in the calendar for 30 AD. The whole account of the Temptation is a supernatural drama: after all, which is less probable in realistic terms, physical survival for 40 days of fast, or conducting extensive conversations with the devil? But even in the midst of narrating a mythical episode, the Evangelists characteristically embed their narrative within the limits of the credible.

So 'hard-nosed fact' is perhaps missing the target here. More perplexing however is the realization that the citation Crace uses to illustrate his hard-nosed fact is in fact bogus, an invented source. The cited text 'Winward and Soule on *The Limits of Mortality*' does not exist outside the novelist's fertile imagination. Both the theology and the science of this debate are surprisingly suspect. Although he purports to pit myth against fact in order to debunk myth, Crace actually sets up a debate between a misread scripture and a phoney, invented piece of scientific evidence, a misheard story challenged by a made-up fact. Even if the novel is conceived more as a clash of alternative narratives than as a duel between truth and myth, the two discourses have been made too similar to one another to constitute a real opposition.

III

The scene is a realistically represented desert, accurately described by a self-professed 'scientific atheist'. It is occupied by people whose bodies consist of an irreducible materiality. It is a landscape devoid of God, in which nothing of the supernatural supervenes upon the interminable and unavoidable biological processes of life and death, birth and decay. Jesus is already dead in his cave. In the midst of this desolate and deathly wilderness, a man has a vision of Resurrection:

> It was not long before Musa spotted movement at the far end of the pans. The sun was in his eyes but he was sure that there was someone coming up towards him, a someone who was light enough to walk across the mud without their sandals sticking . . . it was Jesus walking in the mud, bare-footed, naked, thin and brittle as a thorn. He waited while the man approached, as thinly as an egret, his body wasted to the bone, his too large hands and feet, his swollen joints. Only his genitals seemed unaffected by the fast . . . He'd seen worse ulcers, looser teeth, more hollow eyes. But he had never seen a man appear so weightless and invincible as Gaily seemed to be. When Musa stood and looked again, the man was at a greater distance and almost indistinguishable from the shadows and the bushes. He had taken a lower path, through a sloping basin of thorn and rock, and was walking away from Musa with the confidence of someone who was full of god at last.
>
> Musa watched – relieved, rebuffed – as Jesus set off up the scarp, his body bones combining with the scrub rocks and the sunlight to make a hard-edged pattern which pulsed and slanted all at once. Musa put his hands up to his mouth. 'What do you want?' he called. The Gaily did not seem to hear. He was too far away. He pulsed and slanted, disappeared, became a man again a few steps higher up the slope, was lost between the landscape and the sun.

The air became much colder than it ought to have been. Musa
barely dared to breathe. He could have sworn the man was
glowing blue and yellow, like a coal. (203–4)

The other quarantiners have come to the desert in search of
something: Asaph of healing, Shim of enlightenment, Marta of
fertility. Musa is there by accident, stranded by his caravan, and
brings to the desert nothing more aspirational than hunger for
profit, predatory lust and an instinct of domination. He has, it is
true, been seeking Jesus, but only because he believes 'the Gally'
to have a secret of healing that might be learned, acquired, bought
and used to advantage. Why then does Musa experience this
extraordinary vision of the resurrected Jesus? Science assumes that
there are no transcendent, material forces, and that all forces that do
exist behave in an ultimately objective and random fashion. Nature,
the sum total of physical reality, exists, the supernatural does not.
There are no non-natural events. According to this paradigm, which
Crace persistently endorses, Jesus cannot be simultaneously dead
in a cave, and walking through the desert. The dead do not come
back to life again. How can Musa's vision be explained by 'natural'
means?

Musa has seen Jesus only fleetingly, in the glimpse of a face when
the stranger 'healed' him. Musa has seen many ascetics undergoing
physical extremity, so he would know what to expect if looking out
for one. But what he sees here is exactly the physical equivalent of
the dead body in the cave, yet apparently alive and walking through
the desert. How has he acquired ('he was sure') such certainty of
recognition? More to the point, why does Musa's vision both render
so exactly the physical form of the dead Jesus, yet also assimilate
so precisely to subsequent representations of the crucified one,
wounded yet victorious, victim and victor, dead yet resurrected, 'full
of god at last'?

If there are no supernatural events, then Musa's vision can only
be a hallucination, a mirage, a subjective image created from his
own desires. But what desire of Musa's is it that makes Jesus walk
away from him, absenting his body from the scene in a parallel to
the empty tomb? 'He is not here . . . he is going ahead of you' (Matt.
28.6–7). The behaviour of Jesus's body alternates between mirage,
hallucination and living being: 'pulsed' suggests organic life as well
as a beating in the brain of the observer; 'slanted' the slippage of a

visual mirage; 'became a man' again a restoration to recognizable living form. There seems little difference between these impressions and those detailed in the scriptures to describe the apparitions of the risen Jesus between the Resurrection and the Ascension. His disappearance into the space between earth and heaven, 'between the landscape and the sun', is also the equivalent of an Ascension, and represents to Musa a 'loss' ('was lost') just as it does to the disciples: 'he withdrew from them, and was carried up into heaven' (Luke 50.51). Musa feels a sudden chill, as if this ghostly apparition is cooling the air around it. Finally he sees Jesus's body apparently igniting into a divine flame.

Even more extraordinary and inexplicable than Musa's gratuitous vision is the fact that he is not alone in experiencing an apparently resurrected Jesus. When the two women Miri and Marta (named after the biblical Mary and Martha, sisters of Lazarus) are sent to prepare Jesus's body for burial, they resemble the women in the gospels who come to the tomb. There they find no body to anoint; here they wash and care for an unmistakably lifeless corpse. But in the corpse Marta recognizes the face of the man she has never seen (pp. 224–5), as an image familiar from her dreams. Miri is certain that both the face and the recognition are nothing more than dreams, fantasies that have no purchase on reality. Yet Marta has inexplicably known Jesus without ever having seen him alive. Moreover she believes that he came to her, at the same time as Musa saw him walking through the desert, spoke to her and touched her. Again the encounter is informed by displaced echoes of the gospels. When Mary Magdalene meets Jesus he does not permit her to touch him. Marta has Jesus within the range of her touch, but he touches her instead, with a hand of healing, as the Jesus of the gospels touches those he heals. Where in the gospels Jesus invites Thomas to feel his wounds, here Jesus touches Marta's; and he kisses her feet, as Mary of Bethany had done to Jesus (and possibly with an echo of Jesus's washing of his disciples' feet at the Last Supper). This Jesus knows Marta intimately, knows her husband's name, knows the problem of her infertility: and gives her, apparently, what she came for, a child (perhaps her own – she feels she may be pregnant by Musa – or the child she will share with Miri).

Miri provides the naturalistic explanation that seems implicit in Crace's fictional method: Marta supplies from her own longings and anxieties the features of her healer, and the lineaments of their encounter. If Marta is pregnant, then it is by normal human procreation, not by any miraculous fingertip conception. Yet there are still mysteries here: how does she recognize Jesus? Why does she believe she sees him? How can her vision concur with Musa's?

The death that precedes this miraculous resurrection is narrated by Crace in strongly naturalistic terms, encouraging the reader to perceive it as an ordinary death, from natural causes, and entailing the absolute and final destruction and dissolution of the flesh. Jesus is portrayed as a man afflicted with an excessive spirituality (p. 74). He sees God in everything, and yearns for the absolute. He is depicted as 'a simple-hearted' man who longs for unity with the ultimate being, and is obsessed with questions of ultimate truth. Jesus's death, seen as a willed self-immolation, is prefigured in this characterization of him as oriented to the absolute, and neglectful of the everyday, 'a clumsy carpenter' (p. 75).

Unlike the other quarantiners, Jesus subjects himself to unnecessary and extreme forms of deprivation. He seeks isolation where the others seek or accept community, and punishes his body with an intolerable degree of ascetic renunciation, where they break fast every evening. Rapt in a solipsistic devotion, he mistakes a dead donkey for a divine vision, offerings of food and drink for temptations, the voices of desert neighbours for the solicitations of the devil. Crace presents Jesus as a man who brings about his own death by committing the fundamental error of trusting in a non-existent God, neglecting the laws of nature, believing falsely that the needs of the body can be subdued to the priorities of the spirit (p. 109). In death he encounters not the fullness of divine presence, but a universal emptiness, 'the cold of nothing there'.

Here Crace infiltrates some of that 'didacticism' he declared as one of his objectives in writing the novel. This is how we all die, the common lot of mortality: expiring into emptiness, entering the universal coldness of nothing. The death of Jesus is presented almost as a case-study in the follies of religion, or an object lesson to illustrate the better wisdom of science.

Later passages reflecting on Musa's vision of the Resurrection also seem to strengthen this naturalistic, secular view of death as absolute and final. Musa finds it difficult to distinguish between what he saw and what he imagines of the risen Jesus. As time passes, this difficulty in disentangling the real Jesus from the stories told about him diminishes, and the Christ of faith is seen emerging from the

Jesus of history: 'his outline hardened and his body put on flesh'. The contours of the risen Jesus become more definite as Musa's vision becomes more remote from reality, and the great lie of Christianity takes root. This is the Jesus of the Resurrection, with wounded feet and tangible flesh. But he exists here only in the story-teller's imagination: in reality his corpse is decaying in a wilderness grave. Christianity is a fabrication built on a hallucination, disseminated by a shoddy businessman with a fund of narrative and a knack of persuasion.

Yet the numinous aura of the miraculous continues to cling about these figures and their world. The catalyst of the novel is Jesus's healing of Musa (pp. 25–6), which is given no rational explanation. The man is dying; Jesus gives him water and a blessing. He lives. Critics converge on the natural explanations that lie to hand (since Crace has been careful to place them there): Jesus is not consciously trying to enact miracles; he gives Musa water as an 'afterthought' after satisfying his own thirst; and his words of healing, 'So, here, be well again' are rationalized as 'a common greeting for the sick' (p. 26). But does a miracle of healing require more elaborate wording? In what way is a common language of blessing incompatible with a miraculous act of redemption?

Just before he dies Jesus hears a voice (which we know from elsewhere in the narrative to be that of Shim), a voice that answers his prayers and leads him forth to the scene of others' sufferings in a mission of healing (p. 192). Perhaps this is Shim's voice, the words distorted by the wind, the accent unrecognizable. Perhaps there is a simple explanation for everything, and yet this passage describes something genuinely miraculous. Jesus knows nothing of the other pilgrims and their troubles, or of what is happening outside his retreat. If the voice does take him somewhere, it is in the form of a mysterious spiritual journey explicable by no natural means.

And the miracles do take root in the real. Asaph, dying on his entry to the wilderness, is last seen 'seeming younger . . . and vigorous' (p. 237); Shim walks away proudly with achieved 'tranquillity and self-respect' (p. 229). Miri and Marta escape into an unlooked-for freedom and friendship, 'pregnant with hope' (p. 114), sharing between them the miracle of childbearing (p. 237).

Earlier in this chapter I cited numerous commentaries from Crace himself endorsing a rationalist and scientific reading of *Quarantine* as a counter-Christian polemic. Those observations were in fact detached from a considerably more complex and ambivalent analysis of *Quarantine* and its religious implications. Crace's preface continues:

> Indeed, *Quarantine* did slay Christ. But novels have a way of breaking loose from their creators. That's why they're fun to write. Science does not triumph unambiguously in the book. Faith is not destroyed by Doubt. Jesus does not let me kill him off entirely . . . books have agendas of their own, no matter what the author may believe. Novels and their writers are not mere mirror images.[14]

Here Crace deploys a language commonly used by writers to account for a strange self-sufficiency in writing, a vitality and purposefulness seemingly independent of the creator. Just as he spoke of Jesus wandering into the novel almost in spite of himself, so here he allows space for the novel to set its own agenda, to reveal unanticipated and uncontrolled insights and nuances that arise spontaneously from its evolution. If this is the case then the alternative possibilities of interpretation outlined above cease to surprise: 'despite his own atheism textually he allows a space for the resurrection of Christ'.[15] The novel may disclose something different from the author's own atheism. 'The book doesn't come across as an atheist text, and when you start adopting new scriptural modes, it begins to sound exactly like the thing you are criticising' (p. 117). A reworking of scripture cannot but convey some of scripture's own inherent possibilities.

Not that the novelist himself need necessarily be convinced by the persuasive artifice of the novel. Crace does not find in the novel's narratives of resurrection, healing and miracle any evidence to dissuade him from his scientific atheism. Clearly he can see in his fiction something described by one critic as 'the redemptive power of narrative':

> It's the imp of story-telling at our shoulders, not the Grace of God.

But such redemption as there is remains wholly secular and humanistic:

> So, I'm just as godless as I ever was.

But not quite as confident, perhaps.

> . . . nobody could spend two years writing such a book and remain undisturbed by it . . .[16]

IV

Throughout the Middle Ages and the Early Modern period traditional Christian teaching assumed the resurrection of the body or of the flesh: that the resurrected body was the body of the living person reconstituted by divine power. The gospel language for resurrection is a language of rising or being raised up, standing up or being stood up, which suggests the awakening of a sleeper or the resuscitation of a corpse. One symbolic centre of Resurrection belief is the empty tomb, which is predicated on the absence of the corpse: the crucified body has been raised from the dead and restored to the realm of the living. Tertullian's influential work *De Resurrectione Carnis* taught that the resurrected body was reconstituted in physical form, even though this might involve the 'reassemblage of bits'.[17] The body of life and the body of Resurrection were the same entity, sharing 'an identity guaranteed by material and formal unity' (p. 8).

St Paul, however, in the key Resurrection text 1 Corinthians 15 presents what seems a very different argument:

> Christ died for our sins according to the Scriptures . . . he was buried . . . he was raised on the third day.

> But someone may ask, 'How are the dead raised? With what kind of body will they come?' How foolish! What you sow does not come to life unless it dies. When you sow, you do not plant the body that will be, but just a seed, perhaps of wheat or of something else. . . . So will it be with the resurrection of the dead. The body that is sown is perishable, it is raised imperishable; it is sown in dishonour, it is raised in glory; it is sown in weakness, it is raised in power; it is sown a natural body, it is raised a spiritual body.

> If there is a natural body, there is also a spiritual body. So it is written: 'The first man Adam became a living being'; the last

Adam, a life-giving spirit. The spiritual did not come first, but the natural, and after that the spiritual. The first man was of the dust of the earth, the second man from heaven. As was the earthly man, so are those who are of the earth; and as is the man from heaven, so also are those who are of heaven. And just as we have borne the likeness of the earthly man, so shall we bear the likeness of the man from heaven.

I declare to you, brothers, that flesh and blood cannot inherit the kingdom of God, nor does the perishable inherit the imperishable. (New International Version)

Paul's view of Resurrection does not involve the resurrection of the body, but a replacement of the body by a 'spiritual body', a new type of being (though Pannenberg[18] observes that Paul does not distinguish clearly between 'transformation' and 'replacement' in his model of the Resurrection body).

Both these theories of Resurrection seem to be active in the post-resurrection appearances of the gospels. In some passages the body of the risen Jesus is there to be seen and touched. The disciples 'took hold of his feet' (Matt. 28.10). Jesus invites the disciples to handle him – 'Touch me and see' (Luke 24.39); assures them that he is no ghost – 'a ghost does not have flesh and bones as you see that I have' (Luke 24.39); and eats fish before them to show that he is real – 'he took it and ate in their presence' (Luke 24.42). He points to his wounded hands and feet (Luke 24.39; John 20.20) and persuades Thomas to 'reach out your hand and put it in my side' (John 20.27). All these details indicate not only the presence of a fully living physical body, but also a definite continuity between the crucified and resurrected bodies of Jesus.

At the same time, and even in the same contexts, there are details that suggest that the body of the post-resurrection appearances is more like St Paul's replacement 'spiritual body' than the crucified body restored. Jesus is not recognizable (Luke 24.16; John 20.14 and 21.4), appears from nowhere (Luke 24.36; John 20.19) and disappears at will (Luke 24.31). He declines to be touched by Mary Magdalene.

Clearly for a rationalist and secular mentality neither of these two scenarios is conceivable within the realms of nature. The dead do not reappear, either in the same physical form or transformed into something different: 'For the post-Enlightenment mentality, Resurrection is a very difficult idea to accept.'[19] Jesus is no exception to the universal laws of nature. As Pannenberg drily comments, 'on the basis of present everyday experience it seems extremely unlikely that any dead person will be raised to a new life' (p. 62). His death is a recorded historical incident, his resurrection a fable or myth: 'the death of Jesus can certainly be thought of as history in the modern sense, but not the resurrection'.[20] Given a choice, post-enlightenment scepticism will of course prefer the Pauline theology of the spiritual body rather than the traditional theology of the bodily resurrection, hence as Dahl observes the former began to supersede the latter at the beginning of 'the critical period in Christian theology'.[21] Modern Christologists seek 'an interpretation of the Resurrection that does not require us to suspend the assumptions on which we operate in every other aspect of life'.[22] A typical example would be John MacQuarrie's discussion in *Jesus Christ in Modern Thought*, which begins by dismissing bodily resurrection as an impossibility:

> . . . what is resurrected is not the dead body that has been laid in the grave, not the body of flesh and blood and carbon chemistry by which humans live on earth. (This point raises further problems about the story of an empty tomb.) That physical body is like an automobile – it has a built in obsolescence, and though it may keep going for seventy or eighty or even a hundred years, it will eventually wear out and perish in death. So resurrection cannot be anything so simple as the resuscitation of a corpse, for that would be only a temporary postponement of death, which would come eventually. It would be quite different from the resurrection of Jesus Christ who, the New Testament claims, has conquered death and is alive for ever. To go back to Paul's argument, a natural body of flesh and blood could not be the bearer of a death-transcending existence. (p. 408)

The body known to science, the organism composed of 'carbon chemistry', is mortal and finite and cannot therefore be conceived as the subject of a resurrection. It would probably surprise Jim Crace to learn that some modern theologians have as little belief in the possibility of bodily resurrection as does Richard Dawkins: '"Resurrection of the dead" first of all excludes any idea of a revivification of the dead Jesus which might have reversed the

process of his death.'[23] Such a belief is regarded as untenable in the
light of modern science and philosophy. On the other hand the more
attractive possibilities offered by St Paul's 'replacement' theory of
Resurrection can point towards what is probably the most common
popular conception of post-mortal survival, the ghost or wraith-
like entity that 'goes towards the light'.

Why then does the New Testament contain both interpretations
of Resurrection? The answer is that in order to function as a
central Christian doctrine, without which, Paul asserts, 'faith has
been in vain' (1 Cor. 15.14), Resurrection faith must hold together
the risen Christ and the Jesus who died on the cross. Both are the
manifestation of God's saving intervention into human history,
but it is error to suppose, as did the Gnostics, that the two can be
separated. As Moltmann puts it, 'The original significance of the
Easter faith is that the eye-witnesses perceived the earthly, crucified
Jesus of the past in the glory of God's coming' (p. 172). The body
of the resurrected Jesus must bear the wounds of the crucifixion,
the marks of the nails, the spear's incision, or the saving love of the
crucified God has not been revealed.

Another important strand in modern Christology is to read the
Resurrection as a symbolic language for the undeniable historical
fact of the Christian church. There is an almost universal consensus
among theologians that whatever happened that first Easter, it was of
sufficient power and influence to bring together a scattered band of
broken-hearted followers into a church, a church that declares itself
to be the body of Christ on earth, risen from the defeat and death
of the crucifixion to a life of witness and preaching, evangelism and
proclamation. When Peter first preached the gospel in Jerusalem
(Acts 2), it was the Resurrection that he preached. The church is
the risen Christ: the church is 'the outward, visible, historically
observable aspect of the resurrection'.[24]

V

This sketch of the outlines of modern Christology will enable us to
discern just how conformable *Quarantine* is to the theology of today.
Theologians have pointed out that the empty tomb presupposes a
missing corpse, and that a Jesus resurrected in the spiritual body

on St Paul's model would have had no use for those remains. The empty tomb seems to point in the direction of bodily resurrection. Scholars have suggested that the 'grave' and 'appearance' stories are two separate traditions, and that the empty tomb may have been retrospectively invented to hold the already discovered mystery of the risen Lord. Paul never mentions the tomb or the body: they have no role to play in his schema. Yet it is worth considering that the most impressive proof one could have of Paul's affirmations would be to find in the gospel narratives both a dead body and a resurrected spirit: the natural body sown into the soil of death, the spiritual body risen from the grave. This would allow, as Pannenberg says, 'for the mortal body to decay in the tomb while another one will be provided by the creator God' (p. 68). This is exactly what Crace gives us in *Quarantine*.

The physical death of Jesus is narrated, as we have seen, in painstaking and intractable detail. Crace is as anxious to explain exactly what happened to the body of Jesus as were the Jews who, according to Matthew's gospel, spread the rumour that the body had been 'stolen away' (Matt. 28.11–15). Crace describes the physical signs of bodily decay in absorbed and compelling detail (p. 192). The corpse of Jesus is discovered already prey to carrion birds. It is prepared for interment, given funeral obsequies and decisively buried in a grave of earth, the hole initially excavated by Miri to hold the corpse of her husband. It is as if Crace wants to reduce to the minimum any possible space of uncertainty about the single, absolute, crushing truth that Jesus died a common human death, his corpse 'buried, dead and done with'. [25]

And yet the death and interment of Jesus are threaded with gospel echoes that inevitably prompt in the reader some alternative expectations. The body is laid out in a cave, the entrance blocked with thorns (p. 212). Earlier this place of burial is described as a 'sepulchre' (p. 180). The two women who prepare Jesus's body for burial recall the women who come to the tomb to find it empty (p. 224) but also resemble the sisters of Lazarus who prepared their brother's body for burial only to receive him back resurrected. The women find the body of Jesus still 'beautiful' in its hands and feet (p. 223) and touching it not distasteful, more like a 'blessing' (p. 224).

As Crace observed, 'adopting new scriptural modes . . . begins to sound exactly like the thing you are criticising'.[26] David Jasper echoes this sense of recognition: 'the effect is strangely familiar' as the novel provides 'uncanny resonances' (pp. 99, 103) with the gospels, and Frank Kermode alludes to the 'shadows cast over the characters and events by the original story from which the new fable derives'.[27] Thus the Resurrection narratives seem to flow naturally from this denouement and come as no surprise, despite the harsh and unrelenting naturalism of bodily death. The post-resurrection appearances of Jesus again echo the gospels. He appears to more than one person, and his apparition seems at times physical, at times spiritual. He can be recognized immediately (Marta), or there may be some difficulty in identification (Musa). He can be encountered walking normally towards you, or suddenly and surprisingly appearing in an inaccessible venue. His healing spirit seems to roam the desert, but Marta feels herself physically touched by him. Musa sees him heading purposefully towards infinity, then later returning towards the valley in an apparent reincarnation (p. 243). The Resurrection of Jesus confirms and authorizes the miraculous impact he has had on the small desert community; and is shown (albeit ironically) to precipitate the foundational narrative of a new Resurrection faith.

Why then, finally, should a self-professed scientific atheist engage so closely with key Christian texts and central Christian doctrines as to emerge from the encounter at the very least 'disturbed', and to leave in the wake of the writing process a novel equally disturbed, fissured and fractured by religious revelations that call into question its declared naturalism? The short answer is that Crace the writer, as distinct from Crace the polemical atheist, is by no means as 'scientific' in his perspective on life as he wishes to claim. Much of the particularity, for example, of his topical detail is invented. His manifest love of language leads him to devise linguistic structures that display a 'crystalline' aesthetic beauty, but can scarcely be evaluated by any criteria of objective truth. 'Crace does not proceed by turning reality into fiction . . . he seems to prefer invention to research, making things look right to factual accuracy.'[28]

There are further clues to the solution of this problem in Crace's treatment of the human body. At one level he writes the body as solid and self-contained, the integral sensuous centre of each subjective consciousness. On a broader front he sees the body as part of an eco-system of interrelationships, bound to other bodies and to the earth which sustains their existence. Both appear to be reasonably 'scientific' definitions of corporeal existence, physical and biological: body as matter, body as organism. But already there is a difference. The solid self-contained body, inhabited by a consciousness that can misrecognize its nature as perversely as does Jesus, is the material body subject to the inexorable laws of nature, marked for absolute death and final dissolution. But once we begin to see the body as involved in a network of relations, the death of the individual takes on a different set of meanings. It becomes possible, for example, for the death of an individual to be perceived as a Resurrection by its effecting of Resurrection in other lives.

Throughout the novel the human body is represented as a semiotic vehicle, a site of meaning and interrelationship, as well as a physical organism. Although Jesus isolates himself from community and dies alone on his precipice, most bodies in the fiction live relationally with others and with the land. Miri is conscious of herself as containing another life, the child in her womb (p. 9). The friendship of Miri and Marta grows not only through intimate physical touch, but also through a shared craft of weaving which in turn relates to the contours of the land (p. 103). Musa sees human bodies as inextricably involved with the material substances in which he trades: he fetishizes the female body he desires with his sensuous knowledge of textiles, confusing 'the fabric and the flesh' (p. 89). Above all there is a continual interplay between bodies and landscape: 'Crace's novel', Jasper observes, 'like the desert itself, confuses interior and exterior' (p. 100). The wilderness is able to '. . . replicate through its array of absences the body's inner solitude . . . the empty spaces in the heart' (p. 219). Here Crace is redefining the body in semiotic terms, the body 'mediated through the giving and receiving of signs',[29] the body as a network of signifiers rather than an irreducible material object. In other words he is following the trajectory of post-modern Christology in redefining the body of the Resurrection as a body that can, in Graham Ward's words, 'materialize only in, through and with language' (p. 174). McQuarrie, speaking of St Paul's 'spiritual body', similarly extends the parameters of what a spirituality of the body might mean:

> We have to get beyond the thinking that 'body' means merely or even primarily the familiar structure of bones, flesh, blood and so on. Rather, 'body' is that aspect of one's being whereby one is inserted into a world, and so empowered to perceive,

communicate and act in that world. The bodies that we have insert us into this earthly world of space and time, and empower us to perceive, communicate and act in this world. But may there be other 'worlds', other systems of relationships into which we are differently inserted? Are there, for instance, personal or interpersonal worlds, in which persons would be related in a manner different from that which depends on the bodily senses? Do we already have some hint of the possibility in our present experience, when people claim to be in communion with one another, though not using words or touching or looking at each other? . . . Perhaps resurrection is transcendence to a new level in the being of the human person, a level which eludes our understanding so long as we are seeing it only from below. (p. 409)

In one dimension Crace is entirely closed to these hypotheses, for which, like the existence of God, he has no need. But his fiction is wide open to them. Consider for example the passage in which Miri, herself a sceptical materialist hardened by bitter experience, prophesies the novel's strange denouement, while simultaneously refuting it as logically impossible:

Would the Galilean man or boy, this godly creature who'd crept so memorably into their tent, expel the old man's cancer, fertilize the women's crabby womb, make Shim's heart as handsome as his face, expel whatever madcap spirits had taken residence inside the badu's head, bring god down to the precipice to transform Musa, shrink him to a proper size? . . . She knew that life did not improve through prayers or miracles.

Acting as a proxy for the novelist (and his mentor Richard Dawkins), Miri dismisses the supernatural as an impossibility, a mere 'self-deception' or wish-fulfilment fantasy. Such a wholesale transformation of obdurate reality is literally unthinkable. Yet not only does she think it, something very like it truly comes to pass. At the close of the novel Asaph's condition seems at least to have improved; Marta is literally or symbolically pregnant; Shim has a new-found courage, the badu finds enough common sense to steal Musa's goats, and even Musa himself reaches the novel's closing pages diminished in stature, first by his company's desertion and then by the magnitude of the narrative it is his destiny to convey to the world. 'Certainly' David Jasper observes, 'this young lunatic had effected a justice, for the travellers are shriven and the devil is defeated' (p. 103).

Crace makes no attempt to reconcile the paradox of miracle, but instead lets the supernatural and reductionist explanations lie side by side in mutual discord. 'Crace confirms', reports Tew, 'that the ending is "absolutely supposed to be ambiguous" and that in fiction one can "offer the possibility of alternative explanations"' (p. 133). 'Ambivalent' would be a better word than ambiguous, since Crace seems to present the reader with a much starker choice between naturalism and supernaturalism, the finality of death or the possibility of Resurrection. Jesus's dead body might be 'a discarded page of scripture', or 'Fruit turned back into its seed' (p. 192). The novel opens up some of those gaps that lie intriguingly within the interstices of scientific explanation, exploring questions to which science has not yet found an answer. But whereas the true naturalist like Richard Dawkins remains obdurately confident that in time all such questions will be answered by science, Crace allows for the possibility that quite different answers, in short religious ones, might potentially emerge. The territory of the novel is not scientific certitude but religious doubt, very like the doubt that is threaded throughout the post-Resurrection passages of the gospels. 'Science does not triumph unambiguously in the book. Faith is not destroyed by Doubt'.

> Jesus is separated from form and presence and can be made into something other than factuality . . . [Musa] transforms the significance of the real, using the chimera of the word, requiring a transcendence of the mundane, the referential. He trades the equivocal nature of the miraculous in terms of its effecting belief, especially in its outcome in enabling him to capitalize the aspirational in others. He exchanges hope.[30]

4

Cross and altar: Mel Gibson's *The Passion of the Christ*

I

Only slightly less surprising than Mel Gibson's initial decision to make a Christian film about the Passion of Christ, using Aramaic and Latin dialogue with vernacular subtitles, was the subsequent phenomenon of the film's extraordinary success. *The Passion of the Christ* broke box office records, topped league tables, established itself with striking rapidity as one of the most popular religious films ever made, and even gave mainstream popular cinema a run for its money. '*The Passion* has been embraced by millions as a revelation of biblical proportions.'[1] Subsequent releases on video and DVD sustained this popularity.[2]

But admiration of the film was by no means universal. There was a huge gap between the film's hospitable acceptance by popular audiences, and the critical reception it met in newspapers and magazines.[3] The film won Oscars only in the relatively minor categories of make-up and cinematography. But it did win a Peoples' Choice award in 2005.

It is no longer uncommon for controversy to generate around films before they are seen (in the case of *The Passion*, before it was made). Cynics suspect such debates to be orchestrated as a form of pre-release publicity: 'Gibson appears to have been doing what Hollywood producers always try to do: to get as much positive buzz as possible about his film before the public'.[4] In the case of this film, however, as Rene Girard put it, 'the film precipitated a veritable tantrum in the world's most influential media that more or less contaminated the entire atmosphere in its wake'.[5] Jewish groups alleging anti-Semitism;[6] journalists and media critics, affirming or adopting an atheistic or agnostic distaste; evangelical Christian groups alternately supporting and rejecting the film – all agreed on one thing: they did not like *The Passion of the Christ*.[7] This widely shared aversion could be expressed in a number of different ways: the film was at best flawed and at worst worthless; its religious influence could only be pernicious; it would stir up ethnic and inter-faith hatred; people should not under any circumstances go to see it. Although Christ-films have often courted controversy,[8] never has so much attention been focused on a film by people advocating avoidance. In the words of Isaiah (53.5) they 'hid as it were [their] faces from him'.

II

Those who did unveil their faces and watch the film encountered significant hermeneutic difficulty. Paula Frederickson reported encountering widely a condition of 'genuine puzzlement over the controversy surrounding this movie';[9] and this was due in no small part to a remarkable ignorance of Christian history and theology (or as Nicola Denzey politely puts it, a 'general lack of biblical acumen')[10] on the part of many opinion leaders. Most people who went to see the film could be expected to assume that Christian theology is embodied principally in the quasi-biographical narratives of the life, teaching and death of Jesus to be found in the canonical gospels. Despite their status as divine scripture, the Christian gospels are 'realistic' in style; they are anchored in history; they correspond to Jakob Lother's definition of narrative as 'a chain of events which is situated in time and space'.[11]

They are also of course narratives of events that occur outside time and space, and they include miraculous and mystical materials that would be hard to integrate into any conception of 'realism'. But compared to the scriptures of other religions, the Christian gospels are surprisingly down to earth, a difference arising from their Incarnational theology. Unlike the transcendent divinities of Judaism and Islam, Christ through the Incarnation takes on human form, and thereby becomes accessible to representation. In the Gospels, when miracles occur, they are described in realistic detail; and only rarely do we see Jesus slipping momentarily out of the human frame, and as it were re-appearing to be glimpsed through the lens of divinity, as happens in the Transfiguration (Matt. 17.1–6; Mark 9.1–8; Luke 9.28–36); and of course the Ascension (Mark 16.19; Luke 24.51). Since the early nineteenth century, artists have found it a relatively straightforward matter, whether from a Christian or a non-Christian point of view, to turn the stories of the gospels into prose fiction and narrative film.[12]

But are such narratives the natural or essential language of Christian belief? The canonical gospels post-date the earliest documents of Christian theology, the letters of St Paul. Virtually all scholars agree that the gospels were written later than Paul's letters, that Mark is the earliest of the gospels, and that narrative and discursive elaboration increases with chronological distance from the historical events, culminating in the gospel according to John. A sequential reading of the Bible's books ('*biblia*') encounters Paul's letters *after* the gospels, out of chronological sequence, and the inexperienced reader would naturally assume that Paul is quoting or citing from already formulated narrative sources. He may have been; but Paul's Christology does not depend on narrative. It is anachronistic, *kerygmatic*[13] and liturgical.

III

Paul's 'undisputed' letters[14] contain virtually no narrative representation of the life, actions and teaching of Christ, other than a handful of references to the salient events of Holy Week: the institution of the Eucharist, the Crucifixion and the Resurrection. Paul shows hardly any interest in the story of Jesus's life, and little interest in his teachings. His focus is exclusively on Christ's death and resurrection. Even the famous passage in 1 Corinthians on the Last Supper, which adopts a linear narrative form, is much more concerned with a timeless pattern of sacrifice and redemption than with Jesus's biography, representational accuracy or historical detail:

> For I have received of the Lord that which also I delivered unto you, That the Lord Jesus the *same* night in which he was betrayed took bread:
>
> And when he had given thanks, he brake *it*, and said, Take, eat: this is my body, which is broken for you: this do in remembrance of me.
>
> After the same manner also *he took* the cup, when he had supped, saying, This cup is the new testament in my blood: this do ye, as oft as ye drink *it*, in remembrance of me.
>
> For as often as ye eat this bread, and drink this cup, ye do shew the Lord's death till he come.[15]

In other words Paul's focus is not on the biography of Jesus the Son of Man, but on the transcendent divine actions of Jesus the Son of God, on those events that demonstrate the true meaning of Incarnation, the 'intersection of the timeless/With time'.[16] And in any case discursively Paul is not here recounting a story, but offering a verbal sacrifice: for what is enacted here in the poetic prose of the epistle is nothing less than the sacrament of the Eucharist. This is not an episode in a narrative, but a transcendent liturgical moment that crosses 2,000 years to link the first Holy Thursday, the rituals of the early church and the daily sacrifice of the Catholic Mass.

In a similar way, when Paul cites the post-resurrection appearances in 1 Corinthians 15, he links the unmediated experience of the apostles, who physically encountered the risen Christ, to the apparition that accompanied his own conversion on the Road to Damascus:

> For I delivered unto you first of all that which I also received, how that Christ died for our sins according to the scriptures;
>
> And that he was buried, and that he rose again the third day according to the scriptures;
>
> And that he was seen of Cephas, then of the twelve;
>
> After that, he was seen of above five hundred brethren at once; of whom the greater part remain unto this present, but some are fallen asleep.

After that, he was seen of James; then of all the apostles.
And last of all he was seen of me also, as of one born out of due time.[17]

The ostensible continuity invoked here is misleading, since these apparitions are clearly of a different order. What sounds like a historical sequence of parallel events is actually an anachronistic conflating (as Paul admits with his phrase 'out of due time') of literal encounters with the risen Christ, and the visionary conversion narrative that tells Paul's own story. When God irrupted into Paul's own life, the impact of that event constituted an 'appearance' comparable to those witnessed after the Resurrection. This narrative is not a chronological history, 'one damn thing after another', but the same kerygmatic event repeated over and over again.

Paul's Eucharistic theology corresponds to Rowan Williams's description of the Easter rite as a participatory ceremonial to be experienced, rather than an impersonal narrative to be heard, or a visual representation to be gazed at. This distinction has profound implications for a filmic account of the Passion, and for the experience of its audiences. The Gospel accounts provide the kind of linear narrative that turns itself easily into fictional prose or narrative film. All mainstream Christ-films follow, wholly or partly, the Gospel narrative, often beginning in the beginning with the Annunciation and the Nativity. Franco Zefirelli's *Jesus of Nazareth*, despite its putative link with Anthony Burgess's modernist novel *Man of Nazareth*, nonetheless follows the gospels in strict linear sequence; Pasolini's *The Gospel of St Matthew*, which clearly has links in terms of setting and casting with the traditional communal Passion Play, follows a straight path through the gospel narrative from Annunciation to Resurrection; and Scorsese's radical treatment in *The Last Temptation of Christ* tells the same story, albeit with the interpolation of the famous might-have-been flashback.

Even *The Passion of the Christ*, which spans only the last day of Jesus's mortal life, has a plot that can be traced exactly in the gospels. Mel Gibson has repeatedly claimed, as any obedient Catholic inevitably would, that his film is based on the gospels.[18] But clearly it differs strikingly from the traditional filmed gospels;[19] and in its concentration on one final day, from Gethsemane to

Golgotha, the film truncates imaginary time and space into a palpably experiential, non-narrative concentration, consisting of scenes which do not progress an action, but rather show the same action repeated over and over again. The reason for this difference is that the film's narrative and dramatic structure owes less to the gospels than to a cultural form within which time and narrative assume very specialized meanings: the ritual and liturgy of the traditional Catholic Mass.

IV

Gospel readings are of course part of the Mass, but only a part, and only in the shape of relatively brief passages forming the separate 'doctrinal' element ('The Mass of the Catechumens') that precedes the sacrament ('The Mass of the Faithful'). In performing the Eucharistic ritual, a 'mysterious re-presentation of Christ's sacrifice'[20] the church is commemorating the rite established on the first Holy Thursday, but also, in Catholic belief, reenacting a sacrifice instituted before the beginning of time, which in turn anticipates an ultimate return and reconciliation to take place at time's end. The short affirmation known as *mysterium fidei* or the 'Proclamation of Faith' demonstrates how, in what appears to be a transparently linear sequence of events, time is disturbed and dissociated:

> Christ has died
> Christ is risen
> Christ will come again.

On the face of it this is a simple, textbook narrative sequence constituting a 'story'. But the death commemorated is an event out of time, synonymous with a Resurrection that is ever present ('Christ *is* risen'), and a sacrifice that is renewed daily, for believers, in the Catholic Mass. In turn the Eucharist represents not only a historical sacrifice that took place in the past, but the Eucharistic promise of a final eschaton that lies at the other end of time ('shew the Lord's death until he come').

Profound implications for film narrative flow therefore from Gibson's traditional, many would say reactionary, Catholic faith. As Terry Mattingley observes,

It is crucial to realize that the images and language at the heart of *The Passion of the Christ* flow directly out of Gibson's personal dedication to Catholicism in one of its most traditional and mysterious forms – the 16th century Latin Mass.[21]

And Gibson is cited in the same source as saying:

The goal of the movie is to shake modern audiences by brashly juxtaposing the sacrifice of the cross with the sacrifice of the altar – which is the same thing . . . The script of *The Passion of the Christ* was specifically intended to link the crucifixion of Christ with what Roman Catholics believe is the re-sacrificing of Christ that occurs in the Mass. (p. 2)

The structure of *The Passion of the Christ* is not therefore based in linear narrative, but in simultaneity and montage; it concentrates time and space in order to transcend them; and its style of ultra-close-up realism ultimately serves an anti-realist agenda. To locate the film within the famous Eisenstein-Bazin debate on the nature of cinema, *The Passion of the Christ* works by juxtaposing images to invoke transcendent truth, rather than by delineating space to transcribe the real. Or as Gerald Mast puts it in a useful description of film time, Gibson's film 'imprisons the attention' by using

the cumulative kinetic hypnosis of the *uninterrupted* flow of film and time. Because the art of cinema most closely parallels the operation of time, it imprisons the attention within a hypnotic grip that becomes steadily tighter and stronger (if the work is properly built) as the film progresses and it refuses to let go until it has had its way.[22]

V

The film's juxtaposition of the Passion and the Mass also helps to explain Gibson's explicit indebtedness to the *Dolorous Passion of*

Our Lord Jesus Christ, dictated around 1820 by the Augustinian nun Anna Catherine Emmerich to the poet Klemens Brentano.[23]

The Dolorous Passion consists of a series of dream-visions in which Sister Emmerich imagines herself anachronistically witnessing the events of the Passion. The narrative purports therefore to be that of an eyewitness, positioned in close proximity to the events. Sr Emmerich spoke of her visions as 'shown' to her, in much the same manner as those of the fifteenth-century mystic Julian of Norwich. She does not think of herself as traveling through time, but rather placed in a position of vantage, as a bystander or witness, from which the eternal sacrifice could be clearly seen. She 'sees' the events of the Passion as they unfold; she 'understands' some things and not others; she remembers with formidable accuracy, but forgets details, some of which are later recollected.

The visions were precisely visualized and deeply felt experiences that could be replayed again in the same form, almost like recorded films: 'I have always seen' for example 'the Pasch [Passover] and the institution of the Blessed Sacrament take place in the order related above' (p. 89). Hence the visions are very detailed in their historical representation and physical embodiment, so much so that the book stands as a very early example of the novelistic fictionalization of the Passion story: as John Strohmeier puts it, 'Emmerich's narrative reads in some ways like a skillfully crafted historical novel.'[24]

Take Sr Emmerich's account of the scourging of Jesus, which Gibson clearly used in his film:

> Thus was the Holy of Holies violently stretched, without a particle of clothing, on a pillar used for the punishment of the greatest criminals; and then did two furious ruffians who were thirsting for his blood begin in the most barbarous manner to scourge his sacred body from head to foot. The whips or scourges which they first made use of appeared to me to be made of a species of flexible white wood, but perhaps they were composed of the sinews of the ox, or of strips of leather . . . Then two fresh executioners commenced scourging Jesus with the greatest possible fury; they made use of a different kind of rod, a species of thorny stick, covered with knots and splinters. The blows from these sticks tore his flesh to pieces; his blood spouted out so as to stain their arms, and he groaned, prayed, and shuddered . . . Two fresh executioners took the places of the

last mentioned, who were beginning to flag; their scourges were composed of small chains, or straps covered with iron hooks, which penetrated to the bone, and tore off large pieces of flesh at every blow. What word, alas! could describe this terrible – this heartrending scene![25]

Based on the very brief references in the gospels to the scourging (e.g. Matt. 27.26), Sr Emmerich is extraordinarily precise as to the implements used, the attitudes of the scourgers, the reactions of the victim. 'The appeal of Emmerich's account of the Passion and Resurrection', Strohmeier observes, 'rests in large part upon the author's sensitivity to the inner conflicts of her subjects, and her gift for identifying the significant visual, historic or psychological detail.'[26] In this way her narrative can be imagined as filling out detail absent from the gospels, in the form of a sensuously thick description that provides ample substance for a director's mis-en-scene.

The *Dolorous Passion of Our Lord* can thus be read as a hyper-realistic imaginative account of the Crucifixion, fully and clearly visualized by a floating disembodied consciousness capable of observation, knowledge and compassionate feeling. Mel Gibson's recourse to Sr Emmerich's visions would appear at first glance to intensify the assumed 'realism' of the film, to enable the director to get up close to his historical subject, to 'see what happened';[27] or in the Pope's alleged comment, 'It is as it was'. 'I wanted' Gibson is quoted as saying 'to bring you there'.[28]

Although Sr Emmerich was treated very supportively by the local nobility and clergy who facilitated Brentano's capture of the visions and their publication, there was clearly some potentiality of embarrassment for the church, as is always the case, when confronted with this kind of individual visionary inspiration. Klemens Brentano protested in his preface 'To the Reader', that no deviation from the truth of scripture was intended:

Whoever compares the following meditations with the short history of the Last Supper given in the Gospel will discover some slight differences between them. An explanation should be given of this, although it can never be sufficiently impressed upon the reader that these writings have no pretensions whatever to add an iota to Sacred Scripture as interpreted by the Church.[29]

'The Preface to the French Translation' by the Abbe de Cazales strikes a similarly defensive note, but risks a slightly more open-minded stance. He calls the visions a 'paraphrase of the Gospel narrative', and praises them for their accuracy and truthfulness. But he also acknowledges that they contain material not to be found in the gospels, but which derive from post-apostolic Christological tradition:

> Although [the translator] is aware that St. Bonaventure and many others, in their paraphrases of the Gospel history, have mixed up traditional details with those given in the sacred text, St. Bonaventure professed only to give a paraphrase . . . these revelations appear to be something more. It is certain that the holy maiden herself gave them no higher title than that of dreams, and that the transcriber of her narratives treats as blasphemous the idea of regarding them in any degree as equivalent to a fifth Gospel; still it is evident that the confessors who exhorted Sister Emmerich to relate what she saw, the celebrated poet who passed four years near her couch, eagerly transcribing all he heard her say, and the German Bishops, who encouraged the publication of his book, considered it as something more than a paraphrase.[30]

Mel Gibson echoes these cautious invocations when he writes that 'Holy Scripture and accepted visions of the Passion were the only possible texts I could draw from to fashion a dramatic film.'[31] Elsewhere he revealed his enthusiasm for the nineteenth-century mystic's 'accepted visions':

> When Gibson returned to his faith, he acquired, from a nunnery that had closed down, a library of hundreds of books, many of them quite old. He says that when he was researching the Passion one evening he reached up for a book, and Brentano's volume tumbled out of the shelf into his hands. He sat down to read it, and was flabbergasted by the vivid imagery of Emmerich's visions.
>
> 'Amazing images', he said. 'She supplied me with stuff I would never have thought of.'[32]

What then are the variances between the gospels and Sr Emmerich's visions? What Sr Emmerich observed in her imaginative revisiting of the events of 33 AD was a Passion retrospectively reshaped by centuries of Catholic tradition. Many of the traditional, non-canonical details that confused lay viewers of the Gibson film – the veil of Veronica, the sequence of falls with the Cross, Jesus meeting his mother on the Via Dolorosa – are apocryphal post-apostolic details which in Sr Emmerich's narrative are anachronistically reinstated into the original event. This technique is rendered explicit in a self-reflexive reference to the Blessed Virgin and Mary Magdalene performing the Good Friday rite known as 'the Way of the Cross' before any such ritual could possibly have existed:

> The Blessed Virgin knelt down frequently and kissed the ground where her Son had fallen, while Magdalen wrung her hands in bitter grief, and John, although he could not restrain his own tears, endeavoured to console his companions, supported and led them on. Thus was the holy devotion of the 'Way of the Cross' first practiced; thus were the Mysteries of the Passion of Jesus first honoured, even before that Passion was accomplished. (1862, p. 188)

The 'Stations of the Cross' are seen not as a later Holy Week liturgy, but as specific spots in time and space consecrated by the Virgin's mourning:

> Thus at each station, marked by the sufferings of her Son, did she lay up in her heart the inexhaustible merits of his Passion. (1862, p. 188)

Thus the 'first pilgrimage through the stations of the Way of the Cross' is seen not as a subsequent commemorative invention, but as a sacramental event taking place during the course of the Passion itself. What Sr Emmerich 'saw' in her visions was the concrete realization of a historical martyrdom retrospectively framed by the structure of the Holy Week liturgy, which is replicated microcosmically in the Eucharist. Notwithstanding the richness of detail, her account of Christ's suffering is as firmly focused on death and resurrection as was St Paul's.[33]

VI

The Dolorous Passion divides into two parts, one dealing in four 'meditations' with the Last Supper, the other in 66 chapters with the Crucifixion and Resurrection. Gibson chose to conflate these separate visions by focusing on the 12 hours of the Passion, and interpolating visual allusions to the Last Supper at strategic points in the film. This device of using brief flashbacks to punctuate the Passion proper is a central narrative device in the film, and has drawn much critical attention (though often for the wrong reasons). Most, not all, the flashback episodes are from the Last Supper, which effectively constitutes the 'backstory' of the Passion itself.[34]

Viewers trying to make sense of *The Passion* as another conventional Christ-film have naturally been attracted to flashback details that seem to complete some aspect of the relatively familiar gospel narrative that normally informs and dominates filmic treatment. The unrelenting continuum of punishment that many viewers find unbearable in Gibson's film is, in a sense, relieved by allusions to the longer perspective of Jesus's life and ministry: childhood and adolescence, scenes of teaching such as the Sermon on the Mount, pivotal episodes such as that of 'the woman taken in adultery'. Newspaper and magazine reviews universally homed in on these details, clutching at the reassuring lineaments of biblical narrative elaboration.[35] Some viewers cried for more: 'Nor do the numerous flashback interludes depicting scenes from Jesus's life, ranging from the trivial (his trade as a carpenter) to the portentous (the Last Supper), offer significant respite from the single-minded onslaught of his physical suffering.'[36] In the film it is true that all these references are carefully considered and strategically placed: but they vary enormously in their impact and signifying power, and it is questionable whether some should have been included at all.

For example during the long and painful scourging sequence, the camera alternates viewpoints and reaction shots between the suffering Jesus and the observers Mary Magdalene and the Blessed Virgin. At one point the camera shows a close-up of Magdalene, followed by a subjective camera shot from her viewpoint, which in turn triggers a flashback to the episode of 'the woman taken in adultery'. The two Marys are painstakingly mopping up Jesus's blood with towels given to them by Pilate's wife in an episode provided by Sr Emmerich rather than the gospels.[37] Mary's ground-level gaze recalls the scene of her rescue from execution by Jesus. From her viewpoint we see a foot (several shots of feet, as seen by Jesus himself, have already appeared, so Mary is sharing the same vantage-point of abasement and humility), and then, still at ground level, we see Jesus writing in the sand, drawing a line between Magdalene and the crowd who were about to stone her. We then see her hand stretched out to touch his foot, followed by his hand stretched down to take her up. A clear parallel is established between the bruised and beaten body of the woman, and the scourged and battered body of the Saviour. In the 'woman taken in adultery' episode Jesus saves Mary from the inexorable punishment of the Mosaic Law; now through the suffering of the Passion he offers the same forgiveness to all humanity. The complete parable of forgiveness, reconciliation and transcendence of the old Law illustrates Isaiah's great words of prophecy, which appear as an epigraph to the film:

> Surely he has borne our griefs, and carried our sorrows . . . he *was* wounded for our transgressions, *he was* bruised for our iniquities: the chastisement of our peace *was* upon him; and with his stripes we are healed. (Isa. 53.4–5)

In a later example of flashback, the reactive face of the Blessed Virgin Mary witnessing Jesus falling under the cross is used to cascade a recollected scene of the infant Jesus falling and hurting himself, a scene which virtually all viewers found affecting. The mother's care for her martyred son, which has of course generated some of the most sublime devotional art of all time (the poetry and music of the *Stabat Mater*, Michelangelo's *Pieta*) is part of the essential experience of the Cross; but equally, Catholic art has produced innumerable representations of the infant Jesus which prefigure the ultimate agony of the Passion, from Byzantine icons such as *Our Lady of Perpetual Succour* to Murillo's *Christ Child Resting on the Cross*[38] and Millais's *Christ in the House of His Parents (The Carpenter's Shop)*.[39] The scene is reprised when Jesus meets his mother on the road to Calvary.

Both these episodes are integrated into the concentrated Passion narrative: they enrich its meaning rather than draw the viewer's attention elsewhere. Even these relatively successful examples seem to me however to be distractions from the Passion. In the 'infancy' insert just discussed, and in the sound-bites from the Sermon on the Mount, which though relevant are by no means free from what Philip Horne has called 'the pearly light of TV-evangelist sincerity', it is apparent that Gibson has been seduced by the temptations of narrative into momentary lapses of concentration. Evidence for this analysis is abundant in the reactions of commentators who clearly hated their attention being 'taken prisoner' by the film, yet found interpolations such as the childhood tumble emotionally affecting. Nothing could demonstrate more conclusively that here attention is being distracted, often willingly, from absorption in the central mystery, towards sentimental narrative and relatively innocuous teaching. In the worst lapse of all, the scene where we see a young Jesus at work in his father's shop, engaged in some lame comedy around the construction of a table, the loss of focus is complete. Gibson would have been better advised to follow many other artists who have worked in this medium, and explored parallels between carpentry and execution, between the wood of the carpenter's shop and the wood of the cross. Or better still, to have left this scene among the shavings on the craftsman's floor.

The dramatic references back to the Last Supper, which are dispersed across the film but concentrated around the Crucifixion itself, are of an entirely different order. Here instead of a momentary allusion we have a sustained parallel, with the Last Supper and the Crucifixion running together, interweaving and literally bleeding into one another.

The events of the Last Supper, commemorated in Catholic tradition on Holy Thursday, are narrated in all four gospels, and consist of the Institution of the Eucharist, the 'Lord's Supper'; the washing by Jesus of the disciples' feet; and the 'Mandatum' (hence the name 'Maundy Thursday') 'These things I command you: that ye love one another' (John 15.17). In the church these elements are all commemorated, and the altar is then stripped, with the focus shifting to a symbolic garden of Gethsemane for a ritual of watching and prayer.

In *The Passion of the Christ* 'The Washing of the Feet' is interpolated into the scourging scene, and focuses on the apostle John. Jesus sees the foot of one of the soldiers who is punishing him, which triggers a recollection of his washing of John's feet, accompanied by words taken from John's gospel:

> If the world hates you remember that it has hated me first. Remember that no servant is greater than his master. If they persecuted me, they will persecute you. You must not be afraid.

The helper will come who reveals the truth about God and who comes from the Father. (adapted from John 15.18–26)

The physical detail of the close-up foot serves to anchor this meditation on humility and sacrifice, and the flashback ends with a return to the foot of the soldier. An officer appears and reprimands the men for excessive cruelty: they were not 'ordered' to kill him. *'mandatum erat hominem punire: non eum castigare usque ad mortuum'*. The Latin word 'mandatum' in his speech connects responsibility for Christ's martyrdom with his own commandment to the disciples to practice and preach a gospel of love (*'Haec mando vobis . . .'*, John 15.17).

Later another flashback is triggered by Pilate's ritual cleansing of his hands to clear himself of responsibility for Jesus's death. A bowl is brought for Pilate to wash, which precipitates another flashback to the Last Supper, showing John washing Jesus's hands prior to his taking the bread. In the Mass the priest's hands are washed by a Deacon before touching the consecrated Host, in a rite known as the *'Lavabo'*: *'Lavabo inter innocentes manus meus'*.[40] In the film we then see Pilate drying his hands on a white towel and saying, in Aramaic: 'I am innocent of this man's blood'. Again a verbal echo, together with the liturgical cross-reference, ironically parallels sacerdotal ablution with Pilate's desperate efforts to evade guilt.

With the Crucifixion itself we encounter the most detailed and systematic cross-referencing with the ritual that lies at the heart of the Last Supper, the Eucharist. As Jesus rises to his feet on Mount Golgotha, we see him in an inverted overhead shot, looking upwards, then from his viewpoint we see the sky dissolving into light. In a cut to the Upper Room at the Passover we see bread brought to the table, and Jesus unwrapping it from its enclosing napkin. A cut back to Golgotha shows Jesus's body being stripped of its garments. Body and bread are juxtaposed in a montage of images, as they are united in a single sacrifice. Subsequently Jesus looks at John, and again we are back in the Upper Room on Holy Thursday, with Jesus saying:

There is no greater love than for a man to lay down his life for his friends. (Adapted from John 15.13)

Jesus is laid on the cross, and a nail placed in the palm of his hand.
We see the nail from his viewpoint, and then revert again to the
Last Supper:

> I cannot be with you much longer my friends. You cannot go
> where I am going. My commandment to you after I am gone
> is this: love one another. As I have loved you, love one another.
> (Adapted from John 13.34)

In the scene showing Jesus being nailed to the cross Gibson follows
Emmerich closely, but again allows the Passion and the Eucharist
to interpenetrate. The nail is hammered in, and we see the Blessed
Virgin and Mary Magdalene feeling the blows in their own bodies.
'The Blessed Virgin, Magdalene and all those who had been present
at the Crucifixion, felt each blow transfix their hearts.'[41]

> The executioners did not allow him to rest long, but bade him
> rise and place himself on the cross that they might nail him to it.
> Then seizing his right arm they dragged it to the hole prepared
> for the nail . . . The nails were very large, the heads about the
> size of a crown piece, and the thickness that of a man's thumb,
> while the points came through at the back of the cross . . . When
> the executioners had nailed the right hand of our Lord, they
> perceived that his left hand did not reach the hole they had bored
> to receive the nail, therefore they tied ropes to his left arm, and
> having steadied their feet against the cross, pulled the left hand
> violently until it reached the place prepared for it. This dreadful
> process caused our Lord indescribable agony, his breast heaved,
> and his legs were quite contracted. They again knelt upon him,
> tied down his arms, and drove the second nail into his left hand;
> his blood flowed afresh, and his feeble groans were once more
> heard between the blows of the hammer, but nothing could
> move the hard-hearted executioners to the slightest pity. (1862,
> p. 253)

Similarly in the film Jesus's arm is stretched to fit the pre-drilled
hole in the cross with an audible snap of dislocation. At this point
he cries prematurely:

> Father forgive them . . .

In this tortuous breaking and stretching of the body to fit the cross, the redemptive sacrifice is effectively complete. Jesus has embraced the cross; cross and Christ have become one, 'a perfect redemption, propitiation, and satisfaction for all the sins of the whole world'.[42] The attitudes and expressions of both Marys change during this sequence, from bitter despair to an awed reverence, as mere human suffering gives way to divine transcendence, and the sign of the cross rises against the sky. The offering of bread at the Last Supper, which follows, commemorated in the Mass by the elevation of the Host, is simply another way of putting the same thing, in however many languages.

QABILU LEH AKULU. DNA HU GISHMI[43]

Take this and eat. This is my body (Matt. 26.26)

Hoc ist enim corpus meum.[44]

We see the cross raised with the Christ on it: the body of the crucified has become the Crucifix. The Last Supper defines this offering of blood, again repeated in the Mass as the elevation of the chalice:

QABILU SHTEYU. DNA D'MI

Take and drink. This is my blood (Matt. 26.27–8).

Hic est enim calix sanguinis mei

The primary objective of the film's narrative and dramatic structure is then to confirm the indissoluble identity between the sacrifice of the Passion, and the sacrifice of the Mass. This is a wholly orthodox Tridentine approach, as set out in the pre-Vatican II Missal:

> The supreme act of Divine Worship in the Church is the holy sacrifice of the Mass. This sacrifice is identical with that offered by Christ on the Cross . . . The sacrifice of the Mass is the memorial, the renewal and the application of the sacrifice of Calvary.[45]

The text cited here also quotes from the Council of Trent:

> In the sacrifice of the Mass, the same Christ is contained and offered in an unbloody manner, who once offered himself in a bloody manner on the altar of the Cross.

This juxtaposition is established equally clearly in the book of still images from the film compiled by Duncan and Antonello, where we find on facing pages the Passover meal and the nail placed in the palm (pp. 105–6); the Crucifixion, and the blessing of the bread (pp. 112–13); the pierced feet, and the offering of the chalice (pp. 114–15).[46]

Critics obviously noted that the unrelenting agony of the Crucifixion is punctuated with brief flashback scenes to the Last Supper. But generally they supposed this to be some kind of light relief, to take our minds off the pain by recalling scenes of companionship and love (e.g. Mark Kermode). Christologically the Last Supper is there because it is the first prospective re-enactment of the Crucifixion. It is the same self-offering, the same pouring out of the soul to death, in the breaking of the bread, and the nailing on the cross; in the sharing of the cup, and the shedding of the blood. This is my body, which is given up for you; this is my blood of the new covenant. Bread, wine, body, blood; the death on the cross, the nails and the piercing. As Victoria Messori puts it in one of the best commentaries on the film, 'the blood of the Passion is continuously intermingled with the wine of the Mass, the tortured flesh of the "Corpus Christi" [body of Christ] with the consecrated bread':

> Gibson produced the movie to be 'a Mass', because he believes that the sacrifice of the cross and the sacrifice of the Mass are one and the same, as taught by the Council of Trent.[47]

The use of unfamiliar ancient languages also parallels the Tridentine Latin Mass:

> This film, for its author, is a Mass: let it be then, in an obscure language, as it was for so many centuries. If the mind does not understand, so much the better. What matters is that the heart understands that all that happens redeems us from sin and opens to us the doors of salvation.

The film is ritualistic in its enactment of the Eucharist, as past history and present sacrament: love and death united in one awful moment, but a moment repeated daily in real and eternal time at the holy sacrifice of the Mass.

VII

The Passion of the Christ is something more than, or at least other than, a film. It is also a votive offering, a memorial of the Christian Redemption, a celebration of the Eucharist. The audience is not invited passively to 'gaze', nor even actively to 'watch'; but rather voluntarily to participate in a ritual of shared suffering. 'Gibson is not inviting his viewers into a story, but offering them a visual means by which to contemplate Christ's wounds.'[48]

It is not at all surprising then that reluctance and resistance should be natural reactions from many viewers invited into such unfamiliar, even unwelcome territory. Normally Christ-films address mass audiences by offering a much wider repertoire of interests and ways of engaging: giving to the non-Christian or agnostic 'Jesus the admirable moral teacher', or 'Jesus the compelling example of human self-sacrifice'; offering to the atheist a radical or revolutionary, wholly or partially secularized or humanized Christ. Gibson's film by contrast is unrelenting in its insistence on the divinity of Christ, and on the sacramental participation of the audience. These factors explain both the film's power and difficulty.

For example the film's notorious violence and cruelty have been linked, not with comparable Christ-films, or with traditional representations of the Passion in the visual arts, but with the violence of other films in which Mel Gibson has participated, and with Hollywood screen violence in general. So the film has been compared, not with *King of Kings*; *The Greatest Story Ever Told*; *The Gospel According to St Matthew*; *Jesus of Nazareth*; *The Last Temptation of Christ* – but to *Braveheart* or *Saving Private Ryan*. Mel Gibson as director has been compared not with Nicholas Ray, George Stevens, Pasolini, Zefirelli, Scorsese; but to the characters he himself played in *Mad Max* and *Lethal Weapon*. 'All those who are normally accustomed to spectacular violence' wrote Rene Girard, 'find themselves condemning it in Gibson's film.'

In fact *The Passion of the Christ* challenges rather than reflects conventional screen violence. People are routinely treated in Hollywood films to similar ordeals, but always as a preparation for fighting back. Viewers noted that with a closed, swollen eye acquired early on in the film, Gibson's Jesus resembles Sylvester Stallone as Rocky. He does: but unlike Rocky, Jesus does not retaliate. Rocky always wins.[49] Jesus is not taking a vicious beating that will later justify even more vicious retribution and revenge; He is bearing the chastisement of our peace.

Violence works in this film to subvert Hollywood conventions. The ordeal of the Passion, Latin *passus* or suffering, is an ordeal of subjection, of helplessness, as well as one of violence. Witnessing such voluntary subjection, such willed helplessness, the audience has no choice but to feel compassion, suffering with the subjected victim. By focalizing spectator perceptions through the viewpoints of John, the Blessed Virgin and Mary Magdalene, Gibson's camera guides the audience into a sympathy that is racked with the guilt of enforced helplessness. 'Gibson's camera positions the audience as a spectator to the unfolding drama of pain.'[50] Audiences are accustomed to suffering with the subjected hero, but accustomed also to facilitating his earned manumission from the servitude of pain. In this case the audience is obliged to contemplate the agony of suffering, but is denied the pleasures of resistance and retribution.

This is a painful position for a voyeur to occupy, and explains both the rapture of audiences and the resentment of critics. To witness such agony and to be unable vicariously to help reduces spectators to tears, and critics to uncomfortable silence. 'What you've heard about how audiences reacted is true' said broadcaster John Dean. 'There was no sound after the film's conclusion. No noise at all. No one got up. No one moved. The only sound one could hear was sobbing.'[51] When I saw it the entire audience, mainly of young people, cried throughout the performance. At many points some literally could not look, could not see. 'The viewer is encouraged not to look', writes Mark Goodacre, 'and is often not allowed to look.'[52] They hid as it were their faces from Him.

One imagines this is exactly how Mel Gibson wanted it. He elected to constitute his audience not as detached spectators observing a historical fiction, but as embedded participants sharing in a sacramental mystery. This has nothing to do with sadism, or voyeurism, or attachment to historical realism. Gibson wants his viewer up close to the ordeal of the Passion,[53] not in order to check out the authenticity, or to endure an exploitative shudder, but to appreciate that the occasion of Christ's suffering is the sinfulness of humankind. In Rene Girard's words, 'For Mel Gibson, the death of Christ is a burden born by all humanity, starting with Mel Gibson himself.' We are not even permitted the luxury of loathing the

Roman torturers, though loathsome they certainly are, since Jesus so graciously forgives them. We, as audience, cannot facilitate the cessation of this pain, because we are the cause of it, and because only God has the power to begin and end it (during the scourging the Blessed Virgin mentally asks her son: 'When, where, how will you choose to be delivered of this?'). Again this is an obstinately Christian view that is surely virtually impossible for unbelievers to share. It is strongly present in Gibson's source, where Sr Emmerich sees the procession of her own sins included in the universal guilt that tortures Jesus in the Garden of Gethsemane ('the sins we so frequently commit, and which are, in fact, a species of consent which we give to, and a participation in, the tortures which were inflicted on Jesus by his cruel enemies').[54] And it is also present in the film, where it is Mel Gibson's own hand that we see piercing with a nail the palm of the Saviour.

VIII

Gibson spoke of *The Passion of the Christ* in terms of the Greek word '*aletheia*', 'truth' (literally what is not forgotten in the oblivion of Lethe):

> The film is not meant as a historical documentary, nor does it claim to have assembled all the facts. But it does enumerate those described in Holy Scripture. It is not merely representative or merely expressive. I think of it as contemplative in the sense that one is compelled to remember (unforget) in a spiritual way which cannot be articulated, only experienced.[55]

A parallel Greek word '*anamnesis*' (ἀνάμνησις), used by Plato to denote the soul-memory that survives immersion in Lethe, became in Christian terminology a technical term associated with the Eucharist. Like '*aletheia*', it means more than its usual translation 'remembrance', and suggests a proactive dispelling of oblivion, an insistence on preserving or reinstating the past as a present reality. '*Aletheia*' and '*anamnesis*' are more than just 'remembrance of things past': they are actions of restoration and revivification, 're-collection' and 're-membering'. They are acts of faith.

Gibson also however speaks here of 'compulsion', which may be a spiritual obligation to him, but becomes an onus on his viewer. The compulsion of *aletheia* leaves the disinterested open-minded liberal spectator with precious little room for manoeuvre. In addition this compelled unforgetting is to take place in a 'spiritual way' that 'cannot be articulated, only experienced'. This is entirely in line with the 'contemplative' tradition on which Gibson has drawn through *The Dolorous Passion of Our Lord Jesus Christ*: a tradition characterized by 'vision' and 'showing', the apprehension of images rather than words, things rather than ideas. As Girard puts it, 'Mel Gibson is situated in a certain mystical tradition of The Passion . . . mystics see it as their duty to imagine the sufferings of Christ as accurately as possible.' It also connects the film with the vivid sensuous pictorialism of counter-Reformation visual art, to which Gibson in the same context also alludes: 'I began to look at the work of some of the great artists who had drawn inspiration from the same story: Caravaggio . . . Mantegna'; and to the active devotional contemplation recommended by St Ignatius in his *Spiritual Exercises*. These are all examples of visualized mysteries that defy rational comprehension. As Messori puts it, 'If the mind does not understand, so much the better. What matters is that the heart understands.'

Such contemplation is then essentially visual and deeply filmic. It privileges the image over the word; experience over articulation; immediacy over exposition; repetition over continuity; and where we would expect to find narrative, we encounter instead a timeless domain of inward contemplation. Viewers caught up in this medium, their attention 'imprisoned'[56] or as Gibson put it 'compelled', could find their experience so unlike normal cinematic pleasure as to constitute something other than film:

> This is not a movie that anyone will 'like' . . . There isn't even the sense that one has just watched a movie. What it is . . . is an *experience* on a level of primary emotion that is scarcely comprehensible.[57]

The film's 'compulsion' is also admittedly and unashamedly proselytizing, doctrinaire, evangelical, as Gibson made clear:

> I wanted the effort to be a testament to the infinite love of Jesus the Christ, which has saved, and continues to save, many the world over.

My hope is that *The Passion of the Christ* will help many more people recognize the power of His love and let him help them to save their own lives.

But this Catholic evangelism is quite unlike the more familiar Protestant evangelicalism that dominates modern Christianity, especially in North America. The savagery and splendour of counter-Reformation iconography can only appear as idolatrous to protestant Christians brought up in Reformation iconoclasm:

> Passion Plays and icons were designed, like most visual imagery, to play upon the emotions and stimulate a response; but the ability to evoke an emotional response via imagery or drama is not the same as successfully transmitting the gospel.
>
> When people are *caught up in the emotional plot of The Passion*, all the extra-biblical additions – including each step along the Catholic 'Stations of the Cross' – become as real to the viewer's virtual experience as the factual (but less dramatic) framework from the four gospels.
>
> Is this how God really wants us to evangelise the unsaved TODAY . . . by overwhelming their SENSES in an EXPERIENTIAL display of realistic torture and sadism . . . Experientialism trumping the preaching of the Word?[58]

The logical conclusion of this is to blind oneself to idolatry, as iconoclasts have always done; to repudiate the image and to seek enlightenment in darkness and the light of the word. The cinema becomes what the icon was to Byzantine iconoclasts in the eighth and ninth centuries, or the decorated mediaeval cathedral (described by Melvin Bragg as 'the cinema of the pre-celluloid era')[59] was to fifteenth-century Reformers. In a self-explanatory article titled 'Why I will not see *The Passion of the Christ*', John Legare defines the film as 'idolatrous' in the same way as the Roman Catholic Mass is idolatrous, since it 'misrepresents and denies the complete sacrifice of Christ on the cross by claiming that the sacrifice of Jesus is continued in the Mass'. Legare quotes Calvin on 'the true image of God':

> A true image of God is not to be found in all the world; and hence . . . His glory is defiled, and His truth corrupted by the lie,

whenever He is set before our eyes in a visible form. Therefore, To devise any image of God is itself impious because by this corruption His Majesty is adulterated, and He is figured to be other than he is.[60]

In *The Passion of the Christ* Catholic evangelism has created a new cinematic medium and a new mode of audience participation. Wherever the film seems to harmonize with Hollywood 'normality' it proves instead to be radically divergent. Take as a benchmark Bordwell's checklist of the characteristics of classical film narrative.

- The film has a happy or at least satisfying ending;
- uncertainties or gaps are temporary;
- the source of causality lies in the main characters;
- chronological order is used where possible;
- the viewer sees and hears only what is necessary;
- it is clear whether a scene is objective or subjective;
- the medium does not draw attention to itself as artefact;
- genre defines its presence by adherence to conventions.[61]

The Passion seems systematically to dissent from every precept listed here. Its ending is ambivalent; uncertainties are legion; chronological order is defied; the viewer sees and hears more than is necessary; objectivity and subjectivity break down (some shots represent God's point of view); the medium is full of still tableaux like the '*Ecce Homo*!', and has been described as a succession of Renaissance paintings; and the film invokes and denies every genre convention it touches. What appeared to be normal orchestrated pre-release publicity, with Mel Gibson speaking to church groups, and exploiting or responding to public debates, operated instead, like the Mass of the Catachumens, as a doctrinal preparation for the liturgical event of the film itself:

> The release of the film has engendered a spectrum of fervent responses, becoming in itself a theological event shaped by merchandizing, media and audience reception.[62]

Making an important distinction between literature and film, word and image, Boris Eikhenbaum said that the cinema audience is

> placed in completely new conditions of perception, which are to an extent opposite to those of the reading process. Whereas the reader moves from the printed word to visualization of the subject, the viewer goes in the opposite direction: he moves from the subject, from comparison of the moving frames to their comprehension, to naming them; in short, to the construction of internal speech.[63]

There is no doubt that language is an essential part of *The Passion of the Christ*. The film begins with the prophetic words of Isaiah, and the dialogue, though embodied in ancient tongues, is also subtitled in a script adapted from the limpid transparency of the New Living Translation of the Bible. In both cases written English lies outside the viewer's auditory and visual perceptions of the film image itself.

Clearly this film has an unusual relationship with language. In its Incarnational Christology *The Passion of the Christ* uses the filmed image to represent the Word that became flesh and dwelt among us. The Word to which these densely saturated signs point is the ultimate language of the Logos, the Word of God. But in an Incarnational and Eucharistic theology there is no divergence between signifier and signified. Just as in traditional Catholic theology the bread and wine of the Eucharist become at the consecration the body and blood of Christ, so in cinematic Christology word and image are indissoluble. The unfamiliar ancient languages are there to impede any easy commerce between film dialogue and contemporary colloquial speech, so that words never flutter too far away from the images that enfold them. Even the post-structuralist truism that signs point only to the absence of the thing they signify is accounted for in 'negative theology' by the fact that God is both absent and present in the world.

If *The Passion of the Christ* has anything at all to tell us about cinema then it will be in terms of the way the film problematizes narrative and time. As I have shown by demonstrating the interdependence of the film and the liturgy of the traditional Catholic Mass, conventional assumptions about narrative are contextualized by a timescale of eternity, and normal narrative flow compressed and broken by devices of simultaneity, montage and repetition. Using a medium that is generally held to emulate by kinetic duration the very movement of history, *The Passion of the Christ* redefines history as 'a pattern/Of timeless moments'.[64]

In addition the film calls into question conventional distinctions between the still and the moving image. Whatever technological changes alter the ways in which film captures, records and displays its object, the medium remains of course a sequence of still images that practices on a weakness of the eye, on the 'persistence of vision'. 'When we look at the screen, what we see is not really a "moving" picture at all but a series of frozen ones, *still* pictures'.[65] Usually the film medium does everything possible to maximize the 'phi' phenomenon and its own pretended mobility. But *The Passion of the Christ* by contrast resolves readily into the traditional still images that underlie and inform its construction, such as the devotional paintings with which Gibson began. This challenges for example the distinction Seymour Chatman makes between still and moving image in terms of relative duration. 'Non-narrative communicative objects', he says, do not

> regulate the temporal flow or spatial direction of the audience's perception . . . Temporality is immanent to . . . narrative texts.[66]

This confuses the imagined time of the fiction in which the image is located, with the real time of the spectator. There duration applies equally to both still and moving images.

Film does indeed, then, consist, as Rowan Williams defined it, of 'animated icons'. For centuries the icon was the primary visual resource for Christian worship and belief. St John Chrysostom said that the correct way to view an icon was to stand before it with eyes closed, so that the imagination could perceive the immanent and eternal meanings signified by the two-dimensional image. It is of course impossible to make windows into the souls of all those who saw *The Passion of the Christ*, whether with eyes open or closed; but we can at least speculate that in many cases the film opened up to vision that 'split second of darkness between each image' that normally 'we do not "see"'.[67] It is perhaps no coincidence that the film was made by Mel Gibson's own production company: Icon.

5

God or man? Mark
Dornford-May's *Son of Man*

I

All the works I have examined in this study so far belong to the
religious, literary and filmic traditions of Europe and North America.
Both the Jesus-novel and the Jesus-film emerged from developed
civilizations in the course of the twentieth century, requiring as they
did sophisticated industries of publishing and film-making, mass
literacy and a cinema audience. But Christianity is of course a global
religion, whose centre of gravity, at least in terms of membership,
has shifted significantly towards the developing countries. All
around the world, divergent images of Jesus are constructed in the
light of local religious experience and specific cultural conditions.
Jesus, writes Richard Wightman Fox:

> is perpetually reborn in one culture after another . . . His
> incarnation guaranteed that each later culture would grasp him
> anew for each would have a different view of what it means to
> be human.[1]

There are Jesus-films and Christ-figure films produced from outside
Europe and America, indicating the gradual emergence of a global
cultural form. In this chapter I will discuss one remarkable example
from South Africa, *Son of Man* directed by Mark Dornford-May.
Lloyd Baugh has compared *Son of Man* to Valerio Zurlini's *Black
Jesus* (1968), a classic Christ-figure film set in the post-colonial

Congo of the 1960s.[2] Middleton and Plate set it alongside two
films by the Haitian-American artist Claude LaMarre, *Color of the
Cross* and *Color of the Cross 2: The Resurrection*, which focus on
the idea that 'Christ's true identity, as the Oppressed One, must be
scrutinized and understood in the context of the black experience'.[3]
In addition in the same essay they examine a number of Jesus-films
from Asia and from Cuba. Their cross-cultural analysis is intended
to demonstrate 'the global nature of the Jesus-film tradition', and
'to challenge scholars' predilection for western (and United States)
cinematic constructions of Jesus'.[4]

Son of Man does not sit comfortably inside either of the two
categories that have shaped the preceding discussion, the historical
Jesus-film and the transfigurative Christ-film. At first sight it appears
to be a Christ-figure film, since it is set in a society that, though
fictionally called Judaea, is easily recognizable as twentieth-century
South Africa. The film's world is that of the present, not the past.
The film's Jesus is neither the Anglo-Saxon hero of the Hollywood
Jesus-film, the Jewish messiah of the historical Jesus quest, the
laid-back hippy guru of *Godspell* or the hapless clown of *Life of
Brian*. These diverse figures have little else in common, but they all
purport to be Jesus, and they are all white. The Jesus of *Son of Man*
is a black African, whose life and career are constructed so as to
resemble those of anti-apartheid activist Steve Biko.[5] The preaching
of Jesus is indistinguishable from the activism of Biko: Jesus uses
his words, fosters his gospel of non-violent resistance, and meets
his ultimate fate of clandestine murder. His actions are 'intertwined
with events and public figures of recent South African history,
principally the struggle against the racist politics of the apartheid
regime'.[6] There is no divergence here between the historical Jesus
and the modern world into which he is transplanted, since after all
it was the message of the Gospels – justice, equality, human dignity,
non-violent resistance – that formed the ethical and political basis
of Biko's radical faith. At the heart of African Christianity, in the
words of Reinhold Zwick, lies 'a Christology deeply informed by
liberation theology, deeply rooted in concern for the poor'.[7] The
film's setting is the shantytown society of South Africa: much
of it was shot in Kayelitsha, near Cape Town. Although the film
insistently recalls the struggle against apartheid, and Jesus explicitly
preaches against global imperialism, it avoids the obvious paradigm
of black resistance to white supremacy. All the actors are black, and

speak either in Xhosa, or in English. We hear English voices of a white complexion in voiced-over news broadcasts, but these may be international media utterances, and seem to come from afar. The whites are elsewhere.

So far, then, we are dealing with an obviously transfigurative film. Yet *Son of Man* is unlike other Christ-figure films, in that its narrative is wholly and simply that of the Gospels. All the characters are named characters from the New Testament, and the scripture prescribes their roles. The story of the film's Jesus is the story of the Jesus of the Gospels; nothing happens to him that does not happen to the Jesus of the Bible. His actions are mandated by the biblical narrative. He says and does some things differently, but he is free to speak and to act only within an acceptable margin of scriptural interpretation.[8] So we cannot separate the contemporary narrative from the historical narrative of the Bible, or interpret the relations between past and present as a matter of parallelism and affinity. The Bible and modern-day South Africa are, in the medium of this film, contingent and contiguous. The unmediated, un-transfigured story of the Gospels is enacted in the townships and the deserts of South Africa, under that beautiful luminous sky, among those ramshackle and impoverished dwellings. 'The movie is a radical actualization or "re-contextualization" of the entire Gospel narrative', writes Lloyd Baugh. The film 'does not tell a story of Africa that metaphorically reflects the Gospel; rather it situates that Gospel in the contemporary African reality'.[9]

All the events of the Gospel narrative are presented in a form appropriate to the modern ethnic and geographical setting and context. The Baptism is dramatized as a Xhosa circumcision ritual. Massacres of children by armed government soldiers parallel the slaughter of the innocents. The woman taken in adultery and rescued by Jesus is about to be set alight, recalling the barbaric practice of 'necklacing', a form of vigilante justice used by the black community against collaborators with the apartheid regime. The miracles of Jesus are captured on video camera by Judas, who hands the film over to the elders Annas and Caiaphas as incriminating evidence against him. Jesus delivers the Sermon on the Mount from the corrugated tin roof of a shack. The Deposition is presented as a version of Michelangelo's *Pieta*, with Mary holding Jesus's dead body across her knees in the back of pick-up truck speeding along a modern motorway.

The most striking and creative adaptation of the Gospel narrative, however, concerns the Crucifixion. The Crucifixion of the historical Jesus was a public execution, on a hill for all to see, in which the body of the condemned was humiliated and tortured in order to demonstrate the power of the state. In apartheid South Africa, dissenters were not openly tried and executed, but simply 'disappeared', were killed and concealed in an isolated place. The search for justice that was the mainspring of the anti-apartheid movement involved the demand that these crimes be revealed, the disappeared found and acknowledged (even to the extent of displaying exhumed corpses). 'It was a crucial part of the resistance to unveil the atrocities and accuse the regime by keeping the memory of the missing alive through public displays of photos or even public displays of corpses when found.'[10] In *Son of Man*, Jesus is shot and buried in a shallow grave. It is his disciples, led by Mary his mother, who find him, exhume his body and display it on a cross, at the summit of a hill. The cross thus supplements its historical significance of atonement and reconciliation with the modern emphases of liberation theology: it becomes a protest against injustice and oppression. 'Ironically, the traditional Roman practice of securing peace by instilling fear in their subject peoples through publicly displaying crucified dissidents and runaway slaves has itself here become an occasion for Jesus' vindication.'[11] The police come to disperse the mourners, who enact a non-violent resistance in the form of song and dance. 'Jesus' life and death have led to a resistant human community.'[12]

Thus far the film could be read as a secular modernization of the Gospel story, in which the historical Jesus is alluded to as a first-century political agitator (the 'Son of Man'), who proves to be the spiritual ancestor of the modern anti-apartheid radical. But the film in no way diminishes the supernatural dimensions of the biblical story. Indeed its very opening focuses on one of the relatively few moments in the Gospel narratives where the adult Jesus can be seen operating in a clearly supernatural dimension: the Temptation in the Wilderness. We see Jesus and Satan together in a desert. The face of Jesus is veiled in a mask of white clay, as if he is prepared for a ritual; Satan is dressed in black leather, and carries a goat-hoof cane. Satan asks Jesus to turn stones into bread, and encourages him to leap from a high point. Then we see the two seated together on a sand dune. Jesus seizes Satan bodily and throws him from the summit of the dune, shouting 'Get thee behind me, Satan. This is my world'. Satan disappears into a field of flame, retorting with sardonic laughter 'This is *my* world'. The two figures, the white-faced saviour and the black-clad devil, thus divide the world between them in an explicitly supernatural stand-off. This is clearly not a secularization and domestication of Jesus into the modern world, but a reaffirmation of the Christian belief that what is at stake, in His worldly actions, is nothing less than the struggle of Good and Evil for the soul of humanity. This Jesus surely is the Son of God, as well as the Son of Man.

This acknowledgement of a supernatural context for the human drama informs the entire film. The Annunciation, for example, is dramatized much more explicitly than it is by Zefirelli. Although it takes place in a schoolroom in which a number of children have been murdered, it is nonetheless dramatized as the message of a clearly manifested angel to a shocked and frightened mortal woman. Gabriel is played by a young boy, whose angelic status is signified by a white loin cloth, and white feathers adhering to his chest. He reappears, together with a host of similar angels, at the Nativity. In an extra-biblical scene already mentioned, Gabriel encourages the child Jesus to abandon the nightmare of the human world, and return to Heaven. Simultaneously Satan is omnipresent throughout the film, as he is in *The Passion of the Christ*, clearly sponsoring from the sidelines the incidence of Evil. Although the film makes the Crucifixion in itself a 'resurrection' – the reappearance and public exhibition of the 'disappeared' Jesus – it closes with a joyous Resurrection scene, in which Jesus ascends the hill accompanied by a host of the child-angels. He is more than a political radical whose death can be used as a focus of injustice. He is indeed the Risen Lord.

Unlike other makers of Jesus-films, Dornford-May studiously avoids the use of non-realistic film techniques of lighting, sound and cinematography to adumbrate this supernatural narrative ('special effects', such as the disappearance of Satan into a sheet of flame after the Temptation, are very rare). His actors remain solid bodies, moving in a concrete and clearly represented social landscape. There are some 50 million Christians in Africa: the Christian story belongs to the land. The film's precise observation, and clarity of vision, suggest that the miraculous is firmly rooted in the earth of South Africa, and the supernatural drama is being played out across a soil cherished as sacred by centuries of pre-Christian religious belief and tribal tradition, and sanctified by the Christianity that superseded them. Devils and angels are not creatures of elsewhere, but transcendent beings who occupy the human world alongside us.

This is not however the main reason why the film is so successful in its mediation of a complete Christology to twentieth-century reality. Part of what makes it so different from the other Jesus-films studied here, is that it establishes a different relationship between film and theatre. Dornford-May is a theatre director with a long and distinguished career, beginning with an Assistant Directorship at the Royal Shakespeare Company. In addition, he has a long-standing relationship with the Chester Mystery plays, in which he acted repeatedly, initially as a child-angel, eventually as Jesus.[13] His production of *The Mysteries* was staged in South Africa and London in 2007. It is not surprising that his approach to the making of a Jesus-film was more theatrical than most.

Critics have focused on the way in which the Chester Mystery plays provide a background to *Son of Man*, but more in terms of structure than of style. Zwick calls the Chester plays the 'backbone' of *Son of Man* (p. 113) and enumerates the points of convergence between the narratives of film and play-cycle, listing parallels and omissions. His assessment of this relationship however lacks a truly theatrical consciousness, and is limited to a comparison with the 'second-level naiveté' of another film, Pasolini's *The Gospel According to St Matthew*:

> Like Pasolini, Dornford-May stages his story in the mode of a 'second or second-level naiveté', a seemingly crude directness and simplicity in cinematography that nonetheless reflects a critical consciousness. This second naiveté, as Paul Ricoeur terms it, is particularly important in the depiction of transcendence, which would normally be out of reach for the film medium. For example, instead of representing angels by arrows of light or by off-screen 'heavenly' voices, both Pasolini and Dornford-May blithely present human actors as angels, which in Dornford-May's film are equipped with feathers that suggest wings. This straightforward and only seemingly 'naïve' approach moves the film from the plane of realism to that of transcendence, transforming miracles and mundane events alike into signs and symbols. (p. 115)

What is missing from this analysis is any sense of how this generic shift has been accomplished. How exactly is it, that in this naturalistic film medium, mundane human bodies assume the semiotic richness of 'signs and symbols'? The answer is not within the signifying codes of film at all, but in the dramatic medium imported into the film by Dornford-May's theatrical approach to acting, costume and dramatic speech.

The mediaeval mystery plays are familiar to audiences from some outstanding modern revivals, as well as from the long-preserved continuity of local performance in places such as Chester and York. But it is important to remember that, in their original cultural matrix of production, they were a form of amateur community theatre. Produced and acted by members of local craft guilds, the plays were promenaded round the streets of a town on wagons, and performed to an audience of townspeople. The actors had the responsibility of creating, in an ordinary everyday space, a drama both historical and supernatural, without any of the technological apparatus of modern theatres, let alone the freedom and flexibility of film. Dramatic place was created simply by naming: this street is Heaven, this house is Hell. This stage is the world. Actors stood, acutely visible in the mundane reality of local place and time, under the unforgiving clarity of broad daylight, and called their audiences to witness the divine acts of God and his angels, Satan and his Demons, Jesus and his disciples. This was not artful 'second-level naiveté', but a bold and faithful proclamation of the contiguity of mortality and the divine, through the unique capability of the drama to secure reality through illusion, to both be, and not be, what is being presented on stage.

When, in *Son of Man*, the boy who plays Gabriel appears before Mary, and delivers to her God's message, the dramatic medium is exactly that of the mediaeval mystery play. As a boy, the actor belongs to this context, a South African school-room, just as the Skinners and the Tanners and the Shepherds belonged to the streets and fields of Chester. But he is playing an angel, and in doing so bringing together the planes of the real and the divine, signifying transcendence without ever surrendering his local and quotidian status. He speaks in a declamatory, musical register, appropriate to the rhetoric of the biblical source, but also reminiscent of the heightened artifice of African story-telling. As an actor, he is manifestly and simultaneously both an angel, and not an angel; both a boy, and not a boy. He belongs to his naturalistically delineated context, yet also transcends it. This dual focus enables the spectator to grasp that paradoxical dialectic of identity and difference that is peculiar to the drama: to see a world in a grain of sand, Eternity in an hour. This is not filmic naturalism, of a first- or even second-order kind. It is theatre-in-film.

Despite its adherence to modernity and social realism, *Son of Man* is simultaneously a Jesus-film, a Christ-figure drama, and an essay in Christology. Walsh, Staley and Reinhartz suggest that the film promotes social and political concerns above religious ones: that in it 'Human dignity and community development, not theology, take centre stage' (p. xv). But this is misleading. The values of human dignity and community may sound like the liberal principals of an enlightened secular society, but they are in fact deeply rooted in African Christianity and African culture. Middleton and Plate have written eloquently of the film's theology:

> The 'resurrection' is portrayed as a majestic and meticulous amalgam of celebratory clapping, drumming, singing and stamping. Here, African dance becomes the festive, exultant arena of *communitas*, where the sacred time and space of communion with the crucified and now symbolically resurrected Jesus re-creates the social order and culture, advancing as well as reflecting the solidarity and harmony that Jesus lived and died for . . . the film's final scene thus illustrates Dornford-May's attempt to craft a visual Christology that addresses the contemporary concerns of Africans – concerns for fairness and concord. *Son of Man*'s Jesus represents Christ as the Liberator, and Christ as Reconciler, and, in this respect, the Jesus of *Son of Man* resembles the Christ of Ubuntu (reconciliation) theology, traceable to the work of the South African archbishop Desmond Tutu.[14]

Unlike an actual anti-apartheid campaigner, a Steve Biko, the Jesus of *Son of Man* is seen making the choice to commit himself to the struggle for salvation alongside suffering humanity, rather than return unwounded to His divine home: 'This is my world'. The action resembles that of a modern idealist making the decision to undertake political action against injustice: *my* world, not yours. But the film also confers on the expression its true ulterior meaning: 'for

God so loved the world, that he gave his only begotten son'. This *is* my world: 'for the world was made by Him, yet the world knew Him not'. In addition, by making full use of the resources of African music and dance, overtly and non-naturalistically performed in ways that normally belong to musical theatre or film musical, *Son of Man* roots its Christology in place, as well as in people.

Ecce Homo: A life of Christ

Preface

An important element of this book is that it incorporates a new historical and biographical Jesus-novel, or novella, written in parallel with the critical and theological studies it presupposes. This work, *Ecce Homo*, was developed alongside the literary and theological research. In both style and content it draws on all the texts discussed here, and engages imaginatively and creatively with the Christological controversies they address. Thus the theoretical assertions, and the methods and processes of the critical work, are further tested in a creative laboratory, and the research questions explored in fictional form.

In terms of narrative it largely follows the gospels, with the addition of some non-canonical biographical details used by other writers and visual artists (the narrating of the Crucifixion is for example structured, as it is in Mel Gibson's film and its literary source *The Dolorous Passion of Our Lord Jesus Christ*, on the traditional liturgy for the Stations of the Cross). Where other Jesus-novels try to fill out the sketchy outlines of the gospel story into biographical detail, I have focused only on key 'kerygmatic' moments in Christ's human life, moments that reveal both human and divine capacities, and express both dimensions of the dual nature. Where other biographical works tend to suggest that awareness of a divine destiny only gradually came to consciousness in Jesus, as a vocation slowly dawns on an ordinary man, I have assumed divine knowledge in the human embryo from the very moment of conception.

The creative work thus experiments with Christological problems of subjectivity, such as the 'interior life' of Jesus, memory and pre-existence, divinity and humanity, the relationship between body and spirit. In *Ecce Homo* I have started from the assumption that Jesus was both God and man, and tried to imagine what the experience might have been like. Moreover, although assuming Christ's divinity, I have not regarded this as beyond the scope of modern fiction, and have therefore taken the unusual step of narrating the entire experience of Incarnation from the man-God's point-of-view.

What can it have been like to be both God and man? The question can be addressed historically, or theologically, or philosophically: as dealing with the life and death of Jesus of Nazareth, or the nature of God, or the relations between body and spirit. But insofar as the question is directed towards considerations of consciousness and experience, and to the imagining of God in Christ Jesus as a fully sensate, physical human being, it is naturally a question to be explored in fiction. Where biographers of Jesus frequently struggle with the physical nature, either over-emphasizing its sensual appetites, or suppressing them in favour of a kind of priestly celibacy, I have imagined a Jesus who is, like D. H. Lawrence's risen Christ, a man fully alive in the flesh, a man who knows the pleasures and pains of the body, a man who feels desire, especially sexual desire, as strongly as the rest of us. This a Jesus who is fully human in the flesh, incarnate: a Jesus who eats and drinks, lusts and urinates, encounters doubts and loses faith. But at the same time he is never not God.[1]

In terms of style I have tried to weave together a verbal tapestry using materials from the Jesus-novel tradition, right back to Renan and right up to Jim Crace. Thus the style of the novella is a hybrid of the archaic and the contemporary, and though an original work of imaginative fiction, should be read as a creative improvisation on a critical response to the work of others. The novella is partly what I want to say about the life of Jesus; but much more what I think and feel about what other, much better, writers have already said. The 'Visitation' uses Renan's topography of the Holy Land. The 'Nativity' chapter is indebted for its poetic simulation of an infant perspective to Kurt Vonnegut and Ivan Chernieff, *Sun, Moon, Star* (London: Harper Collins, 1980). The 'Baptism' draws on Zefirelli's film version, with some suggestions on psychology of perception from Burgess's *Man of Nazareth*. The 'Temptation' sequence leans on Crace's *Quarantine*, while the Devil's dialogue is executed in the manner of Burgess. 'Agony' is indebted to both the Kazantzakis and Scorsese versions of *The Last Temptation*, and to George Moore's sceptical Jesus. The 'Passion' sequence follows the 'Stations of the Cross' structure of Mel Gibson's film. The 'Resurrection' deploys a style evocative of D. H. Lawrence's *The Man Who Died*.

In addition the novella uses 'word-paintings', verbal descriptions based on well-known visual representations of Jesus in painting that in turn have influenced the making of the Jesus-films: among them Simone Martini and Lippo Memmi, *Annunication* (1333); John Everett Millais, *Christ in the House of His Parents* (1849–50); *Our Lady of Perpetual Succour*, Byzantine Ikon, fifteenth century; Giotto, *The Kiss of Judas* (1304–6); Stanley Spencer, *Christ Carrying the Cross* (1920); Domenico Fetti, *The Veil of Veronica* (1618–22); Guido Reni, *The Infant Jesus Sleeping on the Cross* (1625); Titian, *Noli Me Tangere* (1514).[2] Echoes of Christian poetry are pervasive, from the Anglo-Saxon devotional poem *The Dream of the Rood*, to St John of the Cross, *The Dark Night of the Soul* (1681) and T. S. Eliot's *Four Quartets* (1944).

To many Christians the idea of trying to imagine the mind of God is a theological absurdity. But all of the works discussed in this study to some degree participate in that unrealizable aspiration. I hope to have shown in the pages that follow that the techniques of traditional prose fiction are by no means inadequate to the representation of divinity as well as humanity, the surreal and the real, the cosmic and the concrete; and that there is no necessary connection between the novel and a purely human Christ. Just as I have argued that the Jesus-novel and the Jesus-film can both encompass humanity and divinity, both sides of the dual nature, so in *Ecce Homo* I have tried to deliver a dual-natured Christ. In doing so I have accepted Hans Kung's challenge that literature is not adequate to the task, and set to disprove it.

Annunciation

I am involved in Mankinde

JOHN DONNE

At first it seemed possible to be in and of all things, as if the integument of flesh had not yet wholly sealed its heavy folds around Him. He was, as he had always been, active and present in everything that lives, moves and has its being: in the delicate wings of the angel which, stirring, shook off a mysterious perfume; in the golden shaft of light which slanted down from above, holding and caressing the tiny motes of dust that floated in its ambience; in the bright air, the incandescent sun and in the modest spirit of the young girl, who bowed her head in deference before the radiant unfurling of Gabriel's splendid pinions.[3] It was his power, and his love, that had created and held the whole moment of annunciation, as a tiny bird can be held, feathers fluttering and heart racing in fear, warm and quivering in the hollow of a man's hand. So for a while he could observe the whole tableau, as if it were a scene in some painting whose frame he fingered: the kneeling angel, bright with unearthly light, gentleness softening the chiselled marble of his features; the maid, shrinking in fear, thin arms hugging the blue mantle about her slender body; the shaft of pure light playing about her head, its source somewhere above in a mass of inscrutable brightness from which fell a sound like the susurrus of gigantic wings.

His newly formed ears were filled with the melody of a music that could have been produced by no instrument, but was exuded from the perfect harmony of this epiphany, a sound as natural as that of running water, but structured by complex chords, a music of light. The celestial odours shed from Gabriel's plumes mingled easily with the common smells of the peasant's house, smells of oil and garlic, the tarry smell of the baked-earth floor and the clean scent of wood-shavings from the adjoining workshop. His tongue still tasted the sweetness of heaven's breath, and reverberated delicately to the soft syllables of Gabriel's greeting, in words that were his words, yet now, with a first sensation of loss, hearing them go away from him, to return spoken, in an unaccustomed language, by one who had become another.

—Hail, Mary, full of grace. The Lord is with you. Be blest among women . . .

It was through the sense of touch that He first began to apprehend what it was to be human, to be the Word become flesh, as the ethereal spirit found itself caged within an intricate structure of cells that sealed the spirit inwards, a tiny but solid body, floating in the dark inland lake of his mother's belly. As the human foetus formed, he found himself irreversibly cut off from the light and space that had been his environment and his nature: sealed into an impenetrable darkness where no sun shines; choking on the bitter iron taste of human blood that began to pump into his newly forming veins. Fold upon fold of flesh imprisoned him: his eyes opening on darkness; ears straining to decipher the strange echoing gurgle of distant human speech; nostrils crinkling in disgust against the offal smells of human organism and function, the body still fetid and rankly reminiscent of the slime from which it had, by his own hands, once and long ago been made.

This was the nadir moment, the point of maximum descent from omnipresent liberty and omnipotent power: to know for the first time, in the body, the fetters of the flesh. But it was also through the sense of touch that he began to know this new world, with its own peculiar grace and beauty, its own propriety of form and design.

This was a different kind of contact from any he had known as God: limited but intense; cramped yet richly textured; a new way of knowing the created world in terms of its shape and form, its ribbed edges and slippery surfaces, its resonant sounds, and pungent odours and sharp, sweet and sour tastes. As a human embryo he could hear nothing of the angel's speech but a deep hollow reverberation, and nothing of his mother's quiet responses save a rippling echo; yet the light that was in him also shed a secret radiance into this, the darkest of all places; and the pulsing anxiety of his mother's fighting heart was stilled by the infusion of this inner grace, as well as by the angel's gentle reassurance.

—Fear not, Mary. Find favour with God.

Her feelings were now his feelings; but at the same time his were hers. His blood thrilled, together with hers, in mingled excitement and fear, at the words of Gabriel's prophecy.

—The Holy Ghost will come upon you. The power of the Highest will overshadow you.

He shared with his mother the surpassing graciousness of trust, flowing like a river of peace through their common blood; joining, in that living red stream, the mind's acquiescence with the body's resignation, as she humbly submitted herself, as every mother does, to her unborn infant's will.

—Behold the handmaid of the Lord.

Her flesh rested in hope. Floating in the warm waters of trust, God fell into his first human sleep.

Visitation

He knew all men, and needed not that any should
testify of man:
for he knew what was in man.

ST JOHN

Much of his time in the womb was spent in sleep, capable now of experiencing the weariness natural to so vast a voyage of transition, so immense a transformation, from heaven to earth, from God to man. Besides, his new humanity required time to repose. The remainder of the time was spent in a restive wakefulness, measuring the sensations of growth, becoming accustomed to the unfamiliar rhythms of a world in which time entails change, and no one moment can ever be identical to the last or the next.

As the little limbs began instinctively to flex and kick, to reach and stretch, he could feel the power and possibility of physical force, however clumsy and limited, to move matter and rearrange space. He became aware of tiny fingers that could grasp and know the external world through the intimacy of touch, the sureness of sensation. Small movements could propel him some relative distance through the dark sea of that amniotic ocean that was now his little world; and his foetal hands, touching the tough curls of the umbilical cord, could feel the force of life pumping urgently through its coiled thickness. This cord, that pierced his middle like a spear, was a chain that bound him fast, prisoner to the placenta; a bond that set limits to his motion, and imperiously pulled him back into awareness of his servitude. Yet it was through the cord that an inexhaustible potency of energy flooded into his new veins and filled them with richness of life. Already he could feel something of the strange dividedness of human nature, its capacity to locate the extremities of love and hate together in the same place, on the same person. He who had never known a mother, had also never felt the irksome tugging of a love that wounds and heals, frees and holds, liberates and enslaves.

The slow rhythm of human development, the gradual accumulation of cells, the imperceptible enlargement of vessels and organs, the extension and strengthening of limbs, all seemed to advance by its own remorseless will, even though ultimately it was his own creative power that had originated the process, his own paternal care that maintained the conditions of its possibility. It was a great source of delight to observe, at first hand, the delicately balanced perfection of the human organism: the way in which each element of its composition supported and facilitated the development of the whole. How the circulating blood spun rapidly and ceaselessly around the tiny system, simultaneously nourishing both physical and mental capabilities; how the growth of tissue and muscle, by extending the possibilities of sensation, expanded the capacity of the brain to absorb and digest information; and how the swelling brain began to instruct and co-ordinate the motions of foot and finger, elbow and knee. The safety and security of the womb, that warm and wet container, afforded both the conditions of successful development, and a welcome period of protection from what otherwise would inevitably have felt like a painful exposure of this delicate weakness to the pitiless harshness of exterior cold and heat, parching dryness and bitter, penetrating frost. Indeed it seemed now vital to know this weakness, this utter humiliating dependence on another body for the preservation of life, this physical vulnerability of the tiny organism to a threatening environment, in order fully and truly to know what man is, and what is in man.

Gradually the sheltering uterine darkness began to seem less like a prison, as he adjusted to the strangeness of being apart from himself, pushing into abeyance those powers of knowledge and vision that had no part in the limited nature of the human creature. The *logos* that was God, and was with God, now translated into another language, was a piece of God broken off from the whole for the purposes of incarnation. A piece of, all of, God, indwelling within the fleshly body; still part of that vast and incomprehensible wholeness, yet broken apart from it in a severance that enabled the unhealing wounds of alienation to begin their long process of bleeding. This, too, was man, and was in man: God all of God, apart from himself, being and not-being, present and absent. Side by side co-existed the assurance of absolute power, immeasurable goodness, eternal delight; with the hunger of homesickness, the yearning inconsolable thirst for reunion with the all.

The sense of separation began to be felt as a human loneliness, being in the world and not of it, enclosed in singleness of being, and knowing only the mother of whose flesh he was also a part. His adoptive father Joseph he knew from across a great distance, hearing only fragments of speech, voice-tones that expressed by turns bewilderment, anger, awe and fear; then resignation, solicitude, patient expectation, quiet pride.

Joseph's thoughts and feelings had been, of course, known in any case to his mysteriously begotten son, this inexplicable gift that had come to him from nowhere by the message of an angel; but known in some abstraction, as a story narrated and overheard, not felt in the blood through the medium of incarnation. With pride and satisfaction swelled the father's heart at the honour granted to his tribe, the ancient and dignified house of David: so much fallen from the days of its legendary greatness, now with this new promise reawakening, perhaps, to a prospect of recovery, stirred by the faint trumpet-call of a distant echo from the past. But that it should be he – Joseph, the simple carpenter of Nazareth, an ignorant and unlettered artisan: who bore with patience and humility the insignia of his tribe, more conscious of its present diminution than of its erstwhile greatness; recognizing himself more in his people's long and patient endurance of indignity and oppression, than in the ancestral magnificence and splendour so eloquently declaimed and sung in the synagogue, through the psalms and scripture of his inheritance, the voices of Moses and Isaiah, the Law and the Prophets – was a more mysterious occurrence in which he could hardly sustain an abiding belief. Although he could trace his ancestry back through the roll-call of 75 generations, to Adam the first-born son of God, yet he felt himself to be of little account in the great affairs of the world, expecting only diligently to do his work, and to care for his family as a just man should; still less that he should be, by manifest choice of God, adoptive father to the Christ-child, the Messiah, the second Adam sent by God to redeem the transgressions of the first.

It seemed more explicable to Joseph that his young virgin girl-bride Mary should have been the first choice of divine providence, since such was his love for her that he could imagine not a moment's hesitation on the part of any god looking for a womb to nestle in. To Joseph, his espoused seemed the perfection of womanhood, though scarcely yet a woman: beautiful, yet virtuous; quiet yet strong-willed; pious yet practical; unassuming, and unwilling to seek public advantage, or even recognition, for her manifest intelligence and learning.

That God, the God of his fathers, the God of Abraham and Isaac and Jacob, should have chosen for his medium of passage, from all the women in the world, a virgin, whose young flesh remained chaste as ivory, uncontaminated by the rank stain of human seed, seemed entirely natural. What cleaner or more fitting sheath for a God's protection than this tight, unstretched uterus, this unpenetrated womb, which seemed in his imagination a nest of spices, smelling as sweetly as her ivory skin, faintly scented by the crushed flower-petals that passed among the poor as perfume. Yet Joseph also knew that this clean, unpolluted body was no rigid chamber of chastity, but rather a lively flame of female sensuality, only too eager to give itself over to lawful passion and the pleasures of the marriage bed. Although neither he nor Mary would have considered breaking one of their community's most rigorous taboos, they had already known, in brief exchanges of kiss and embrace, the power of sexuality, drawing them together into an intimacy of the body that seemed deeper and more binding than any convention of affiance, or ceremonial ritual of joining. In the event, however, Mary's flesh had become not the vessel of transmission, through Joseph's eagerly jerking loins, of royal David's seed, but a body breached by the flame of incarnation, opened up to receive an angel-child before the slim thighs had parted to admit a mortal man's urgent desire. Joseph had quickly outgrown his initial angry suspicion of Mary's possible infidelity. But still he could not help feeling a certain jealousy, a deeper realization of his own marginal role in this great process of divine conception, gestation and delivery. Not only was this child not his child: neither was it the blossom he had hoped would spring strongly forth from the root of Jesse's stem. Not a son of David, not one of those children of Israel glimpsed in Abraham's vision, as innumerable as grains of the desert sand; but the God of David's ancestors now slept quietly under his wife's delicate ribs.

The baby's habitual sensation of floating in a weirdly echoing isolation tank, insulated from exterior contacts, was then one day as suddenly interrupted by a violent intrusion from the outside world, a sudden shock of encounter that brought him into intimate awareness of another human being beyond himself, and beyond his human family. A period of suspension, induced by the rhythmic motion of his mother's walking, intimated to him that she had been prompted to undertake her journey into the hill-country to visit her cousin Elisabeth, not seen since Mary had received the apparition of the angel, but spoken of then by Gabriel as the vessel of another miracle: all her life barren, considered well beyond child-bearing, yet now inexplicably pregnant with the God-given gift of a son. Certainly, with God, Mary had reflected, nothing is impossible. Reluctant to expose Elisabeth to the prying eyes and wagging tongues of the village community, her husband Zacharia had secretly conveyed her away to a remote hamlet perched up on the rocky heights above the plain of Nazareth. Carried passively along the steep winding mountain-track, feeling by soft absorbed tremors the slipping of his mother's sandalled feet on the uneven path, he sought from his condition of blindness and deafness to orientate himself on the map of this country which was to become his human world, the scene of all his earthly joys and sorrows. With the eagle vision of imagination, from the windswept plateau above Nazareth, he scanned the horizons.[4] Far to the west, he saw the outline of Mount Carmel, with its abrupt peak that seemed to tumble into the sea; then the great double summit that towered over Megiddo; the mountains of the country of Shechem, its holy places sanctified from patriarchal history; the hills of Gilboa, and the rounded breast of Tabor. Through a gap between the slopes of Shunem and Tabor he could see, in his mind's eye, the valley of the Jordan and the high plains of Peraea. To the north around the flank of Hermon he glimpsed the edge of Caesarea-Philippi; to the south, the Samaritan hills foreshadowed the desolation of Judaea. These would be the places marking the scene of his life and death: the hills and lakes and valleys; the wooded mountain slopes and the dreary sun-bleached plains; the villages of square white houses; and the thronging streets of the cities. From the narrow crossways of Nazareth to the paved courts of Jerusalem; from the fertile shores of Galilee to the bald slopes of Golgotha. These places he would come to know not as spots on a map, but roads to be travelled, where sharp flints wounded the feet, and in the dry season white dust filled the eyes and choked the nose and mouth; and as roadside dwelling places where the stranger would be welcomed in to wash his feet, slake his thirst and sit to talk with the people over a skin of wine. Points of the compass, distances and directions, black ink-marks on a chart; thirst on dusty roads, the cool trickle of a fountain in the village square.

Then, breaking in upon his reverie, the overwhelming sensation of someone else, someone like himself and yet different, someone he partly knew, someone he knew would recognize him. The sound of women's voices, a sensation of embrace, an outpouring of great joy: and then as Elisabeth caught the sound of Mary's voice, he felt that violent leap of the foetus in the other mother's womb, like a salmon leaping the rapids and falling back into the frothing foam, a bound of joy that could be felt like a pulse through the whole fabric of the universe, the supple energetic twist of a body feeling itself too full of the Holy Spirit to be contained, to stay still.

John. With a shock of knowledge the Baptist made himself known as a powerful stream of energy that rippled like a great wave through the waters of his little sea; as a voice, eloquent though yet knowing no words, ringing through the stillness like the pealing of a bronze bell; as a light, a piercing brightness that lanced through interior darkness like the heaving up of a sudden unlooked-for sunrise, light breaking where no sun shines upon his blind, all-seeing eyes. It was not only the common possession of that spirit which had presided over both their conceptions, and filled each full of an inward spiritual grace, that brought this keen companionship. It was the bond of humanity, the mutual indwelling of incarnation, sealed in the flesh yet enlivened by the spirit, that enabled this perfect reciprocity of greeting, this common knowledge.

John, who came for a witness, to be a witness of the light, that all men through him might believe. John, who from the shelter of his mother's belly saw the visitation of the dayspring from on high, as clear as day, and leapt in the womb for joy. John, the harbinger; John, the voice crying in the wilderness; John, who would urge the people of Jordan to prepare the way of the Lord, to make his paths straight. John, who would rage like a lion in the deserts of Judaea, now skipped like a newborn lamb at the sound of his aunt's voice. Cousin, John.

Nativity

This birth was
Hard and bitter agony for us, like a Death, our death.

T. S. ELIOT

The agony of parturition was again a reminder of dependency, as well as a foretaste of comparable agonies to come. Not one of the human strengths and capabilities he had developed in the previous months was effective in resisting the series of deep seismic shocks that rippled uncontrollably through the mother's body, wave after wave of powerful contractions, taut muscle alternately relaxing and tightening with an irresistible impulse of expulsion. Fighting against the pressure exerted by the spasming uterus, he pulled himself away from the yawning darkness that spiraled above his head into a whirlpool of magnetic force, dragging him outwards towards the light. Then the comforting waters of his habitual haven suddenly rushed, as it seemed, vertically upwards, like an underground spring that has worked its way to the surface and explodes into a fountain, and gushed through the aperture, leaving him exposed to a sudden inrush of cold air, sharp as the breath of daybreak on his naked skin. By an unstoppable power he was pulled in the same direction, his head engaging painfully into the tight neck of the uterus, his body following as the head squeezed impossibly through the tiny, reluctantly expanding ring of muscle. His mother's cries of pain, short shrieks of agony reached him from the outside, increasing in volume and intensity as the contractions became more rapid, and the baby's head pushed inexorably against the pelvic floor, seeming to cleave her body in two. As if a sword had pierced her womb.

At first the unpredictable combination of sensations produced an overwhelming confusion. Near his eyes a bright source of light blinded his widely stretched pupils, while beyond the light lay a great darkness; his ears still rang with the yells of his mother's labour-pains, now diminishing into tired sobs of relief, and were soothed by the comforting voice of his father, who knelt by Mary and wiped the sweat and tears from her face. The strong smells of straw and animal fodder, together with the warm pungent scents of the beasts themselves, located the stable in his sensory map of the world: four rough walls, a dirty pavement, a penthouse roof of beams and slate. Other people were there too, just beyond the circle of light shed by the lantern, bedding down in the straw with the asses and camels. He registered a sense of pity, the sympathy of the poor for the poor.

From the darkness beyond the swinging lantern's fitful and flickering light, where grotesque shadows tossed on the roughly whitewashed walls, came the contented snuffling and champing of animals at their feed, the running clink of a chain, the hoarse grunt and squeal of a tired camel. What lay within his human vision was what his eyes could see, since his rubbery little neck could not raise or control the heavy, lolling head.[5] So it was a confusing scene: in the foreground rough faces swelling into vision; beyond, the softly illuminated courtyard of the inn, thickly populated with the sprawled exhausted bodies of sleeping men and women; and nearer still the humped shapes of tethered beasts. From the corner of one eye, he could see the smooth white slope of his mother's breast, broken by the distention of a rosy nipple, already beginning to ooze a white cream of milk; from the corner of the other, he could glimpse, above the white walls of the compound, an immense blackness of sky, powdered with a haphazard sprinkling of stars. He felt his mother's hand cup the warm delicate globe of his head, and press his face towards her breast. Instinctively his mouth opened and received the taut nipple, his tongue probing experimentally at its strange soft hardness, his lips closing around it as the sucking reflex began to draw into his mouth, and to send trickling down his throat, a thin thread of warm milk. Quickly, after a few choking snorts, he adjusted his breathing to the rhythm of suckling, alternately drawing cold air through his nostrils, and warm milk through his lips. His right hand rested against the full breast, tiny fingers flexing in folds of crinkled skin. Then as his eager sucking subsided to a contented lapping, and Mary's head fell back in exhaustion against the pile of unloaded baggage on which she lay, his lips released the nipple and his head lolled back against the crook of her arm, from which position he was able to look straight up at the sky, and to see it with a double vision: as the cold inhospitable spaces of a vast desolation, lit by the hard glitter of unfriendly stars; and as an outer, material shell of his own empyrean home, fuming with festive lights of celebration, and (beyond the reach of human vision) filled with a company of the heavenly host. The cold brightness of a waning moon rode easily through whitened clouds, and their frosty phosphorescence seemed like clouds of incense rising from some sacrifice. Directly above the inn stood, in glory of glittering brightness, the star that heralded, for those that had eyes to see, the time and place of his arrival.

Where now was his home: beyond that dark infinite immensity, or here against this soft hospitable bosom? What now was the essence of his being: spirit or flesh? Who was he, Son of God, or Son of Man? For in order to accept the responsibility of incarnation, he had had to divide himself, to leave himself behind, so that the Godhead whose ambience he could glimpse, glittering above him in supreme brightness, was that of himself that he, together with his fellow-men and women, would learn to name and recognize as the Father. At the same time, lying helpless and vulnerable in the arms of his earthly mother, replete with the comforting kindness of her generous milk, his cheek nestling against the soft living and breathing rise and fall of her breast, he could not imagine it possible to feel more human. To be human was to see that sky also from this perspective, as a void of infinite emptiness, rather than (as he saw it through his own inner eye) an inverted, concave blackness, pierced by starlight, as if a sheet of black metal were punched with holes and held up to blot out the unbearable brightness behind. It was only the one bright star of epiphany, pulsing with a soft radiance, that seemed from his earthbound position to be a living piece of heaven.

He was awoken by a chatter of excited voices speaking to Joseph. He felt, rather than saw, rough weathered faces, lips parted in wonder, dark eyes glittering with a kind of hunger. Among the shepherds was a young boy who had carried on his shoulders a newborn lamb they had been reluctant to leave overnight in the cold fields. Hesitantly he laid the lamb beside the baby, so the little hand could explore its physical contours. The baby's fingers played experimentally with the thickly twining clusters of grey hair, and with softly pressed fingertips felt the rough smoothness of animal skin. This again was for the child a new sensation, the soft tangling texture of wool. Strange that the living creature consisted of this too, and that through this exterior integument it was possible to acquire a differential engagement with the life force within. There were revealed to him two distinct forms of knowledge: that which was his already, the creator's awareness of the creature, derived from a process of design and execution, shaping the manufactured object from within; and this new acquaintance with the body as both an extrusion of the spirit, and the shell that protects and contains it. So alive it seemed, this warm quickening mass of skin and fur! And he too was alive in the same way, incarnate, embodied. Yet at the same time the lamb's helpless bleating pierced his heart with pity of those he came to save, and for the sacrifice he himself, the Lamb of God, would have to endure.

After a while the shepherds withdrew. He could hear, from the adjoining stall, the excited voice of a child, recounting to his mother, who had slept throughout, the events of the night. He had seen, he told her, the arrival of strangers, who grew in his imagination to the stature and magnificence of kings. They had knelt, he said, to worship the child, and to proclaim him as the Messiah. They had offered him gifts of infinite riches, including a lamb with a fleece of pure gold that had shone in the gloom of the stable as brightly as the light of the sun.

He saw the woman peer over the stall. There was nothing unusual, nothing but a young mother asleep with her baby in her arms. A lamb lay in the straw, but although the lamplight touched its fleece with a golden glow, it appeared to be no extraordinary creature, no bearer of the Golden Fleece. But mother, lamb and baby must have afforded her a touching sight, since he saw in her eyes disenchantment give way to tenderness, and she continued to gaze at them as, over Bethlehem, the dawn of a new day began to break.

Presentation

And a sword shall pierce thorow thy soul, thine also.

ST LUKE

The streets of the city afforded some relief from the unmitigated harshness of the Judean wilderness. Here the air seemed more hospitable after the bitter desert nights, since the mild winter sun was reflected from the hard pavements, propelling from their shiny metallic surfaces currents of warm air.

Progress was slow through the crowded streets, clogged as they were with bazaars and markets, choked with a plenitude of human and animal traffic and trade. On the dry trek from Bethlehem, his mother had kept the child's head covered from the air, holding his face to her breast, and swathing his little body in the folds of her garments. Now as they pushed their way through the slowly undulating crowd towards Herod's Temple, he peered out from the sheltering cloth, screwing up his eyes against the harsh vertical light, watching the constant movement and infinite multiplicity of a city crowd. In the packed streets a tightly pressed mass of humanity, all the social diversity and multi-coloured ethnicity of Jerusalem's chequered population, went noisily about its everyday business. Rich Phoenician merchants haggled over goods in the markets, their white turbans nodding above the heads of the crowd. Beggars crouched against the wall, skinny hands alternately fluttering to wave away the flies, and thrust out towards the passer-by in urgent importunity for alms. Everywhere the dusty air was thick with several dialects and with many languages: Greek, Aramaic, Syrian, Roman. Close to his face the dark eyes of a woman stared at him from within the folds of a veil; then he recoiled in shock as the vacant misery of a leper's ravaged face eyed him closely. An off-duty Centurion of the Roman legions lolled against a doorpost, avoided by most of the crowd: far from home, isolated in his misery, drinking down his loneliness.

Jerusalem of Judaea, City of David. Jerusalem of the golden courts, fair hill of Sion. Jerusalem, foretold of by the prophet Daniel as destined to become a desolation of abomination, whose children would flee into the mountains to escape a suffering never seen since the beginning of Creation.

They entered the Temple precincts through the Benjamin Gate, and stepped gingerly over the crippled forms of the sick and disabled who lay, sprawled around the Pool of Bethesda, waiting for an angel to stir the miraculous healing waters. Then they were circumventing the massive stone walls, their bases in deep shadow, their high tops yellow in the winter sunlight. As his mother was pushed by the crowd close against the wall, he perceived, close to his eyes, one of the great joins where the rough-bossed stones of Solomon's ancient Temple met the smooth, precisely jointed blocks of Herod's modern masonry. Mounting the great stone steps, they entered the outer courtyard, the Court of the Gentiles. Ahead, occupying an elevated position, could be seen the walls of the Court of Israel, within which was the Priest's Court, containing the inner sanctuary, the holy of holies: his Father's house. At the south-east corner he could see the pinnacle of the Temple rising in golden splendour above the valley of the Kidron. Strategically positioned at the opposite corner, the fortress of Antonia dominated the enclosure, its military garrison diplomatically invisible. The colonnades of the Royal Porch echoed to the noisy disputes of the scribes, and the rattle of coinage on the moneychangers' counters. The two pigeons carried in the wicker basket at his father's side cooed persistently.

They passed through the Gate which was called Beautiful, with its doors of exquisitely sculpted Corinthian bronze, and entered the Court of the Women, then threaded their way through the crowd and reached the entrance to the Court of Israel. Here Mary was obliged to halt and hand over the baby to her husband. No woman could penetrate further into the Temple, and so it fell to the father to carry in the boy and present him to the Lord. Reluctantly Mary released the baby into Joseph's outstretched arms. The child could feel his mother's unwillingness to part with him expressed in the fingers that tightened around his legs. He could see, gathering in the corners of her eyes, a shadow of fear at the prospect of his physical pain; but also a certain wounded dignity and hurt pride, as she acceded with some manifest reluctance to this enforced abandonment of her son, this larger sacrifice on the altar of Jewish motherhood. For had she not submitted in dutiful obedience to the Law of Moses, patiently waiting out the time of her purification, though she had known no man, and though God Himself had spoken to her through the message of an angel, and though it was written in that same Mosaic Law that every male child who opens the womb shall be called holy to the

Lord? She had no desire, as a woman, to follow her husband into the holy of holies, into the Court of Priests, into the Tabernacle. Let those mysteries remain reserved for men, and for the priests of men: the sons of that Moses who had seen God face-to-face, and spoken with Him on the slopes of Mount Sinai; and for those who bore the sacerdotal mantle of his brother Aaron. But hers was the womb that had opened to admit this little God-child into the world. Then who, if not she, had the right to offer him in presentation to the Lord; to hold up his little body to receive the blessing promised to Isaac and his seed; to watch the blood flow from the secret wound of his circumcision, and to still his sharp little cries of agony against his mother's breast?

*   *   *

Filled with smoke from the altars of sacrifice, the sanctuary echoed and reverberated to the throaty harmonious singing of men's voices. Lined entirely, floor, walls and ceiling, with boards of fragrant cedar wood, the acoustic properties of the space enriched and amplified the sound to an unearthly beauty like that of angels' song. Everywhere on the wooden walls were carvings of natural forms, palm-trees and fruits and open-petalled flowers. Thin chains of gold veiled the inner from the outer sanctuary. Two huge cherubim, carved from olive wood and decorated with gold leaf, spread their massive wings from wall to wall, seeming in the thick perfumed smoke to hover in protection over the holy of holies.

The mellifluous tenor voice of a cantor sang, in ancient and familiar words, of King Solomon, dedicating the first temple:

The Lord said that he would dwell
In the thick darkness.
Blessed be the Lord God of Israel
Who spoke with his mouth unto David.

Acrid smoke from the bronze altars fumed towards the cavernous panelled ceiling; incense of burning flesh.

The priest took the baby into his arms, and in a sonorous bass voice began to intone the liturgy of circumcision. The child's fingers became intertwined in the hairs of his long white beard, and the great sacerdotal voice boomed in the infant ear. The priest sang of Abraham and Isaac; of the Covenant, of the Law, of the holy ritual by which each male of the tribe is purified, and the badge of God's people signed in his flesh.

The ceremonial knife, elevated towards the inner sanctuary, gleamed brightly in the light of a hundred petal-shaped, beaten copper lamps. The naked child himself was then held up towards the sanctuary, presented to the Lord. The priest handed the child over to another priest, and with swift and skilful expertise pulled the tiny foreskin away from the penis, and sliced it off. Holding the bloody little prepuce in one hand, and the sacrificial knife, speckled with blood, in the other, he held both aloft, and called God's blessing on the new son of Israel.

So this was pain: pain experienced in gradations, from mild discomfort to acute agony. The priest's thumb and forefinger had clamped firmly over the foreskin, and the sensation of skin, with its limited elasticity, being pulled away from his body was hurtful enough. But that quick slice of the sacrificial knife, cutting pitilessly through the soft tissue, sent jangling through his nerves a bewildering sensation of agony. With pain also came a feeling of violation, of having been taken in his weakness and wounded in his most vulnerable part; and with that a violent reaction of indignation, as if at some injustice or unfairness. He felt the corners of his own mouth twitch uncontrollably downwards into a peevish grimace, and heard from his own throat the desperate bawling yell of a hurt child.

For the first time he felt the possibility of pure physical anger, provoked indiscriminately by real injustice, routine suffering or arbitrary injury. Nothing could protect his flesh from the lancing fire of pain, nor from the violence of resentment that he felt against the priest, nor from the momentary bitterness of disappointment against his father who had delivered him up to this ordeal.

Looking down at his groin, he could see the ragged rim of his severed prepuce, seeping blood over his fat little thighs. This was the first shedding, the first drop into an inexhaustible cup. Blood poured out for many.

For this he came: but all he could feel when his father took him outside and handed him back to Mary, who was waiting in restless impatience at the Temple door, was the cruel soreness of his inconsolable little wound.

Baptism

Behold the Lamb of God.

ST JOHN

The queue stretched from the river's edge all the way back to the road, taking in its course a number of meandering turns and dogleg bends. Despite the numbers of people, the assembly stood and shuffled patiently forwards in virtually uninterrupted silence. A woman's baby cried, a thin voice of protest in the great quiet valley, until she plugged its mouth with a full, olive-skinned breast. An old man, head covered with a fringed prayer shawl, muttered under his breath quiet invocations. The heat swelled and quivered in the valley, buoyed up by a slow hot breeze that moved sluggishly in from the south, breathing the parched dryness of the Negeb. A constant undercurrent of sound was provided by the uniform buzzing of innumerable flies, and the swishing of sleeves as listlessly flapping hands attempted to wave them away. All longed to reach the coolness of the river, but none broke the disciplined conformity of the queue: thirsting, it seemed, after righteousness more than for water.

He stood in line, waiting his turn, sandalled feet scuffing the dust as he shuffled slowly after his immediate predecessor, an Essene who stood bare-headed under the cruel sun, as if welcoming its violence. Jesus could see on the almost black, sunburnt skin of his neck runnels of sweat, greedily lapped at by thirsty flies. He could feel, sympathetically, the maddening itch of their quivering little legs on the twitching skin, and had to control an impulse to swat them away, guessing (knowing, if he chose to admit the knowledge) that endurance of such petty irritations was for the ascetic a strict point of personal discipline.

The sun was riding low over the west bank, and dribbling molten gold over the waters of Jordan, by the time he reached the dried clay of the river's edge, and scrambled down the steep dusty declivity to reach the stony shallows. Directly ahead he could see, now silhouetted against the setting sun, the grizzled head and naked form of the Baptist, waist-deep in water, his great voice booming across the shallows, prophesying the coming of the Messiah, and the apocalyptic terrors of the wrath to come. Each catechumen, having

forded the shallow reaches to stand before the Baptist, was seized
in powerful hands, and subjected to his penetrating stare. His head
resembled nothing so much as a lion's, unkempt hair standing out
like a mane in matted curls, tangled beard jutting fiercely forwards,
eyes burning with intensity. As Jesus's dusty feet entered, with a
delicious shock, the blissful coolness of the water, only two or three
candidates ahead of him, he could see clearly in the yellow evening
light the crudely constructed face of his cousin, with its broad
cheekbones, wide snub nose and thick red lips thrusting through the
auburn clusters of his beard; so different, he knew, from his own pale
features and dark hair and beard, just as the refined, small-featured
beauty of his mother had contrasted with the rough peasant face of
her cousin Elisabeth. The Baptist's body also, despite the privations
of his wilderness diet of locusts and wild honey, seemed surprisingly
strong, with powerful shoulders and arms ribbed with muscle. The
physical strength was apparent as he grabbed the next catechumen,
a well-built man, by the scars on his shoulders a former soldier, taller
by a head than John, and swept his feet from under him, catching
him by the neck to immerse him in the water. The man's feet could
be seen kicking in a flurry of foam, and his arms reached up to clutch
the Baptist's shoulders. Unperturbed, John raised his eyes to heaven
and bellowed out the formula of remission:
   —Be clean, for your sins are forgiven you.
   As his grip relaxed, the man's head burst blindly out of the river,
water cascading from sodden hair and beard, and coughed and
spewed from the constricted throat. But half-drowned as he was, he
knelt in the water, seized John's hands and kissed them.
   —Master.
   John pulled him to his feet, and spoke with kind firmness:
   —I baptize you with water: but one shall come, mightier than
I, who will baptize you with the Holy Spirit, and purify you with
fire.
   When his turn came, Jesus shook back his headdress, and
approached John with his face bowed towards the river. He could
see, through the rippling waters, the rock-strewn sand below, while
the surface danced with brilliant points of light. He saw below him
John's sunburnt hands open and cup together beneath the water,
then lifted, out of his sight, to pour over the hot, bowed head a
trickle of the cooling liquid. With drops of water chasing down hair
and beard, he raised his face to look full into John's eyes.

Joy unspeakable; terror uncontrollable; wonder, fear, adoration, all in a flash traversed the Baptist's face, jaw dropped in slack amazement, eyes pierced through with rapture, pain, pity and awe. Struck by the vision of a new life, quelled at the prospect of his own death; flooded with a great relief at this arrival, saddened by the certain knowledge of his own demise, John slid to his knees in the water and raised his hands in petition. His voice, subdued by wonder to a hoarse whisper, yet reverberated loudly across the still water, filling the whole sunlit valley with words of adoration and welcome.

—Behold: the Lamb of God, who takes away the sins of the world.

Jesus laid his hands briefly on the shaggy head, leaned forward and kissed John on the cheek, then drew the Baptist to his feet, and in turn knelt down into the water before him. John's face was eclipsed into darkness, while the rays of the setting sun flamed his hair to a golden aureole. A man sent from God.

—Come, cousin, said Jesus, familiar, reassuring. I am here to be baptized.

*   *   *

It had been the news of John, reaching him in the quiet village of Nazareth via the stories of passing travellers, which represented to him the signal he had awaited, through 30 years of uneventful provincial life: the sign predestined to inform him that the way was prepared, the good news proclaimed, the world ready to receive and reject him.

He could recall the decisive moment that had marked the end of his pleasant period of Galilean obscurity, and dispatched him on the brief journey towards his final destiny. Rumours had circulated throughout the towns and villages of Galilee concerning a prophet, who had arisen in the valley of the Jordan, preaching a strange new gospel of purification, a baptism of repentance for the remission of sins. Some said he was Elijah, still living on the holy mountains, or Isaiah, reborn into a new time, since his inspired rage against the corruptions of Rome and Jerusalem echoed the old prophet's righteous anger, flung against a generation of vipers, warning of the wrath to come. He used Isaiah's words, it was said, as if they were his own, words of unearthly beauty that moved all hearers to remorse, to discontent with the emptiness of their lives; filled them with hunger and thirst for a reign of righteousness to come.

But it was some time before Jesus encountered witnesses of the prophecies of his coming. He had left his father finishing a job in the workshop, washed his hands and face at the well and gone to the village inn to hear the gossip that brought echoes of great events from the major centres of the civilized world: Rome, Alexandria, Athens. In Nazareth these places were cities of remote magnificence, that shone in the obscurity of the provincial imagination like jewels set on the rim of a great wheel, circling around the far horizon, always remaining at a distance from the undistinguished, almost absent, centre.

He sat on a bench outside the inn, under a clustering vine that luxuriated across the front of the house, and enjoyed the warm rays of the declining sun reflected from the old yellow stone. He softened his dried flesh with a little bread dipped into a basin of olive oil, and sluiced the sawdust and wood-shavings from his throat with a cool cup of purple wine. It had been too dark in the workshop to continue working by natural light, and candles being precious, he had swept the floor, put away the tools and urged his father also to knock off for the day. Pity had searched at his heart as he saw Joseph, now a frail old man, continuing to plane smooth a knot in a plank of wood, his sight too weak to register the deepening twilight, his work guided by touch rather than vision. He himself would never reach old age, would never share with his father this gradual but inexorable deterioration of the body: the slackening and wrinkling of the skin, the veined hands with their tremulous grip over the carpenter's tools, the stiffening of the joints that gave the inflexible walk of an elderly man, the mumbling toothless mouth, the pigmentless rough hair sprouting undisciplined from nostril and ear; the deafness, the diminishing sight, the slowness of wit and lapses of memory. From his observation of the old artisan, continuing his work because it had been promised for the next day to a neighbour, Jesus considered that old age, with its undignified dependency, might well be one of the hardest things his human children had to bear, harder even than the long-drawn out suffering of a painful death. Responsibility lay heavy on his heart.

Voices reached him, rumours from the desert, speaking in tongues.

—A man sent from God. He came from nowhere; some say his father was a priest.

—He keeps to the wilderness, lives in a cell carved out of the rock in a mountain-side. He never sleeps in a bed, fasts and prays and wears goatskin garments. A holy man!

—There are those who say he is Elijah. I think he may be the Christ.

—He cannot be the Christ.

—Did he say he was the Christ?

—No. He said that another would come, and that he himself would not be fit to unbuckle the other's sandal.

—A greater one than Johanaan!

Jesus thoughtfully wiped the last drops of oil from his bowl with a crust, and rinsed it down with the dregs of his wine. As the liquor slid over his tongue to chase the crumbs of bread down his throat, he could feel a fine film of oil moistening his lips. He rose from the table, and strolled back through the streets to the house of his father. Silent white-robed figures flitted through the darkness, ghostly and anonymous until they came close and gave Jesus a word of greeting. As he passed an open gateway he could see into a courtyard, where a family sat around in a circle beneath a spreading fig tree, digging their fingers into a huge bowl of cooked cereal and meat, looking very close-knit as they drew together into the circle of orange lamp-light. Everywhere the air carried the smells of cooking, garlic and oil, and the smoky perfume of burning cedar-wood. Looking up, he could see, framed between the white walls of the narrow street, the sky, a blue-black setting for the pulsing radiance of a hundred stars. He felt at his heart the sharp sadness of leave-taking.

At home, his father had dropped asleep on a bench against the wall, his grizzled jaw hanging open, his slack mouth mumbling sterterous snores. Jesus eased his body gently down so his head rested on one of the rolled mats that served them as pillows, and he slept more easily. His mother sat on a leather stool beside the fire, watching their dinner cooking. As she looked up at him, the glow of the firelight flattered her small features, and softened the grey in her hair. Her face opened with the smile of uninhibited joy that always greeted the return of her first-born son, the angel-child. As soon as she glimpsed his face, bearing a look of sorrow she had seen before, but never so deeply etched on his features, she knew the time had come to release him to the world. Without a word she stretched her arms towards him, and caught him tightly to her breast. He could feel the silent tears moistening his face, taste their saltiness as he kissed her cold cheek. Silently, with no effort of attention, he read her inner thoughts.

*   *   *

Now, as he prepared to leave his old life for ever, and sat on the edge of his mattress turning over the images of the past, as one would browse through a scroll, he reflected that the most intractable memory of all was that expression of pain on his mother's face. His mother, who had nurtured and protected him throughout his childhood, rubbing his bruises and salving his little wounds. To whom had he showed every cut and contusion, every breach and indentation of the vulnerable flesh. When, in his father's workshop, playing on the floor among the curled, sweet-smelling wood-shavings, his father busily at his bench fashioning a door from clean planks of cedar, his open hand caught on a protruding nail that tore the skin and embossed his palm with a vivid blossom of blood – horrified then for a moment at the sudden vision, breaking in upon his infancy, of stigmata still held tightly in the closed hand of the future – who had kissed the soreness of his ripped hand, and whose soothing words of comfort had pushed the future back into the remote distance?[6] Who had succoured him when, as a toddler, become so absorbed in the rich and fascinating world of childhood that he had almost forgotten his true identity, he was suddenly again assailed by the vision of his own death: from the corners of each eye an angel, holding towards him the cruel implements of his destined execution, the cross, the spear and sponge of vinegar? Then the face of his mother, hearing his cries, had loomed towards him, in an exaggerated perspective, so that the angels diminished to manageable size, and his field of vision was filled with her great pitying eyes, full of pain for his distress.[7] In terror he ran towards her, one of his sandals flapping loose, and she caught him to her lap. Always he retained that image, formed into a picture in his memory: his mother's face, hooded against a golden sky; the angels with their fierce little battery of instruments receding into the distance; himself seated sideways on her lap, her hand comfortingly enclosing his. Confronted with the requirements of his father's work, he had been only too grateful then to avail himself of the infinite succour and solicitude of his mother's love.

*   *   *

John took the sacred head in his hands, and pushed it beneath the water. As his eyes closed instinctively against the aching coldness of the stream, Jesus watched his baptism through the medium of his cousin's vision. Neck strained back, throat stretched forward, the Baptist faced the heavens. Eyes screwed tightly shut, from behind the lids he could see only a bright flame of sunlight, laced with an internally reflected network of red blood vessels. As he opened his eyes, each retina recorded its own separate field of vision, so there seemed to be two skies, each separate and integral in its uniform cobalt blue, as if the heavens had opened. In the space between these two skies, the point of invisibility where human eyes only imagine they see, he perceived a searing white radiance, like a fork of lightning blinding the eyes, but to the inner vision soft and delicately textured as the feathered breast of a dove. Then his senses dissolved into unintelligible sound and incomprehensible vision, as the wings of the Holy Spirit beat about his head, and the voice of God thundered at him from the clouds.

Just as suddenly all was silent again. The world tilted slightly on its axis, and righted itself. The heavens closed; the sky welded seamlessly into pristine singleness; the cold waters still flowed about his thighs, the people continued to stand on the shore, waiting patiently for remission from their sins. There before him, as clear and tangible as his own baptising, sacramental hands, was the reassuring smile of Jesus, echoing the words he believed he had heard rumbling in thunder from the riven skies.

—You are my beloved son, he said: in whom I am well pleased.

Temptation

Neither death nor life, nor angels, nor principalities, nor powers
. . . shall be able to separate us from the love of God.

ST PAUL

In the early morning, after the sun had shouldered itself above the
mountains, the desert's elaborate pattern of angular shapes was
pervasively punctuated by short black shadows. The visual relief
provided by this variation and contrast of light enabled the eye to
explore a rigorously designed, inscrutably chaotic chequerwork
of lines, squares, triangles and rhomboids, a parched and peeling
structure seemingly built on principles of classical aridity and strict
chastity of form. As the sun moved slowly zenithwards, this stark
geometry gave way first to an appearance of softened crumpling, as
if the surface of the desert were an immense cloth flapped out to dry
into a solidly textured parchment of uneven folds and fissures; then
this effect in turn gave way to the annihilation of all perspective,
as the sands dissolved under the heavy midday glare into an
incandescent white uniformity of heat and light. A cooler air from
the north collided with the quivering haze of heat, and whirling
little dust-storms danced haphazardly across the plain, shifting the
sands, subtly altering the contours of the landscape. A great space
of desolation, constantly changing by modifications so slight as to
be invisible to the observing eye: an arbitrary artistry continually
sculpting into mobile shape this sun-bleached crystal plenitude of
fluid form, still yet still moving, as time plays imperceptibly across
the surface of eternity.

Most of the day he spent on a rocky plateau above the sandy
plain, directly exposed to the sun, his white headdress pulled
right over his head to shield his scalp from the unpitying rays.
Cocooned inside this little tent, its interior brightly illuminated
by the strong white light that forced through the thin material,
he watched and waited, observing the sensations of his body,
preoccupied with the labyrinthine ramifications of his thoughts.
During the first week of his fast, the suffering of the body had been
almost intolerable, as the starved flesh cried out for nourishment,
his stomach racked and contracted by acute spasms of unsatisfied
hunger. Thereafter the griping agonies diminished as the body

surrendered its unanswered clamour, hunger reduced to a dull aching, and increasing physical weakness reduced the capacity of the nerves to feel. He kept by him an earthenware jar of water, cooling beneath a little cairn of stones, and from time to time moistened his cracked lips with a few drops of that liquid without which, so fragile is the human system, the body would be unable to survive at all.

As each day flared uneventfully past with the insouciant rotation of the sun, he was aware of a gradual but inexorable emaciation of the flesh, of his ribs beginning to stick out from the skin of his chest, while in his hands the skeletal structure became clearly visible as the dehydrated skin desiccated to the texture of parchment. Looking into his water-pot, he would see reflected in the liquid surface a face unrecognizable as his, hollow cheeks drawn tightly around the bones, dry broken lips a mass of sores, eyes smouldering fiercely with an animal's stubborn endurance of physical extremity. After a while he was almost too weak to move at all, so it was just as well that with lack of food his empty bowels had ceased to function, and the little liquid his body absorbed was exuded through his pores in sweat, so his dry bladder had no moisture left to give back to the earth.

As the sun westered downwards towards nightfall, the shadows returned, pointing the opposite way, but apart from a dreamlike impression of inversion, indistinguishable from the shadows of the morning. The light softened again on the rocky slopes, delineating crease and crevice, highlighting pinnacle and declivity. To the east the elevated slopes began to dissolve into a blue haze, as, in a misty wash of colour, the higher peaks began to fold away into the darkness. The great white desert moon rose without ceremony, barely waiting for the sun to vacate the premises before swinging over the mountains and flooding the empty plain with a patina of chaste ivory. As the moon rose he would hear the sharp barking yelp of the jackals as they gathered at the base of the rock for their invariable nightly exploration of his solitude. Each night, ever more hopeful, they would come closer up the slope, sniffing downwind at the unwashed stink of the man, registering with a drooling howl the scent of death exuding ever more strongly from the enervated body.

Throwing back his headdress to scent the cool night air, he saw before him the huge yellow disk of the moon, and silhouetted against it the face of a jackal, red eyes staring directly at him.

Wearily he closed his eyes to shut out the vision, but could still see it lodged behind his eyelids: the sharp pointed ears, tufted with obscene grey hairs; the mouth open, and the long red tongue sliding across the sharp yellow teeth. When he heard the beast utter a sharp snickering whine that sounded like nothing so much as sardonic scornful laughter, he knew the time was very near. He hid his face again beneath his headdress, and his cracked lips moved soundlessly in prayer.

*   *   *

As soon as he awoke from an unaccustomed sleep, he knew the other was there. He looked around to see the morning already far advanced, the sun beginning to gather its strength for the day's uninhibited ritual of inflammation. Opposite him, seated on a rock, was a young man of extraordinary physical beauty, with a face of classical precision, hair clustered in yellow curls that hung on the nape of the neck in the Grecian manner, and with wide blue eyes full of irony and humour. He wore a white tunic pinned across with a gold clasp on the shoulder, leaving the slim arms bare, and just revealing a few sprouting blonde hairs in the centre of the chest. A carefully studied appearance of Hellenistic beauty and charm, modelled on a Ganymede or Hyacinthus. The sun flamed on his curls, but the face remained impassive in cool, chaste ivory, with a strange light playing about the features.

—I thought you were never going to wake up, he said, in a tone of exaggerated solicitude. Thought you'd got tired of all this and decided to go back where you came from. It's a harsh world down here, I can tell you (he gestured around towards the spreading desert). What some future poet will call 'inhospitable', I think; a world in which to 'draw your breath in pain'. Perhaps you didn't realize just how *awful* it can be down here, never having, as an absentee landlord, had to live here yourself? Power without responsibility, I think that's the phrase: the prerogative of the whore.

—Cleanse your mouth, whispered Jesus, licking his ulcerated lips.

—Well I'm glad you brought up the subject. There's nothing I'd like better than a cool cup of water to swill round my mouth, and wash out the dust of this Judean shit-hole. You'd be on the dry side yourself, now, by the look of you. Let me help.

From the ground at his feet, breaking through the thin crust of dried sand, burst a spring of fresh water, lancing into the sunlight, running on all sides into the parched earth, then settling into a little cascade that clucked and trickled over the lip of the rock and fell towards the arid plain below.

—One drop would save your soul, I think?, said the Devil. A cheap trick, I know: I apologize for its crudity. But the demonstration makes the point, don't you think? If it's as easy as all that, *can all this really be necessary?*

Jesus looked at the mirage, and could not conceal his body's desperate cry for water.

—I thirst, he said.

A malicious expression seized hold of the Devil's face, and for a second transformed it into the mocking mask of the jackal.

—A little premature, I think, for that particular catch-phrase. Let's not be too hasty; why rush matters? Don't we have all the time in the world?

—Why do you do this, asked Jesus, when you know the outcome?

—That's a little more than I would care to admit just at the present stage. Rash of you to say it's already over, when to my modest perception it hasn't even started yet. If it were just the outcome you wanted, you could make it happen. Turn back time; unravel everything; roll history back to that delightful little garden suburb in Eden, and – undo the fault. Make me an offer; perhaps I'd agree to go away and live quietly somewhere on a pension. You could even, if you really wanted to set things right, rewind everything right back to the beginning. Get me back on your side. Think what a team we'd make – 'Father and Prodigal Son' – if you were only prepared to settle that little matter of promotion . . . Or you could do it the other way. Roll everything forwards, and bring about your kingdom. Think of it: unchallenged power; absolute obedience; everything and everybody in its place; yours truly safely chained on the burning lake; your little pet, man, forgiven and so *extremely* grateful for your *inexhaustible* mercy and your *abounding* grace. You could do it; you know you could. So *why don't you?* Give me one good reason. Don't give me that crap about expiation and atonement. It's so – Jewish. So you have this odd preference for the seed of Isaac, opted to enlist with the Chosen, and had your little knob mutilated by some unsuspecting old Rabbi. But don't tell me you haven't moved on a bit from animal sacrifice and – what is it again – an eye for an ear? There is no universal law that says sin has to be paid for. Create something weak, and in its weakness it will betray you. Surely you have the power to forget, as well as forgive – *noblesse oblige*. Forgiveness can't be conditional; the quality of mercy is not strained. If you detest evil, why countenance it? You have the power to destroy evil for ever: then do it. Do you really think that *I* want to go on with this pantomime, in which – assuming the *denouement* is consistent with your plans – I don't even get a decent part?

Jesus closed his eyes, wearied by the pressure of thought, his bodily weakness obfuscating the operation of his mind. The Devil took the opportunity of moving closer.

—I don't believe for one minute, he went on, that you're here to fulfil some big plan of redemption. So what's it about? Do you fear failure? I'm mightily encouraged if you do. But how can you fail, O Omnipotent One? Help me out: I'd genuinely like to know. Or let's approach it from another angle. This is all very worthy and admirable, reducing yourself to human frailty, clothing yourself in weakness. I'm sure your little creatures will ultimately appreciate your sharing their shitty little lives with them, born in a pigsty and all that. Personally I take it as an enormous compliment that you're prepared to meet me here on what I believe will, at some time in the future, be called a level playing-field; that you're prepared so sportingly – to persist with the anachronistic athletic metaphors – to play an away match on an alien turf. But you've made things very difficult for yourself, you have to admit. Face one fact: *every human being that's ever lived on the face of this earth has at some time renounced or betrayed you.* That's what they're like: weak. They don't know any better. Why should you, Jesus of Nazareth, be any different? You'll forgive them, for they know not what they do. A nice phrase, that one. You can have it. For free. So why not give yourself a break, by the same rules? Charity begins at home. Surely you know that it's your weakness that summoned me here in the first place? If you were fighting fit, I wouldn't come within three leagues of you. I'm not looking forward to any of that casting-out stuff: you know, 'Begone from him!' Nor do I want to be forcibly deported into the stinking belly of some swine.

The point is simply this: *people who've fasted for forty days start to see devils.* The news of your vulnerability ran round the universe in two shakes of a Paschal lamb's tail. How could I help, thinking I might be in with a chance, flying straight here on the wings of the wind? Even I can see it's unfair. Let's even things up a bit. All you need is something nice to eat, and you'll feel much more yourself. Get your strength back. Be a man again. Here: do yourself a favour.

Bending down, he picked up a round smooth pebble, and held it towards Jesus on the palm of one hand.

—Here. Turn this into bread.

Despite himself, Jesus could not control the automatic operation of his own appetite, and for a second all he could see on the devil's palm was a freshly baked loaf, round and yellow and sprinkled with sesame seeds, leavened to a light fluffiness that in imagination could be apprehended melting in the hungry mouth. The bakery smell arising from the phantom bread twisted his bowels in an agony of desire. He closed his eyes to shut out the vision, but the delicious scent kept wafting into his nostrils and bringing again the pains of hunger. His body twitched with the effort of self-control, and tears of frustration and self-pity forced themselves from his eyes. The Devil was very close to him, now, whispering in his ear; on his breath Jesus could smell the sweetness of chewed herbs, masking a sour undercurrent of decay.

—But *I can't do it for you,* you know that, he said. It must be by *your* will. God feeds his people: he fed the children of Israel in the wilderness. Would any father whose child asked for bread give him a stone? How can He leave you hungry? How can you do this to yourself? Here (holding the bread close to Jesus's face, the crust touching his mouth, his tongue tasting flour and salt). All good things are gifts from God. Receive this, as your present to yourself. This is your body. Take. Eat.

Jesus opened his eyes. The agony was past. In the Devil's hand lay a round, worthless stone. Observing it restored to its true condition, Satan dropped it with an air of disgust, and rubbed his hands clean from the clinging grains of sand.

—Not bread, said Jesus, but the spirit. Men can endure all extremities if the spirit is strong. Man cannot live by bread alone, the scriptures tell us: but by the word of God.

He heard the leathery creaking of bat-like wings, and as he slipped into unconsciousness his dreams began immediately with a vivid sensation of flying.

*   *   *

He was woken by the bitterness of a cold more intense than any he had ever experienced, a cold that cut through the skin and knifed into the bones, infiltrating them with a dull ache. He could see nothing but an impenetrable white mist that swirled around his head. The air was thin, and his lungs panted rapidly to draw in what little oxygen there was in the rarefied atmosphere. With accelerated respiration the circulation of the blood also quickened, and his sensation of lethargy fell from him. His mind felt cold and impersonal, his thoughts clear-cut and diamond-sharp.

The other stood behind him, and when Jesus turned to observe him appeared much older, a man in late middle age, his face lined with mature authority and imperturbable confidence. He was dressed in the Roman fashion, in a military uniform covered by a tunic of patrician purple. His eyes gazed at Jesus with impersonal objectivity.

The Devil raised his right hand as if in greeting, and suddenly a blast of wind sent the curls of mist reeling and spinning skywards, opening up before Jesus's eyes an immense, dizzying, dazzling prospect. They were on the summit of a mountain that rose impossibly high from the vast rolling plains below, its ice-fanged pinnacle lancing at the heavens, its slopes precipitating downwards into an infinite series of black fissured valleys and ragged-rimmed crevasses. This was no mountain of reality, but a peak of dreams, a great construction of the imagination, as insubstantial as the thin air that surrounded its frosted summit. Far below, the surface of the earth lay shimmering in the sunrise, stretching away to the furthest horizons and beyond, mountain and valley and forest and plain, river and lake and sea and ocean, continent upon continent, country after country: Syria, Cappadocia, Armenia stretching to the Mare Caspium; Cilicia, Galatia and Bithynia rolling away to the Pontus Euxinus. Delayed amidst the scattered islands of the Greek archipelago, the eye took in Thrace and Macedonia, and followed the Dalmatian coast to Italia, then beyond around the square mass of Hispania, north to Gallia and Britannia's chalky cliffs. Due west lay the whole coast of the African continent, Egypt, Cyrene, Mauretania, to the narrow straits of the Mare Nostrum; to the south unfolded the deserts of Arabia. Set among the rolling hills and plains like so many jewels rose the great cities, beacons of civilization: Damascus; Alexandria; Athens; Rome. All the wreckage of great past cultures, the Egyptian, the Assyrian, the Babylonian, lay scattered untidily around the world, while the golden towers and palaces and temples of Rome and Jerusalem shone like torches in the darkness. Beyond the fringes of the Empire, civilization could be seen slipping away, in the dark bristling pine-forests of the North, or in the bleak arid deserts of the South, into barbarism.

—Power, the Devil began.

Jesus half-turned his head to listen, keeping his eyes focused on the vast panorama that undulated all round him to the very margins of the known world.

—What holds all this together, and prevents it from disintegrating into meaninglessness? What is it that has left the traces of civilization across the face of the wilderness? What maintains, throughout all this great melting pot of peoples and languages and cultures, the possibility of civilization? I will tell you: power. All the great empires have advanced civilization, brought peace and order and the rule of law, only through the exercise of power. The Pax Romana extends now from the Atlantic to the Mare Caspium, from the northernmost shores of Germania to the Cyrenian desert. The enemies of Rome will tell you that their legions bring only fire and sword, cruelty and destruction. Yet the fire and the sword were there before the Romans, and are now in abeyance throughout the empire.

—My kingdom, said Jesus, is not of this world.

—But nonetheless, said the Devil quickly, *here you are*. If you were content with the unalloyed bliss of your empyrean domain, you would have remained there. The fact that you are here is evidence that you hope to win this world back for your empire. You want this world for yourself. But it belongs, if it belongs to any heavenly power, to me. You gave it to me. I am the prince of this world. I speak its language, and I know how it works. Its language is power. It operates by the exercise and implementation of power. So if you genuinely hope to recover this territory, lost to you by my success and by man's treachery, then you can do so only through power. What other methods lie to hand? Do you really believe you can persuade the Jews to accept you merely by

words, by nursery lessons and children's stories? Do you think
the Empire will tolerate your preaching and your activism? The
Jews will sell you down the river, and the Romans will crucify
you before your mission gets off the ground. Your followers will
go the same way, dangling from crosses. But by means of power,
you could do it. The Zealots of Jerusalem would revolt against
Rome at the slightest provocation. That in itself would be enough
to destabilize the Empire. If all Rome's subjugated millions, from
Britannia to Egypt, were simultaneously to rise and throw off
the Roman yolk, Rome could not survive a year. Tiberias is not
immortal: he sleeps, and men have knives. With a vacuum of power
at the centre, you could march on Rome with a few thousands of
your Sicarii at your back, and assume control of the whole known
world. It's only what your people expect. They look for a Messiah.
They remember David and Solomon, the great kings of Israel. Are
they hoping for some anonymous Galilean carpenter to come to
them empty-handed, with no weapons but words? This world is
mine, and only I can give it you. I would do so: in exchange for the
supreme power you have arrogated to yourself. For you, power
is inseparable from action. You are not prepared to sit there,
replete with the capability of infinite power, knowing that you can
make and unmake worlds, create and destroy, by the insignificant
flexing of a finger. Until it is exercised, until it issues in action and
consequence, your sort of power remains mere potentiality, the
possibility of power, not power itself. What could it mean, out
there in the human world of reality and truth, to say 'I can do
this', and not do it? And your creatures, those ungrateful vermin
whose treachery, so like mine, you so freely forgave (though mine
you marked down in the book of transgressions as the sin for
which there can be no forgiveness): could their belief in your very
existence have been sustained for more than one minute, without
ample and abundant demonstrations of your power? You *need*
to be mixed up in all this. I don't. It's immaterial to me whether
your children do good or evil, whether they live or die. You can
have complete control over their destinies: do with them what
you will. But let me have the Power. Kneel, and worship me. Make
me God. Stay here and work at building your kingdom. I promise
never to interfere. Passive power is all I want: the light of heaven,
the pleasure of the senses, freedom from pain. Give me back my
pride; and I'll give you everything you want. Kneel. Call me God.

Worship me. I will give you (with a sweeping gesture of his arm he took in the countries and cities and mountains and seas) all this. The whole world.

For a moment Jesus pondered the Devil's words. The world lay shining below him.

—You will never understand, he said. My power is vested in weakness. I could crush the Empire and all its peoples, you and all your ministers, with a wave of my hand. Power of the kind you describe means nothing to me. Obedience secured by subjection, obligatory worship, forced adoration: I want none of these. Those who serve me with love, and desire my kingdom; those who hunger and thirst after righteousness; those who, of their own free will, endure everything for my sake – these I seek, these are my people, among them is my kingdom. The scriptures tell you that you shall worship the Lord your God, and Him only shall you serve. You cannot be God, Satan, and I cannot worship you. Get behind me, for there you belong, and I must go forward to accomplish my mission.

He was alone, and around him the peak was bare. His eyes closed, and again he drifted off to sleep.

*   *   *

He opened his eyes, and in reaction against a surge of sickening dizziness grasped feebly at a protruding chunk of masonry. Fragments of mortar, dislodged by his hand, fell rattling and tinkling into the valley of the Kidron thousands of feet below. As he looked down, a horror of height overwhelmed him, and he sobbed aloud as he clung for dear life to the pinnacle of the Temple.

All his feebleness and giddiness had returned, as the euphoria that had given him illusory strength on the mountain-top evaporated, and he knew then for the first time, as a man, an ungovernable terror of death. Again he glanced downwards, and the valley-floor seemed to reel sideways as if the temple itself were falling. He could feel his precarious grip relaxing, and his mind began to blacken over with the swooning unconsciousness of a fall, when he felt his wrist gripped tightly by the strong fingers of another's hand. Possessed by instinctive gratitude towards the one who had saved him, he clasped his rescuer's hand in both of his, and slumped at the stranger's feet, bunching his body tightly inwards to protect it from the horror of yawning space that screamed at him from above and from below.

The Devil had re-assumed his own shape, which was no single definite form, but a continually mutating physical transaction between the various modes of his being. As Jesus looked up at him, what he saw was the face of the Fallen Angel, a face of breath-taking beauty marred by marks of suffering so deep as to deal a blow to the heart of the observer: the face of a spoilt child, peevish and resentful, but heart-rendingly beautiful in the strange dignity of its trivial sorrow. Then as the demon held the man's hand tightly to prevent his fall, as if unwillingly and against all instinct, or under the force of some resented compulsion, for a moment through the lineaments of ruined grace appeared the ugly long snout, the black mouth with its short yellow incisors, the long tufted ears and the eyes that glowed like apertures opening onto the furnaces of Hell: the face of the Beast.

The brutal mask was as suddenly gone, and the grey eyes of Lucifer again were looking down on him, clouded over with self-pity and indignation.

—I loved you once, he said. I was the fairest of all your followers, the brightest angel in all the heavenly host. My beauty shone in perpetual glorification of your power; my voice sang ecstatically the song of your praise. You betrayed me, though the official story twists it the other way. You should have advanced me as I deserved, accepted me as your partner. We could have become as one all-powerful being. I never hated you: it was servitude and slavery I hated. You made me hate you by refusing me my rightful inheritance . . .

A spasm of fury distorted the lovely features, and again as the brows blackened and thickened with rage, the upper lip lifted from the lower in a snarl of anger, the pale grey eyes reddened over with an uncontrollable passion of hatred, the devil began again to resemble himself.

—Now, he said, shortly: to business.

Violently he thrust Jesus's body outwards with his arm, so the feet lost their purchase and the body slid inexorably downwards with a ringing cry of terror. But the Devil tightened his grip on one wrist, the falling body was dragged up short to dangle awkwardly over the abyss. A hard dry wind blew round his head, and his feet kicked helplessly to find their footing in the insubstantial air. A loosened sandal, detached, sailed lazily downwards and was lost to sight in the depths of the ravine.

—You can come to no harm, said the Devil from above him: for it is written in your scriptures, that the angels will bear you up, that you may not dash your foot against a stone. If I let you go, the prospect of your injury would tear a hole in the fabric of the universe, and at that summons ten thousand angels would appear to catch you before you hit the ground. Call them, now: let your fear cry out to the empyrean, and be saved.

—I will not, gasped Jesus, as he swung to and fro in the wind. I would die as any ordinary man dies, and you would gain nothing. I will call no angels at your behest.

—Well then, yelled the Devil, his voice breaking into hoarseness as he shouted over the monstrous wind: Go to your death sooner rather than later – what's the difference? The supreme sacrifice will have been enacted, the price paid. Why not get it over with?

—I will not rise from the dead, said Jesus, with a broken body. Not a bone of my body shall be broken. I will die in my own time, and under my own conditions. You will not be making my funeral arrangements.

—You are lost already, shouted Satan. As a man, you have no strength left. The snares of my world have caught and defeated you. You can escape only as God. Become God, now, at my insistence, and be in my power. Give in. Surrender. Put an end to all this.

Jesus pulled his hand free, and as the devil scrabbled to seize it again, launched himself from the pinnacle into the air. As he sailed down towards the ravine, the stuff of his garment flapped and fluttered in the wind of his descent. He seemed to fall slowly, having time to observe the tower from which he had precipitated, and the earth towards which he was racing, pivot and wheel and change places in dizzying rotation, as his body twisted and turned in its fall. He felt all around him the possibilities of rescue and safety: the air clamoured to assist him, willing itself to thicken with viscosity and bear him up; behind the skies he was aware of angel-legions gathering to catch him in his flight. By enforced passivity he pushed away these pressures, so that no miracle or supernatural aid could be summoned to assist him at the Devil's request. Just before he dropped from sight into the ravine he glimpsed, now far above him on the pinnacle of the Temple, wide as the sky itself, an expression of open-mouthed amazement at this turn of events, a twist of the plot that left the Devil helplessly disarmed, as he saw the Son of Man drop through space like a falling star. Just as he himself had fallen, the Son of Morning, falling like lightning from heaven, flung ignominiously down cliffs of immensity by the irresistible blast of divine anger. But Jesus fell of his own accord, choosing to renounce, in a moment, all power, that supreme power might be eternally retained.

Like some great white bird wounded in flight, Jesus dropped into the darkness of the crevasse, and with a cold shock that obliterated his consciousness, plummeted into the icy waters of the Kidron. Down he sank, his garments floating and undulating about him, his nostrils stinging as the cold water forced its way into his nose and mouth. A huge bubble of air, the breath of life itself, escaped his mouth and belched and rippled its way towards the surface.

Here in the sunless depths, with the light of day floating inaccessibly above him, it seemed as good a place as any to die. But with no decision or act of will on his part, the body chose to seek life. As his lungs filled, his arms and legs kicked instinctively against the cold waters of death, and pushed him back towards the light. In a flurry of foam his head broke the surface, and with clumsy movements he splashed and scrambled his way to the river's edge. Lying on the muddy bank in his sodden garments, he coughed and spewed the water from his throat and lungs, his chest heaving in uncontrollable spasms as he fought to receive the restoring air.

As his breathing returned to normal, he looked upwards to where the cliffs of the ravine delineated a ribbon of empty, cloudless blue sky.

—Do not tempt me, he managed to cough out through rasping breaths, to the Devil who had departed from him for a season: do not tempt the Lord your God.

Agony

Eternity is in love with the productions of Time.

WILLIAM BLAKE

The wood of the ancient olive-trunk felt cool against his fevered forehead. Its bark long since stripped by the gnawing incisors of rats and tree-squirrels, the venerable old wood showed, from a distance, smooth and grey in the softening twilight; but close up, patterns of age, etched as deeply as the lines in an old man's face, fissured the gnarled and knobbed contours of its weathered surface. Here the trees grew so close together that their dusty grey-green leaves interwove to form a tent of foliage that canopied the grove and stippled it with shade. In the umbrageous coolness, sweat formed a clammy layer on the skin of his face and neck. As the warmth of his body dissipated into the cool air, so the comforting warmth of companionship also began to fade away into the evening chill. Further down the slope he could hear the disciples making their way behind him up the Mount of Olives, their voices loud with wine and friendship; occasionally taking up snatches of a hymn, then breaking into rowdy laughter at some subtle or witty remark or observation. Relaxing into the welcome temporary chill, he let the hot urine flow in a bright arc that splashed against the tree and blackened its grey trunk.

And so he gave to the earth that had no part in his genesis the waste of his body.

—Earth: mother of my human part; mother who never bore me, yet whose surface has willingly borne these thirty years the tread of my feet: receive back from me now what little I have to give you, the foul water and waste of my entrails. In death I will not even bequeath you my corpse for the work of your creative corruption; for this body will ascend into heaven, and in my flesh shall I see God. I have cheated you, great mother, for I have taken every advantage of your hospitality, yet I repay you with nothing. Worse still, I must, to fulfil my mission, convert those who worship your powers from their natural faith, destroy their confidence in the familiar gods of forest and stream, mar their pleasure in these fair and spirit-haunted groves. My service is a chaste discipline, and my church must be founded by men of stern ascetic disposition, who will need to deal ruthlessly with

your shrines and idols, turning the hearts of the people from rocks
and trees, towards heaven and the things of the spirit. Later, when my
kingdom is strong enough here on earth, men and women will again
turn back to you, their only mother, and acknowledge your ancient
power: just as I, before I go, must speak at least a few words of
comfort to my own poor mother, Mary, the handmaid of the Lord.

He moved away from the shelter of the olive tree to join the
band of disciples, who now sat or lay at leisure, their white robes
flickering through the shadows, around the trunk of one of the
two great cedars of Lebanon that dominated this slope of the hill.
The bazaars and merchants' stalls that in the daytime rendered
this part of Olivet a busy concourse of trade, had been struck and
carried away for the night. The doves that filled the leafy cedar
branches with the flapping rattle of wing against leaf, and with the
urgent, insistent bubble of their voices, were settled for the night,
betraying their presence only by an occasional restless flutter, or
an isolated cooing sob. Looking up into the high branches he
could see their white feathers glimmering ghostly in the twilight,
as they nestled in the branches, a mute cloud of witness. With
them, the Holy Ghost brooded over Olivet, shedding through the
gloom a peace as soft and quiet as the falling of a feather through
the olive leaves.

As he sat down with his followers, their spirits still cheered and
quickened by the party mood of the preceding hours, he could
distinctly feel the presence of that spirit that seemed to sit in the
cedar branches with the cloud of doves, as the dew of Hermon
which falls upon the Hill of Sion, keeping a protective watch over
the little company below. Facing them, across the valley of the
Kidron, stood Jerusalem, its walls and gilded roofs and towers
golden in the evening light. Sion, city of dreams, a sacred mountain
rising in ancestral splendour of snow and gold; that Sion of the
imagination, which may not be removed, but standeth fast for ever.
But his vivid apprehension of the spirit, hovering in solicitude over
the earth, depended on the strength of this little band of followers,
camped at their ease under the cedar tree; and on his power as a
human leader to keep them bonded indissolubly together. Although
their unity was already sealed in mutuality by their love for him,
and consecrated in the covenant of bread and wine; yet it was
buoyed aloft only by sustained confidence and unflinching faith, as
the dove's wing is held aloft in effortless flight only by the kindness

of the hospitable air. Their unity, though strong enough to challenge empires, and to bring much of the world to its knees before the insignia of his power, was nevertheless as fragile as the bones that fashioned the delicate architecture of a bird's wing. Outside the charmed circle of this little band lay the forces of darkness, ready to strike back at them when the moment was right; and within the group, notwithstanding the gaiety of their fellowship, lay the seeds of division, the conflicts of belief and policy that would resolve into treachery and schism, and give to the world, together with the dream of global unity and the hope of the heavenly kingdom, a divided church, and an abiding archetype of treachery. The hills stand about Jerusalem: even so standeth the Lord round about his people. But Jerusalem would fall; and the temple of his body, rebuilt, would not stand within those walls. As the sun set behind the city, touching the tallest towers and terraces with white and gold, the courts and temples of Jerusalem dissolved into obscurity. Over the olive trees behind them, the great white Paschal moon began to climb the skies, frosting with phosphorescence temple and tower. Gradually, as the evening chilled towards night, and as the city's lights began to glow softly through the gloom, the sense of a protective spirit haunting the hillside began to withdraw, and the company's cheerful demeanour likewise began to ebb away. Peter peered nervously around into the obscurity of the olive groves. Instinctively the group drew closer together around the shelter of the great auburn trunk. The young John again crept closer to Jesus, laying his head in the Master's lap. Judas sat slightly apart, his brooding gaze continuing to remain fixed on the lights of the city across the Kidron. The power of darkness was abroad.

The group had fallen silent, and all now looked to Jesus for some sign or instruction. Jesus looked down at the boy's head in his lap, and for a moment fingered the dark hair, the delicate curve of the ear, the soft rounding of the cheek, still flushed with the wine and warmth of the feast. The moon silvered Jesus's face, the pale brow, the downcast eyes with their dark lashes, the black hair falling across the cheek, the lips pressed tightly together with some preoccupation or decision.

Then almost roughly he pushed the boy's head from his lap, and rose abruptly to his feet.

—Take care, he said to the company at large, that you are not drawn into temptation. Keep watch. I go to pray.

John tried to take his arm, but Jesus shook him off and strode away into the olive trees. After walking for a few minutes through the plantations of fig, palm and date-trees, Jesus found himself at the gateway to Gethsemane, a garden adjoining the olive-farm. He entered, and immediately found his nostrils assailed by the overpowering scent of flowers, jasmine and rose, hibiscus and mimosa. Here the shrubs and bushes, watered by an elaborate network of irrigation trenches, grew to the height of a man, and bent under the weight of their blossoms. He buried his fevered face in the cool calyx of a flower, drinking in its perfume, rubbing the smooth petals against the roughness of his beard. Finding a grassy enclosure surrounded by bushes, he sat down and looked back across the moonlit slopes to where his companions could just be glimpsed, still grouped around the cedar tree. He observed that Peter had taken up a position of observation at the head of the path that wound up from the city; and that his brother James, from the other side of the cedar's trunk, was watching the olive groves further up the slope. From each figure he caught the occasional flash and glint of a sword.

Apart from a line of azure fringing the western horizon behind the city, the sky was darkened to a deep blue-black, and the stars were beginning to appear. Jerusalem stood in the unconcerned moonlight, her courts and palaces unnaturally silent, as if with some foreboding of menace or danger.

Cross-legged, elbows on knees, head bowed, Jesus clasped his hands and began to pray.

—Our father, which art in heaven, hallowed be thy name: Thy kingdom come. Thy will be done, in earth, as it is in heaven. Give us this day our daily bread. And forgive us our debts, as we forgive our debtors. *And lead us not into temptation*, but deliver us from evil. Amen.

A small wind scattered faint starlight through the olive-groves. The experience of prayer was more than ever like talking to himself, the words echoing inside his head so that it became difficult to disentangle speaker from listener, interlocutor from eavesdropper, quotation from hearsay: what he said to himself, and what he heard himself say. On occasions, when he had prayed, bare-headed on the mountain-tops, where the crests of the cedars bent in the heaving wind, or under the brightly punctuated blackness of the night sky, he had felt himself perfectly in balance: at one with the rotating earth and with the wheeling heavens; bridging the dividedness of his broken nature by speaking directly across the gulf of alienation separating him from himself. At such times he could feel the testimony of his humanity flowing across the universe, all its meaning and witness immediately absorbed into that great, quiet, considering and caring mind: each fragmentary experience of pleasure or pain, registering as a pulse of significance, slightly modifying the repository of divine knowledge. Simultaneously he had felt, as a man, the grace of divine blessing and consolation falling upon him, as the mountains shed their dews over the desert, so that reassurance and power seemed to enter into him, strengthening the body and steadying the mind. At such moments of divine communion, God and man co-existed in a perfect symbiotic relationship, two in one, speaking to each other not with one voice, but in a common language so imbued with mutual familiarity as to resemble a dialogue of complete understanding between the soul and itself.

Here, now, in the moonlit garden, at a most critical conjuncture for himself and his followers, he found this balance and propriety disoriented, the channel of communication within himself fraught with howling interference, the commonality of language ruptured into a cacophony of unintelligible dialects, just as the language of Canaan fragmented into a plurality of tongues, when the towers of Babel toppled and crashed to the earth.

His lines of communication thus interrupted, he found himself forced back onto his own loneliness, and stranded on an island of disillusion. He had entered a dark wood of depression so deep and threatening that he felt as if he had strayed into the borderlands of death itself.

—I am sorrowful: even unto death.

The moonlit, flower-strewn shadows of the pleasure-garden seemed to gather and coalesce into the darkness of some mythological wood of suicides, some forest of despair. Was that the screech of a night-haunting bird of prey, or the howl of some tormented, tree-bound human soul? The landscape changed with the colour of his mind, to a blue–grey expanse of swampy ground, pitted by potholes and muddy pools, wreathed about with rank and noxious mists, hiding and revealing the skeletal delineation of a shattered wood, trees stripped leafless and riven into fractured shapes. To the west, where Jerusalem had stood, he saw a shapeless heap of ruins, ruptured roof and toppled tower, the abomination of desolation from Daniel's prophecy. Beyond the jackal-haunted ruins rose the ugly bulbous protuberance of a bald hill, surmounted by three stark crosses, black against the livid streaks of a false dawn: three gaunt gallows on a hill of skulls.

What was this strange condition of dejection and despair? Was it merely apprehension of what the morning was to bring? Was his human nature simply seized by pure physical terror of the coming pain, that instinctive aversion from the harmful and dangerous that serves as a mechanism of protection for the body in its hostile environment? Was his flesh, burdened by a knowledge no flesh should ever have to bear, overwhelmed by mortal dread, wincing and shrinking from the fearful prospect of the scourge, the nails, the sponge, the spear?

Or was his mood rather supernatural in origin, an aversion of the divine spirit reluctant to subject itself to humiliation and mockery? To be God, and yet to stand by and observe himself, buffeted and spat upon, mockingly arrayed in purple and crowned with the thorns of the desert, beaten by the indignity of stripes and riveted on the rack of a malefactor? Isaiah had said of his suffering servant that none had seen sorrow like unto his sorrow. Yet if the flesh of man could hardly bear such affliction, then how should God offer himself to a yet more humiliating sacrifice? Was it within the capability of power to submit itself in weakness, for authority to kneel in subjection, for a king to doff his crown and bow his sacred head beneath the piercing mockery of thorns? Would it become necessary, at the eleventh hour, to cast aside his vesture of frailty, and to rise as the Son of Man in a cloud, with power and great glory, and bring the wrath of the heavens tumbling down on the heads of his accusers?

No; it was neither human dread, nor divine hesitation, that infiltrated his soul with this corrosive toxin of despair, just as the mists of his mental landscape introduced a chill into his shivering bones. Mortal fear could be isolated and overcome by divine contemplation; divine aversion corrected by the guiding hand of the omnipotent will. This was something else, something deeper and darker than natural reluctance or a venial shrinking from destiny. For what he had encountered, here at this final turning-point of his mission, the point at which his liberty of independent action was to be surrendered and exchanged for passive suffering and victimization, was a sudden and unexpected loss of faith in the entire enterprise. It was on this ground of disillusion that human demoralization and divine disappointment met and merged into a last temptation, a dark midnight of the soul. For after all he had done, all he had shown, all he had accomplished throughout the length and breadth of the Holy Land: all the teachings and parables and exemplifications of doctrine; all the cures and healings of the blind, the lame, the sick; all the castings out of demons, and the pacifications of mental frenzy; all the miracles and marvels and wonders he had performed – still there were but few who believed in him; many who believed not at all; and some who hated him with a hatred that would never be appeased until they had accomplished his death. Even his disciples, in whom he reposed an absolute trust, were still fashioned of the same unreliable materials as all mortal creatures; even his beloved Peter, the rock on whose solid foundation his church would be built, would betray him that same night.

His bitterest disappointment was focused on Jerusalem. He thought again of the city that had already, in his fantasy, fallen into ruin, like the sacked city of prophecy, compassed round about by enemies, trodden down by the Gentiles. He thought of all the hopes that had been focused on that great citadel of faith, on the Hill of David, the Temple of Solomon, the city of Sion. All the great laments and poems of longing and nostalgia, sung by those in exile, testifying to the power of this holy place to hold the human imagination in rapt contemplation of the beautiful and the good. All the prophecies and aspirations that built Jerusalem again, in the mind, as the City of God, *Civitatis Dei,* the rallying-point of the nations and the home of the Messiah, whenever he should choose to come.

And when he came, his coming remained unnoticed. Although the world was made by him, yet the world knew him not. Although he had entered the city, in the manner prescribed by prophecy, offering himself for recognition by the custodians of the faith; yet the priests and elders, the Scribes and Pharisees – those most deeply imbued with the language of his scriptures, those whose religious observance entailed a responsibility to look out for his arrival – yet failed to recognize him, looked at him and saw him not. Although they had heard him speak, and were fully furnished with the means of understanding his gospel, they yet refused to listen to him, or listened without understanding; rejected his word, and clung by preference to the threadbare wisdom of their traditional beliefs.

Jerusalem had rejected him; Jerusalem would kill him. The people who had welcomed him as a king, casting their palms and garments in his way, would be only too ready to change their cry from benediction and welcome to a baying for sacrificial blood. He beheld the city, and wept over it.

—Jerusalem, Jerusalem: killer of prophets, stoner of missionaries: how often would I have gathered your children together, as a hen gathers her brood under her wings. But ye would not! Now, behold, your house will be left desolate.

Disillusion, disappointment, demoralization, sapped his strength and weakened the substance of his will. Earnestly he prayed to be delivered from the terrible demons of doubt. In the perturbation of his spirit, tears ran down his face; in the extremity of his beseeching, sweat poured from his forehead like great drops of blood, and fell upon the ground.

—My God! he cried. Take this agony from me!

While he had been thus wrenched apart from himself on the rack of his grieving, his vision of the city destroyed had dissipated, and once again the flowers of Gethsemane surrounded him with their innocuous beauty, and the moonlight still fingered with a chaste illumination the towers of Jerusalem.

A fitful, flickering light appeared before him, indecipherable as a mirage, a blurred and wavering spiritual body forming itself into visibility. His imagination could make it into an angel, though he knew there was no angel there, kneeling in obeisance, wings furled backwards in dutiful homage. Before his face there formed the likeness of a chalice, held in invisible hands, a cup, an offering, the vessel brimming with some dark viscous liquid whose surface trembled with the broken reflection of the moon.

A strengthening cup to quicken his fainting spirit? His own answer to his own prayer? Fingers touched to invisible hands, an elevation of the spectral chalice tipped its brim towards his mouth, and he took a deep drink of the liquid it contained.

Retching against the poisonous sourness of the draught, his gorge heaving in spasms of revulsion, he spat the liquor out onto the grass. Its taste was as foul as wormwood, as bitter as gall; a foretaste of death itself. He hawked the poisoned phlegm from the back of his throat and spat its burning corrosiveness vehemently from his lips.

—Take this cup from me!

The night was silent. No trace remained of the vision; but beside him the grass lay stained with a dark contamination of blood and bile. That was all his cup contained: pain and death. Unthinkingly he had dashed it from him, and spat its contents contemptuously on the ground. But the cup was of his own making, the liquor of his own mixing. If he rejected it, then with it he had renounced his mission, his sacrifice, the very reason for his being in this place, and being at this time.

Suddenly he realized that he was alone, and wholly human. The godhead had gone, the divinity departed, with a strange sound of farewell like distant pipes playing under the earth. He was a man, take him for all in all. He was no longer afraid, since there was no longer any reason for fear: he was a man, and master of his own destiny. His thoughts ascended in silence, and no echo returned from the indifferent skies. The Word had become flesh, and dwelt among us.

*   *   *

This, then, was the eventuality that had escaped even omniscience: the twist in the tale that an all-seeing, all-knowing providence had yet somehow failed to predict, or managed to overlook! What had been apparent to the wide eyes of celestial vision was the fate of divinity incarnate in man; and those eyes, though they saw all, had not foreseen the possibility that the God who could occupy man could also depart from him, leaving him alone and single in his humanity. God could embody himself in Jesus of Nazareth; but that Jesus of Nazareth might voluntarily alienate God from himself, he could not recall as having formed any part of the foreknown future. This unconceived operation of free will seemed to have torn a hole in the fabric of time, through which the human being could unobtrusively slip away and escape his allotted destiny.

Was he, then, as a man, sufficient unto himself, capable of standing alone, solely responsible for his coming and going, his beginning and end? Did he have any ultimate need of a God whose service had signified for him little but pain and punishment, dolour and death? Surely man could live without God, since His divine anger could be no harsher or more rigorous than the privations of his service. What was there to fear in God's displeasure, if his blessing brought no benefits except suffering and extinction?

Why, indeed, should God have thought to involve himself in human affairs in the first place? Could He not have enjoyed, like the gods imagined by Epicurus, an existence of uninterrupted pleasure untrammelled by responsibility for the trials and tragedies of humankind? Why should God have any need of man?

What, after all, is man, that God should care for him? What value did man possess that he should cost his maker the exorbitant price of divine immolation? Was God in any way diminished by man's fall? Surely a thing of so little value was not worth the price of this exchange, in which a commodity valued at nothing was bought at the cost of everything.

What difference would it make to God if man did not exist at all? Heaven would still be heaven, and cries for help from the deepest pit of Hell need not disturb the tranquillity of its quiet courts. The heavenly bodies would still perform their celestial dance; the unsleeping Seraphim would continue to keep their wide-eyed watch; Heaven would still ring with the singing of eternally youthful spirits, and the ministers of light would burn for ever just as brightly, bowing their flaming heads in worship; Angels and Archangels and ministers of grace would still adore him, and the flames of praise would be kept alight by the wakeful sons of fire – even if man were left to weep alone over his own self-inflicted wounds.

Let man then be abandoned, since to God his existence could be of no discernible benefit, his extinction no conceivable loss. Let the children of dust follow their corrupt inclinations, and return to the dust from whence they came, which would blow away as insignificant detritus before the proud winds of heaven. Should the great universal mind reduce itself to the narrow confines of the human brain, since that God-given intellect had been permitted by corruption of the will to lapse into madness? No king would abdicate his power on the grounds that one of his petty subjects had compassed his own ruin. The Lamb, being innocent, does not deserve to die; still less should his innocuous blood be shed for the sake of the wolf who would, in his madness and fury, seek to destroy his peace for ever.

Here, then was the solution: God had no use for man; then man had no need of God. It had happened before, and it would happen again. Millions of human souls had passed through their earthly existence with no knowledge of God, their spiritual needs satisfied by submission to dark chthonic powers, content to bow before the grinning bloodstained mask of some heathen deity, or to prostrate themselves before the squat, powerful ugliness of some mute stone idol. In the future, men and women would more resolutely set their faces against God; some brave enough, knowing the truth and reality of His power, but too proud, like Lucifer, to accept a subordinate place in the universal hierarchy, to face existence, themselves alone, without His assistance or succour. Others would simply choose, as he himself had now chosen, the solid tangible reality of earthly life over the abstract and tenuous dimension of the spirit. Men and women would prove themselves capable of goodness, fidelity, creativity, though even the concept of God would come to mean virtually nothing to them. Such creatures might, he reflected ironically, value life that much more highly, given the certain knowledge that death ended everything. Might they not seek to end the reckless violence of war, in which human life becomes cheap and expendable? Might they not seek with greater dedication to combat illness, defeat disease? If life is a unique and unrepeatable gift of nature, would not is its recipients wish to prolong it and enhance its quality? The belief that the human world, without God, would immediately descend into a nightmare of barbarism was a convenient fiction designed to consolidate divine power and prohibit human liberation. Perhaps human beings, left to their own devices, would be able to create a better world for themselves and their descendants. Had he not, in their composition, provided them with that capability? Had he not made them that way?

He would walk away from his destiny. But not, as he had initially contemplated, into the desert, seeking the seclusion of the anchorite. He would find some role in life, as a teacher or healer, a doctor or counsellor; and by using his human capabilities, with no subterfuge of divinely assisted miracle or marvel, help to bring peace and wisdom, health and hopefulness, to the human race.

He would begin now, right away, delaying the decision no longer. He would return to his companions and explain to them this new choice of direction, this newly defined ministry, this reoriented mission. Perhaps some of them would agree to join him, adjusting their expectations to his new-found faith in mankind. Although he knew in his heart that for some of them, attachment to his Messiahship, a fanatical belief in his charismatic powers, a reckless hunger for his heavenly kingdom, might well prove too firmly lodged to be detached by a few words of explanation. Perhaps he would take with him a chosen few, Peter and John, and his brother James, and Mary of Magdala, advising them, indirectly in the first instance, only of some change of plan; then seeking gradually to instil into them this new humanist faith, this new world of well-being without God, based on belief in the value of human existence, and the dignity of man.

He would give them a new commandment; that they should love one another, as he had loved them.

Love! Love was the essence of the gospel he had come to teach to mankind; and yet of all his teachings, this was the one men and women seemed to have found most difficult to comprehend.

—Love the Lord your God, he had said to them, with all your heart, with all your mind and with all your soul. Love your neighbour as yourself. If you love me, keep my commandments.

What could be simpler? A love that linked gratitude for the undeserved gift of creation with compassion for the fellow-creature; a love that kept its focus on God, and out of love for God found it easy and natural to do God's will; a love that could sustain obedience, not as a humiliating dependency or subjugation, but as a loving discipline of respect and self-respect, charity and self-control. Yet human beings had seemed incapable of dissociating this simple universal charity from the appetites of the body, the petty jealousies of possessiveness, the mercenary ownership of civil marriage. Again, and again, he had tried to explain to them: that true godly love, the love preached in his gospel, incorporated the desires of the body and yet was not bound by them; and that the love he offered, the charity of grace, could not be measured and parcelled out to fit any human rules for governing the disposition of property and land.

He had tried using different words, in different languages – *eros, amor, caritas, charis* – to convey to them the simple truth that there were many kinds of love, but that in his love, the love of Christ, men and women would find abiding solutions to their perennial problems of sexuality and relationship. The Scribes and the Pharisees had bickered endlessly over the exclusivity of marriage, unable to understand the possibility of a different kind of association, in which the little life of the body, with its tyranny of greed and possession, gave way to the bigger life of the spirit, in which one could love freely without anxiety of possession, and feel, in every little tremor of sexual nerve or emotion, a tiny echo of that great music that harmonized the universe into one ecstatic whole. He had shown them, over and over again, that the sins of the body could be forgiven, and, absolved, would leave no abiding contamination on the soul.

—Go, he had said to the woman taken in adultery. Your sins are forgiven you. Go, and sin no more.

Perhaps, he reflected with new-found clarity, they had mistaken his nature: blinded by the sheer beauty of their cherished ideas of chastity and virtue; deafened to the words he spoke by the plangent music of their ancient poetry and prophecy: 'Behold, a virgin shall conceive . . .' Did they believe, in truth, that he, though fully a man, was impervious and immune to the same promptings of desire as those that tormented them, keeping them awake through long hot restless nights of love-sickness, driving them to obsessive violence of punishment and revenge?

Had they not observed, both his friends who knew him best, and his enemies who were always so vigilant for signs of weakness in him, how his lips had parted, and his cheek coloured, when the Jerusalem crowd had hauled before him Mary of Magdala, her garments ripped and torn where they had dragged her from the rank sweat of an adulterous bed?

                              *   *   *

He pictured the scene again, the portico of the Temple, sleepy and silent in the afternoon heat; the little group of listeners gathered on the cool pavement in the shade of the cloistered court, as he spoke to them wistfully and gently, almost with homesickness, of the Kingdom of Heaven, and of the coming of the Son of Man. Then the commotion of an excited crowd, a woman's screams, a turbulence of dust and violent motion. Suddenly she was flung to the ground at his feet. What he noticed first was the sheen of sweat that glistened on the brown skin of her back, showing through her ripped and tattered gown, as she cowered against his knees to escape the mob of angry men, who still continued to shout and spit at her, to aim at her ineffectual blows or spiteful kicks. Just before the leaders of the demonstration, Scribes and Pharisees and elders of the Temple, had advanced forward to address him, he had observed, within the crowd, heavy, sharp-edged, stones being purposefully weighed in the hands of both men and women, rocks as yellow in colour as their teeth, cruelly bared in moral disapprobation.

—Master, this woman was taken in adultery, even in the very act. Moses in the Law commanded us, that she be stoned to death. What do you say, Master? What would you have us do to her?

Then in the pregnant silence which awaited his answer, she raised her face towards him, and he knew for the first time the lawless importunity of desire. It was more, far more than the instinct of pity provoked by those wide-eyed, thick-lashed, dark-irised eyes, that stared up at him in mingled hope and terror; more than his compassion for the torn, bruised body, or the swollen contusion from a glancing blow that bloated the red, painted lips. It was more even than a natural desire for a beautiful woman, though that too shook through him with a seismic jolt, as he noticed a strand of dark, perfumed hair pasted with a crust of dried blood to the skin of her cheek, and observed the sharp red point of a rouged nipple, maculating the smooth olive skin of a loosened breast, that protruded through the ripped fabric of her clothing.

No; the emotion that seized him, with an overmastering power and an unprecedented shock of knowledge, was compounded indiscriminately from beauty and abjection, from pity mingled with lust, the smell of female vulnerability urging him, despite himself, to desire her in further violation. In his imagination he could taste the kisses of her bought red mouth, see the skin of her throat stretched tight away from the sliding pressure of his jerking chest, smell the rank sweat of another man's semen soaking her trembling thighs. To know so suddenly the want of a woman would not, in itself, have surprised him: many lovely women had desired him, sometimes in embarrassing extremity of prostrated desire, and he would, if he could, even in courtesy, have desired them in return. It was only that he could not, without compromising both his universal love of all creatures, and his gospel of charity, choose to become intimate with one human being rather than any other. Since to engage in physical intimacy with all humankind was an impossibility, though one his nature deeply desired, he had no choice but to eschew physical intimacy with anyone. With these principles clear in his mind, and his body balanced in equipoise of promiscuous friendship and indiscriminate affection, sexual desire had never troubled him until now.

But as Mary knelt before him, and the crowd, their devious leaders watching his every move and gesture, eagerly awaited his reply, he felt the want of her like a pain at his heart. His desire towards her had in it no trace of virtue or legitimate affection: what he wanted was to take her, there on that crimson-covered, scented bed, in the cocooning boudoir of a Jerusalem brothel; to lie across her, stretching his limbs luxuriously into the acrid trace of another man's sweat; to bruise with harsh kisses and sharp bites her swollen lips; to take that red-painted nipple, like a ripe strawberry, between his lips and taste of its fruitfulness; to feel his penis engorging against the shaven smoothness of her vagina, excited both by the sharp smell of her female extrusions, and by the painful knowledge, across his genital nerves, of the familiar path traced in slime across her yielding flesh by other men's wetness; to feel his virgin manhood irresistibly tickled by the irritating rub of love.

To cover his confusion, he had leaned sideways away from her, and with pale, shut face and inscrutable gesture, with his finger traced invisible words on the unblemished stone. The Elders watched his action, some leaning forward and craning their heads to see what it was he was writing. Mary's lips were close to his ear, and as he signed off his incomprehensible message across the empty air, she whispered to him, in agony of self-presentation, words of sexual promise, impelled by a hot breath of fear and desire, that exceeded even the extravagance of his own heated fantasy.

It was that offering of herself to him, not in surrender of self-sacrifice, but in an offering of barter, promising to repay his mercy with the only commodity she owned, her used and abused body, that released him from the dangerous moment of obsession. In imagination she had appeared as the passive victim of his mastering embrace, the soft and vulnerable flesh that yielded to his entry and folded around him in ecstasy of violation. Through the woman's words of negotiation and self-abnegation he was able to envisage the encounter for what it would truly be: a trade of flesh for safety, in which, let him root as deeply as he could in the fertile soil of the woman's penetrable body, he would yet never reach his goal, the inaccessible substratum of her being, the soul. He knew then, with a gift of prophetic percipience, sadly denied to men, that the attempted intimacy would be a failure: and that while soft arms and clinging legs could wrap him around, soft mouth welcome him in, strangled shouts of ecstasy draw him deeper and deeper into the cavity of the flesh, yet would the woman's soul be kept aloof, hard and brightly burnished, untouched by all that wasted energy of masculine ravishment and penetration.

I will love her, he had said to himself, as he stooped down and wrote upon the ground: but not in that way. My knowledge will not permit me the illusion of believing I can reach the spirit through the body, if the body is offered as a commodity in exchange of trade, and if the spirit is held aloof and unviolated. I will love her, as she deserves to be loved, for herself, and for what she can give, not for what I can take from her.

—Master, repeated the chief of the Scribes: do you hear us? What is your verdict?

Fully composed, Jesus turned to them again, and laid a protective hand on Mary's head.

—He that is without sin among you, let him cast the first stone.

As they backed away, sheepish and silent, Mary took one of his hands, held it to her mouth, and softly and rhythmically lashed the palm with the wet sweetness of her tongue.

*   *   *

His spirit flowered with optimism as he walked back through Gethsemane: his eyes comforted by the stars of white blossom that gleamed through the garden gloom; his nostrils blessed with the perfume of bud and petal; the skin of his face occasionally feeling a pleasant sting as a thin twig bent against his cheek, and whipped smartly across his ear as he pushed past. This was his world: it was made for him, and now at last he would occupy and enjoy it, as God had intended he should.

His thoughts returned again to Mary, who after his rescue of her from the Jerusalem mob, had devoted herself body and soul to his service. When he had explained to her, that his action of deliverance had not been taken in the hope of possessing her flesh, but as a prototype of the redemption he offered to all mankind, she had at first recoiled in suspicion, thinking him another fanatic, interested only in making her an example in one of his parables. Who but a madman would refuse unlimited access to her person, when so many men would give the wages of a week's work to lie with her for an hour? Coupled with this perplexity, though, and clearly visible to him in the expressions of her changing face, was a deep sense of hurt and rejection, that he did not seem to want her as she was accustomed to be wanted. It appeared that of all the crooked, twisting paths to her heart, whether you traversed them with money or affection, violence or pity, there were none that did not pass through the medium of her body; that she possessed no sense of self-worth distinguishable from her powers of sexual allure.

Thereafter Jesus had sat with her for many hours of quiet, patient conversation, explaining to her the nature of his mission, seeking to reassure her that her value to him, as a lost human soul, was far greater than the richest material gift she could imagine being paid down as the price of her body; leading her gently towards the realization that the joys of the spirit far exceeded the pleasures of the flesh, and that a free association of human beings held together by bonds of charity, such as that exemplified by his followers, offered a far more fulfilling environment of communality than the harsh cash-nexus of exploitation. Gradually she listened to him, the darkness of fear and suspicion, and the hardness of calculation, fading from her eyes, and being replaced by a new softness of unselfish desire, a new yearning for righteousness and freedom. With this dawning realization of a new hope, he was painfully aware, came a yet more dangerous attachment to her liberator, potentially more disruptive than her initial greed for possession and control. Now when she looked at him, it was with eyes of such self-abasing hunger that again his soul liquefied in helplessness of compassion. So, gently, he drew away from her, softly disentangling from his emotions the fine filaments of love she had begun to spin around him. He gave her into the keeping of his disciples, who showed towards her the same insouciant attitude towards her past, the same burning enthusiasm for the life of the spirit, that she had seen in Jesus himself, and who, seeming almost blind to her sexuality, respected and valued her as a comrade in fellowship, bound to them by her share in a common adherence to the Master. Deliberately he distanced himself from her, so the perilous bonds of intimacy did not bind him too closely to one person especially favoured above others. Eventually she accepted this change, and seemed to understand the need of it; certainly she did not return to her old life, but stayed with the community, worked with the other women at common household tasks, sat quietly in the crowd and listened when Jesus taught the people, modestly served him at supper as he ate, drank and laughed with his disciples. Occasionally as she moved around the room, bearing herself with a new-found grace that only enhanced her loveliness, he would catch her dark eyes looking at him, and would look away with a corresponding sense of incompleteness, of a small wound in his heart that would neither close nor heal.

Now, he reflected, with gathering excitement, at last the prohibition keeping them apart from one another, distanced in the formal relationship of master and disciple, had evaporated, and there remained no reason why he should not, as a man, take her to him as his lover, his wife, the mother of his children. At last he could be whole as a man; at last that ancient injury of insufficiency could be cured, man and woman cleaving together as one being, bone of his bone, flesh of her flesh. At last he would be able to enjoy the simple, everyday pleasures of marriage, that close, private, breathless intimacy he had never known, but vividly remembered from the times he had lain awake, as a child in his parents' house, listening to the soft sounds of love-making from his parents' bed: the long-drawn out stillness of kiss and embrace, the eager panting of intercourse, the gasps of agonizing pleasure as the two bodies, humped blindly together in the darkness, drove deeper into one another in search of the final ecstasy. More than anything he remembered the quiet, wondering silence afterwards, as hammering hearts stilled to a regular rhythm, and as exhausted, sweat-drenched bodies lay cooling into a blissful sleep of satisfaction.

How many times had he, as a man, heard the same sounds, in houses where he had rested and sheltered, hearing men and women brought closer together by the perfume of love his presence exhaled, and finding that closeness consolidated in a mingling of bodies; and how often he had felt in his human nature the unfairness of his virgin destiny! All this now would change, and he would take Mary of Magdala as his lawful wedded wife, and with her bring forth and raise the children of their love.

He quickened his step as he approached the place where he had left his followers encamped, eager to share with them the good news of his acquired enthusiasm, induct them into the principles of his new gospel.

Uncertain of the exact spot, he cast about him in the darkness, and at least glimpsed a faint ripple of whiteness through the interlacing leaves. He was half aware that the light barely revealing their whereabouts was the first light of the sun breaking over the

Mount of Olives, in what was to have been the dawn of his last day on earth.

There they were, sprawled around the girth of the cedar trunk, an ungainly huddle of assorted humanity. Here a bare leg stuck out untidily from the jumble of limbs; there a lose-flung arm lay uncomfortably across another sleeper's face. They could have been a heap of dead bodies, corpses slaughtered on a battlefield, but for their restless stirrings and uneasy snores.

The sentinels too had out-watched their wakefulness: James sat upright with his back against the tree-trunk, but his mouth hung open in exhaustion of vigilance; Peter also remained at his post, drawn sword across his knees, head resting on folded arms, consciousness dead to the world. There was no sign of Judas.

His heart moved in pity for their weariness, their unpreparedness, their lack of any reliable defensive precautions. He had chosen them, from among millions of ordinary men and women, to support and sustain his ministry; they had devoted their lives to his service, and he would in turn remain faithful to them. He knew they were capable of great courage, immense determination, selfless dedication, and he admired them for those qualities; but what moved his heart to its depths with compassion was the sight of them, thus displayed so nakedly in their human weakness, exposed and unprotected, prey to all the violence they sought to extirpate from the world. Although he knew them to be brave and strong, some handsome or beautiful, full of nobility and virtue, loyalty and faith; yet it was the sight of them in their defenceless weakness that caused his heart to go out to them in tenderness of love. Already, from the direction of the city, he could see, flaring in the darkness, a glare of flickering torches moving across the Kidron.

Instinctively he stretched out his arms crosswise, his palms extended towards his followers in a gesture of acceptance and protectiveness.

—Could you not watch with me one hour? He murmured.

In that moment all the power of God flowed irresistibly back along his body, through his extended arms, and was shed from the palms of his hands in a perfume of invisible benediction and grace. No, they could not watch with him even so long; for they were human, fallible men and women, whose eyes could not help but close in weariness, and whose best intentions of charity and goodness were all the more beautiful in the purity of their aspiration, so at odds with the limitations of the human organism, with man's incapacity to attain or deliver even a fraction of those lovely images of moral excellence dreamt of in his deepest imaginings.

No, God could not after all desert man, his latest offspring, his best-loved son, his cherished daughter. Their fates had been inextricably intertwined with his since the time of their creation. God had been involved in the life of mankind since the moment of mankind's making, from a time before the necessity of incarnation – when God would become man indeed – arose, by man's treacherous but venial, noxious but forgivable, fault.

He had made a mistake, an error of judgement that had perhaps, after all, been foreseen and provided for, lying hitherto unperceived in some amnesias of the divine memory, now perpetrated and resolved in a way calculated to involve him ever more closely, as Himself, in the lives of his children.

—Son, he commented ironically: I have sinned against you; daughter, I am not worthy to be called your father.

The lights were close now, the clink of armour, and the rattle of spear against shield, announcing the presence of soldiers accompanying the officials who had come to arrest him. Hearing even that first faint sound, Peter was instantly awake and on his feet, dews of the mountain shed from the blade of the sword that rose in his hand. Again Jesus stretched out his hands in the gesture of deliverance, this time to welcome Judas's embrace. A forest of spears bristled against the early morning light. With infinite tenderness and love, he took betrayal into his arms, and gathered it to him with a kiss of peace.[8]

Solitude

There is but one God. But was that God ever alone?

JOHN DONNE

His eyes snapped open onto palpable darkness. Tangible opacity pressed against his stretching, questing eyeballs. Where was he? Had it all happened – all the suffering and endurance; all the passion of bloody sweat and bitter tears; all the shame of public humiliation, and the brief sharp agony of the cross – all gone, passed, in the twinkling of an eye, as if he had slept through it all, alive but dead to sight and feeling, in some blissful state of impervious unconsciousness? All around him the blackness closed in, sometimes seeming to wrap him around like a shroud; sometimes like soft black earth covering his face, and filling his nose and mouth; sometimes like the shadows of the tomb, where no light falls, that hollow space that reflects in on itself nothing but darkness. It was the soreness and hurt of his body that was forcing him awake. Had he died, and risen, and was he risen to this? The same fragile human body, flesh crying out against the affliction of wounds, waking to the darkness of the grave, as if buried alive, and lacking the power of self-resurrection? God was to have raised him from the dead, on the third day, as it had been spoken of by the prophets, and as he himself had predicted to his disciples. But where now was God, apart from himself? What remained to him of divine power, or even ordinary human strength, sufficient to roll aside the massive obstruction, and bring the Easter daylight flooding in?

But gradually, as he came to himself, there broke upon him the bitter realization that it was not yet by any means over, that it was all yet to come. The pain that throbbed and lanced through his body, pain the retreat from which had crushed his consciousness tightly into a corner of his skull, and that had made him feel again, for a time, wholly a man, all flesh, all pain – was nothing more than the discomfort of a body subjected to a cursory beating at the hands of the Roman soldiers who had taken charge of him from the officers of the Sanhedrin; nothing personal, nothing specific, only the generalized routine administering of a few turns of the boot, a few glancing blows of the spear-butt, casually meted out to any prisoner, whoever he might be, and whatever his offence. The aching of his arms and legs came not from limbs racked and contorted on the splintered wood of the cross, but purely from the irritation of sitting in a space so confined as to prevent him lying down. The darkness that veiled his eyelids, and filled his imagination with a horror of the tomb, was only the blackness of night turning his narrow chimney of a prison-cell into an imaginary grave.

His initial sense of disappointment, that the ordeal was yet to come, disappeared, as he screwed tight his nerves, and gathered together the strength of his spirit. Yes, his passion was as yet unsuffered, and its intolerable pain still before him; still there remained no sorrow like the sorrow that remained for him to endure. But it was not thus, surely, that he would rise from the dead on the third day; not still sick with weakness and exposure, not still wincing and throbbing with pain? He trusted in God, the God that was himself, yet not present with him here in this narrow cell, to raise him to newness of life, in a body washed clean from the stains of torture and punishment, and healed from the hurt and humiliation of his Passion. Indeed, as he sought, with imperfect human vision, to penetrate the blackness surrounding him, he could dimly see, or believed he saw, directly above his head, what must have been an aperture giving onto the open air; for hovering in the darkness, almost like the dusky glimmering of an angel's wings, he could see a faint misting of cloud cross the blackness, and even, if he stared long and hard enough, the pin-point brilliance of a single star.

This, then, was the finality of loneliness. He had often sought loneliness, as a necessary condition of meditation and self-knowledge; it was a horror of loneliness that had possessed him during his agony in the garden; and it was loneliness he had feared, during that brief abdication of his godhead. After those three-and-thirty years of human existence, was it after all surprising that he should have become subdued to what he worked in, like the dyer's hand; inured to the human condition, engrafted to the body, its pains and pleasures, its desires and fears; that he should have become, through that process of learning to know and love his creatures, almost a fellow-creature, almost one of them? To be one of them rendered him capable of experiencing what, to the gregarious and social spirit of humanity, seemed more than anything else unbearable: solitude, exile, friendliness. This, to men and women, was how the reality of hell could be imagined; not in visions of the tormented soul, burning in unquenchable flame of incandescent fire, or lodged tight in the freezing ribs of a glacier; but the condition of absolute isolation, the state of being cut-off from God, sundered from family, severed from friends, set apart from those fellows with whom one shared the agonies and ecstasies of mortal existence. No man is an island, entire of itself; every man is a piece of the continent, a part of the main.

Jesus had come to understand, through these experiences, from the inside, the true nature of human brokenness. For that original and inescapable state was the condition to which all those other words – alienation, separation, loneliness (each with its particular implication of what was needed to restore the absence – belonging, community, friends) – endeavoured to speak, and finally alluded: the condition of a creature who was born whole, and whose wholeness was fragmented; who was born a part of his world, and was wrenched away from it; who was born free, and is everywhere to be found in chains.

He had known loneliness, as an inner wound, from his mother's womb; he had sucked the milk of alienation from the maternal teat; he had felt, in the cutting of his umbilical cord, and in the soreness of his circumcision, painful little replications of that great primal separation of himself from himself. But as he had grown deeper and deeper into humanity, so he had come to fear loneliness and to avoid it: keeping in the midst of human society, always surrounded by friends and disciples, always interacting with other human beings, who – friends and enemies, bearers of love and promulgators of hate – all alike served to reinforce the reality of human companionship as the essential medium of existence. He had almost forgotten that his destiny was not to eschew loneliness, but to embrace it, and to take it with him into the darkness of the tomb. To be with them for ever as God, dwelling in them and they in him, he needed to go through with the process of removing himself, as a person, from the world. He knew that for them, this would seem an inconsolable bereavement, and that his departure would leave behind him an unappeasable aching of unsatisfied love. Only by separating himself from those he loved, could he be with them forever, as he had explained to them: a little while, ye see me not; and again, a little while, and ye shall see me. Only God knows how to wound us into love.

The real danger implicit in his temptation in the garden was not that, by engaging with human beings in carnal congress, he might suffer contamination of the flesh, and damage to the spirit. It was rather that, out of the fear of loneliness endemic to the human condition, he had momentarily lost sight of the true necessity of solitariness, of facing the radical insufficiency of the human soul as yet reunited with the divine spirit. Human beings feared dying more than anything else, it seemed, less from a fear of pain and weakness, and more from an instinctive aversion to the loneliness of the journey every man and woman must needs take into the mysterious obscurity of death.

Somewhere outside his cell, from which direction he could not discern, he heard the tread of approaching feet, a rattling of keys, a sound of whispering voices. Instinctively his hands tightened in apprehension, broken nails cutting into the soft skin of his palms. As the noise of his jailers' movements ceased, and gave place to a harsh scraping of rusty iron bolts, he tried to fix his eyes on the opposite wall, preparing his dilated pupils for the sudden onrush of light. But it was from behind him that the warped wood of the cell-door creaked open, and the blaze of torchlight that broke into his darkness washed the opposite wall with whiteness, cutting his own shadow into a black silhouette: shoulders hunched, as if flinching from some burden of indignity; unkempt hair knotted and wreathed in interlacing spikes that pricked with prescient wounds the incandescent air. The absurdity of his misapprehension, graphically illustrating the limitations of human sensation, was compounded as they seized him under the arms and dragged him roughly backwards out of the cell, leaving him sitting in undignified awkwardness on the cold flagged floor. Slowly, painfully, he bent forward, drew up his knees, gripped with the bruised soles of his feet the icy stone, and with trembling hands pushed himself upwards off the floor. He stood for a moment in silence, looking at his shadow on the wall of the vacated cell. A man of sorrows. Then he turned to face his captors, and in the concave mirrors of their glittering torchlit eyes he saw, with startling clarity and definition, himself: white and wavering as a ghost, Lazarus come back from the dead; the suffering servant, standing in patient subjection, his wrists crossed one over the other, though they were not bound; his head bowed as if in courtesy or respect. At the same time there played about his marred features an unearthly light that seemed to absorb the flickering torchlight, and to quench its tributary brightness. The light of the world. As the expressions in all their eyes passed, from contempt and mockery, through fear and suspicion, to a terrified wonder and overmastering awe, he read in the map of their vision the cartography of his own power. On the viscous optic surfaces of their eyeballs there floated the fragmentary, distorted image of a broken man. Yet deeper within those microcosmic orbs, he could detect a scattered brightness that was beginning to disperse earth's darkness with the unquenchable light of heaven.

Passion

Ecce homo!

ST JOHN

I

Pilate sweated. On his smooth face Jesus could see drops of perspiration chasing one another down the pampered flesh of his cheeks. Pilate leaned forward from the judgement seat and searched, with frightened eyes, the ravaged face. On his breath the sickly sweetness of Lydian wine; in his eyes, agonies of indecision and fear. Fear of the Emperor; fear of the Jews, their Elders waiting in a threatening silence for his ruling; above all, fear of this strange, silent prisoner, a mockery of purple thrown about his shoulders, blood from his pierced head all but effacing the lineaments of his face. This man who, unlike any other criminal brought before him for judgement, had no plea for mercy, no word of exculpation, no curse of defiance. Only a profound, immobile silence, speaking volumes of meaning; a massive, palpable sense of resistance, contrasting with his passive subjection; and an inexplicable aura of power, at odds with his position of weakness and captivity. Pilate leaned close enough to whisper so that no one else could hear.

—What do you want, man? Do you hear how many things they accuse you of? Do you understand the seriousness of the charges?

In the urgent vibration of his voice, and in the rank smell of sweat penetrating through the mist of perfume that anointed his body, could be heard the anxiety of his longing to defer decision. Jesus looked at him and saw, through smarting blood-filled eyes, not a bad man, as Roman governors go; sensual and lazy, wanting only a quiet life, unfairly trapped here in this inextricable political dilemma. For whatever he decided, difficulty and inconvenience would inevitably ensue. If he pardoned the man, the elders of the Jews would be furious, and would try to cause trouble for him all the way to Rome: at best conveying to Caesar a sense of ineffective government; at worst, a whiff of treachery and disloyalty to the state. If he fell in with their wishes, and condemned the Nazarite, there would be, just as surely, a mob of angry zealots to contend with.

Jesus could not help him, though he wanted to, by breaking silence. With a barely audible hiss of frustration and contempt, Pilate sat back and appealed beyond the prisoner to the Elders of the Jews, opening his arms and pointing to Jesus as if in disbelief.

—Behold your King!

A dissatisfied murmur arose from the crowd that had pushed its way into the Praetorium behind the elders. Hearing these mutinous voices of sympathy the priests quickly moved to exercise control.

—No king of ours. Crucify him, we say: crucify him.

Pilate assumed a stiff smile and tuned his voice to a note of sweet reasonableness.

—What? Should I crucify your *King*?

—We have no king, shouted their spokesman, triumphant at having manoeuvred the governor into a trap. No king but Caesar!

The smile died on Pilate's lips as quickly as it had formed, and his round face became the blank, impassive countenance of a civil servant. He would not expose himself to charges of treason for this crazy fool, who would not even speak up in his own defence.

—Very well, he said, coldly, without looking at Jesus: let him be crucified.

Immediately soldiers took him by the arms and swung him round to face the Elders. As he was wheeled about, he caught a glimpse of Pilate, who had turned aside, and, while pointedly not observing the outcome, was nervously rubbing his hands together as if seeking to rid them of some spot or stain.

The Elders stepped aside to let the soldiers pass. Other troops pushed the crowd down the steps of the Praetorium, and held them back with their lances to clear a way for the prisoner's escort. Before him Jesus could see the road running straight ahead across the square, disappearing into the dark streets of the city, and re-emerging as a hillside path leading to the spot where, just outside the city walls, there rose the ugly black hump of Golgotha. *Via Dolorosa*: the Way of Sorrows. At its end, the Place of the Skull. I am the Way. The truth. The life. But first, the hard cobbled causeway that leads to death.

II

Anchoring his right shoulder into the angle of shaft and cross-beam, shoulder tightly locked into the joint, cheek pressed against the rough, unplaned surface, right arm stretched around the beam to steady and balance the shaft in an equilibrium with his body, he attempted to rise, and to raise, with his ascension, the squared bulk of the cross. For this, at least, he had some modicum of training: familiar from his childhood with the ways of wood, hatch and cross-grain, mortise and dovetail; used to heaving and hauling, with nothing more than stretch and sinew, timber and plank.

His knees shuddered and buckled under the weight, but once he had shouldered the shaft erect, and locked his knee-joints into position, the volume and mass of his burden became bearable to biceps and back. He wondered, idly, what type of wood it was, since his brief frequentation of that which was to be his instrument of torture, the vehicle of his vanishing from the world, had not permitted so close or curious an acquaintance. It was certainly not as heavy as it looked, once you had it across your shoulders and had settled and balanced the weight. As he started to walk forward, feeling the foot of the shaft bumping and sliding across the cobbles behind him, the long journey seemed feasible. He could do it. Surprising how strong it was, this skinny angular frame with its clumsy joints and weak extremities. Yes, he would make it. If only the strength of his spirit could sustain his physical powers. If only all of it were over.

III

His first fall was a mere trip, as his foot caught on a cobble and slipped sideways, his body thrown off balance by the weight of the cross. The beam went down with a jarring jolt, and he went with it, grazing his hip on the rough stones. For a while he flailed in an awkward struggling, trying to extricate his pinned arm.

The soldiers turned their backs on him to face the crowd, their jutting lances forfending pity. Among the jumble of faces he could see some of them laughing, the poor in spirit tickled by another's indignity; some moved to compassion, their impulse to aid blocked by a sharpness of javelins; and others gathering their brows in a red rash of anger against the conqueror's cruelty.

Make it stop, he thought. I can make it stop, this circus show, this Lenten entertainment. Unassisted, he hauled the heavy beam back onto his shoulder, and staggered upright to resume his slow procession.

IV

Something prompted him to look up, raising his eyes from their fixation on the floor. From the ambiguous field of faces loomed one all too familiar, a face whose double suffering redoubled his. *Mater Dolorosa*. Every line of pain ingrained on her face cracked another whiplash across his back. Every tear that coursed down her cheeks rammed another thorn deep into his skull. He could hear, in the audible beating of her heart, the hammer-blows of his crucifixion; he could feel, in the agony of the sword that pierced her womb, the final spear-thrust that would pierce his side. Weeping and mourning, the salt tears burning her blue-veined eyelids, Mary's sad gaze never for an instant turned from the spectacle of her tortured and tormented boy.

Although he had known it was to come, this final farewell to his earthly mother; though he had known it would be the hardest pang of all, the heaviest cross, the deepest wound; yet no prescience or preparation had adequately equipped him for this. No, he could not bear it; could bear anything but that she should see him thus. Through cracked lips his swollen tongue mumbled terse words of recognition and dismissal:

—Woman, behold your son.

Then as hastily as he could, as John drew her aside and hid the unbearable agony of her tear-stained face, he moved on past her, unable to watch, with mortal eyes, the breaking of his mother's heart.

V

He began to feel light, light-headed, light in the body; a strange force of levitation lifting the soles of his feet from the ground. The cross seemed like some great eagle that had swooped down and rapt him in its talons, and was now rising on the wind, lifting and tilting and wheeling, reversing gravity in its effortless heavenward flight.[9]

Or else it was his own broken body, prematurely giving up the
ghost, unstably dissolving and transmuting from fragile corruptible
flesh into pure and ethereal spirit, unerringly following its own
remorseless proclivity to ascend. It was too soon, the tragedy had
not been played out to its symbolic denouement. He was not to rise
here, God incarnate vanquished by mere human weakness, the coarse
clay of the body melting into helpless evanescence, the splintering
wood of the cross whirled and fragmented in the rushing mighty
wind of His resurrection. Such capability of instructive violence
He had shown innumerable times, in the rage of the tempest, the
shock of the earthquake, the power of the wind: and yet the sons
and daughters of men had persistently hardened their hearts against
Him. Now, when his earthly pilgrimage had brought him so close to
the completion of this drama, when the sign of the cross would be
reared eternally upon the hill, and the still small voice of voluntary
suffering would cleave the hearts of his hearers more surely than
any lightning rending the Temple's veil; was he to be betrayed by
the body that had for so long kept him securely anchored to the
earth's spinning and slippery surface?

It was some time before he realized that the great thundering
reverberations echoing through the chambers of his sense were not
the noise of celestial rejoicing at his triumphal return, but only the
banging of blood through his heart, still tenaciously pounding in
his exhausted chest; and that the sensation of lightness derived,
not from any gravity-defying flight of the spirit released from its
fleshly integument, but from the helping hands of pitying fellow-
creatures, some of whom had braved the Roman lances to duck
under the transverse beam, and take up the weight of the cross.
Already others were risking their freedom and comfort to follow
him, and to share his burden. Although we are many. The cross
moved forward through the crowd as a corporate being, bound in
sympathy of suffering into one body. By the time the soldiers moved
in to beat back the bearers, he had regained, from their assistance,
sufficient strength to press forward on his way.

VI

At a street corner the soldiers allowed him to stop for a brief rest. For
the first time he had leisure to look at their faces, and to read in their

expressions of boredom and indifference the shabby lineaments of their private thoughts. If the prisoner became too exhausted to continue, they would be left with the bother of pulling the cross themselves, while the sun was growing hotter, the crowd more restless. If he died on the way, they would still have the added responsibility of dragging his corpse along to the place of execution. It was in their interests to keep him alive, and equipped with at least enough strength to bear his burden over that last few hundred yards.

The shadow of a figure fell across him. Looking upwards, he could see only a slender shape silhouetted against the blazing light, and a nimbus of saffron brightness encircling a carefully cultivated coiffure. Shielding his eyes from the sun, he could make out the form of a woman, richly attired, a Roman lady whose social prominence evidently protected her from the attentions of the guards. In her lovely face he could decipher a confusing range of emotions, from pity, through piety, to an intense curiosity and an excitement of discovery. Bending down towards him, she held forward a swatch of silk, and in a gesture of compassion, pressed it over his ruined face. The soft coolness of the material momentarily soothed the soreness of his bruises, and he breathed in the incense of an exotic perfume. Gently she patted the silk around his face, modelling the nose and eye-sockets with artistic precision. An edge of the cloth caught on a thorn, and the shreds ripped as she eased it carefully away from his face.

Before him was his own image, etched in blood and sweat: drawn cheeks, bruised mouth, scarred forehead; the matted beard, forked at the chin where she had tucked in the cloth; the plaited corona of thorns, whose absent barbs seemed still to be tugging at the ripped and ragged shreds of silk.[10] The woman carefully folded the cloth and secreted it, as if it were some treasure, within the folds of her dress. As she turned away into the brightness, her face, in its chiaroscuro of darkness and light, seemed to reveal signs of both tragedy and triumph.

VII

His second fall surprised him. At first he hardly knew he had fallen, feeling no particular change in the volume or intensity of his pain, virtually oblivious to his sudden lack of progress, surprised at the shout of shocked sympathy he heard from the crowd lining the

dark, narrow street. Gradually he became aware that his knees were
scraped and wedged against the cobblestones, his shoulders pressed
hard down under the weight of the wood. As his vision cleared,
he could dimly discern, through a field of vision misted by blood,
edged by the sharp points of protruding thorns, and confined by
the falling canopy of his sweat-greased, matted hair, the uneven and
variegated colours and contours of the ancient cobbles that lined
the street, focused now with hard and clear definition and intensity.
In a great sudden silence he stared with fascination at the subtle
beauty of the stones, tracing with his eye their textures and shapes,
revelling in the exquisite artistry of their composition. For God so
loved the world. Stones of the old city, more various and complex
than the flat chiselled slabs with which the Romans had paved
the Praetorian precinct: their surfaces glistening with the sheen of
quartz and mica, or hiding in dark polished depths tiny twists and
traces of precious silver or gold. So much exquisiteness of structure
and detail; so much beauty habitually forgotten and ignored, as
millions of sandalled feet scuffed and slapped insouciantly across
their surface. Yet now, seen thus at close quarters, how much more
deserving of closer study and contemplation!

A sharp lash flicked across his back, smarting through the
purple of his robe, and with a wince of pain he came to himself
again. This time lifting the cross was not so easy: its rough familiar
surface seemed less answerable to the guiding grip of his soaked and
slippery fingers. Where initially it had elevated easily with the rise
and lift of his body, this time its gravity seemed deeply settled to the
earth's surface, almost like a root buried in the soil, resisting with
a grim, unbroken tenacity of purpose all efforts to wrench it loose.
Eventually it gave way with a sudden sharp loosening that almost
toppled him sideways. But he was upright; the cross was again safely
shouldered in a perilous equilibrium. He could move forward again
and resume his slow, painful progress towards the final agony.

VIII

—What have I done to thee? Wherein have wearied thee?

Compressed to a dry whisper, the voice still vibrated with that
familiar tone of hunger and reproach. As he had lurched sideways,

almost falling into the crowd, Mary Magdalene, who had threaded her way to follow his progress, now thrust herself between the bystanders to grasp at the hem of his garment. To render herself unobtrusive she had resumed the scarlet robe of her former occupation. No one would give a second glance to a prostitute, plying her trade among the crowd inflamed to excitement by a public execution: unless it were with the intention of slipping after her into some narrow alley, and there in the furtive darkness to test the sweetness promised by her full lips and breasts.

But now as she detained him, clinging to the edge of his purple robe, she courted peril: she of all his disciples, prompted by her passion to a reckless disregard of safety. Again he felt the same irritant of impatience against her: she for whom everything, despite all his efforts of instruction, remained personal, even to the carelessness that urged her to this sword's edge of danger. Was her bravery that much greater than that of Peter or John, her heart growing in strength of purpose as their courage ebbed away, that passion should put her to this risk? Or was it the old attachment, that which in the past had caused him so much awkwardness and pain: to the man in him, to the creature of flesh that very soon the earth would see no more? It was as if his crucifixion were nothing but a grand drama of renunciation, in which he could finally put himself beyond the reach of those seductive, clutching arms.

—What could I do more for thee, she protested, that I have not done?

He looked down at her, her face reflecting in his the transfiguration of pity and love.

—*Noli me tangere, Maria*, he said, gently disentangling her fingers from the folds of his robe. For I am not yet ascended. Stay behind and wait for me: my choicest vine.

Reluctantly she let him go, still unable to resign herself to the prospect of his absence.

His choicest vine. What fruit could she bring forth, other than the dark grapes of sensuality that ripened in her perfumed body? Since he had not been able to crush from her flesh that sweet vintage, in her thirst he had given her vinegar to drink, mingled with gall. O my people. What have I done unto thee?

IX

His third fall was more like a relapse into oblivion than a conscious descent from the perpendicular, resembling that blissful moment when the mind, stretched to extremity on a rack of painful thought, apprehends the advent of unconsciousness and dives with alacrity into an ocean of peace. He slept, as a baby that has cried itself to sleep, hearing in his mind's ear, as if from elsewhere, the catch of a sniffling sob, as one hears, from inside the insulation of half-slumber, the alien ratcheting sound of one's own snores.

With a double consciousness, both sensory and visual, he felt his own body stretched on a soft couch of slumber, and at the same time saw, as if from above, an image of himself, as a sleeping infant, plump little belly and thighs lying vulnerably exposed. His face, cheeks flushed and lips parted, was averted towards the observer, and shut into blind oblivion. Under his body, and swathed about him, was a rich blue cloth, ruched folds lapped about his groin and pillowing the softness of his cheek. So perfect an image of childish slumber, drawing the sweet breath of infant peace! He had become again, in the words of his own parable, as a little child, recovering, in a moment, lost years of relapsed time. An opportunity, maybe, to defer the final agony; or time regained, to repeat his earthly ministry, doubling and redoubling its scope and power. Or perhaps his life was reverting to a moment back beyond the call of destiny, giving him again a choice of fates: whether to remain God, or to become man, whether to sustain immanence unaltered, or seek a new immortality through the mortal mysteries of life and death.

But as his dream-eyes focused more clearly, he became aware of other objects hovering in the background of his mental painting: two cherubs, watching protectively over him, one with hands joined in prayer, the other whispering in his ear, as if warning him to wake. Naked newborn babes, they strode the blast of a gathering, thunderous sky. In the distance, a patch of livid light revealed that same bald hump of a hill that haunted all his dreams. Looking more closely at the sleeping child, he observed with horror that one rosy, plump little arm rested on the smooth curve of a skull, already yellow with the corruption of age; and beneath the languid infant body (strange bed to sustain so sweet a sleep), the rough surfaces, and harsh angles, of the cross.[11]

Dream touched reality, and he came to. It was his frame that lay prostrate, it was true; but not fleshed in the delicate skin of a slumbering child, but loosely wrapped in the torn skin and battered bones of his own ruined body. Around him were no folds of delicate drapery, but the bloodstained purple of his mockery robe. He could still feel, under his empty right hand, lying open on the soil, the cold contours of death.

They pulled him upright, and dragged the cross the last few yards up the slope. Looking around him, he saw that all the yesterdays and tomorrows, all the imaginative spaces of his dream landscape, had become nothing more or less than today, and Jerusalem. He stood at the foot of the hill, and above him swelled the skull-shaped curve of Golgotha.

X

He stood on the hill's summit, and surveyed what was left of his little kingdom. Throngs of observers crowded the slopes, held back by a steel ring of armed soldiery, pressing forward to obtain the best possible view, to smell blood, and to hear for themselves the groans of the dying. More and more people flowed from the city gates, swelling the crowd, until the hill seemed in itself a living thing. Some distance away, he could see a little group of mourners, kneeling at the hill's foot, hands clasped, faces to the ground. Pray for us now, and at the hour of our death.

Looking back along the road he had travelled, he found himself marvelling that so short a distance should have been prolonged to what seemed an endless avenue of agony. The high walls of Jerusalem insulted the empty sky, presenting to him a blank, harsh surface of hostility and exclusion. King of the Jews; Messiah; son of David: cast out from his inheritance to die on a hilltop in the afternoon sun. Although, at this elevation, a soft breeze stirred the folds of his garment, and cooled the fire of his lacerations, the sun, just passing its zenith, burned downwards with an inescapable heat, drying the sweat of his face, as it parched the sands of the wilderness away to the south.

A centurion stepped forward and brusquely snapped the cord that held the robe around his throat. Its folds fell and curled about his feet, a last vestige of ironic dignity. In a gesture of instinctive modesty, he cupped his bruised hands over his exposed genitals. The shame of Adam. Ah, the pity of that ancestral punishment, that made human loveliness an object of fear and derision! Yet also fitting that he should now, in person, reap the legacy of his own righteous anger. Why seek now to conceal that which had always been hidden, that instrument of affection no man or woman had ever handled in tenderness of love? Let all now see, at least, that he was in all respects a man; though set apart by virgin enclosure, yet bonded to all in commonality of flesh. He dropped his hands and let them hang loose, exposing his humanity to the world.

Divested now of borrowed robes, clad only in the garment of flesh, he felt no indignity or shame. Having shrugged off, with the imperial purple, all false pretensions to worldly power, his newborn nakedness figured forth what God had given: his only begotten son, the Son of Man, willingly bound over in proud humility of sacrifice.

Ecce homo. My kingdom is not of this world.

XI

He raised his arms crosswise, presenting to the people his open palms, offering to his executioners slack wrists of subjection. Soldiers seized the outstretched arms and pushed him over backwards, onto the cross that lay on the ground, ready to receive him. As his vision tilted, he glimpsed, below him, thousands of onlookers suddenly fall to their knees, caught in the tide of a great dawning realization.

For a while he lay prostrate, looking for the last time at this side of that intense blue sky. The sun's brassy radiance fogged his eyelashes with dancing sparkles of light. To his left he could just see a gathering of dark thundery clouds building up from the west. Here, at this almost final moment, he felt fully prepared, virtually without fear. How much easier was this passion of subjection to certainty, than the hard road he had just travelled, or the agony of indecision endured in the garden? Although the worst was yet to come, all but the worst was over. No worst; there is none.

He could hear the executioner preparing his instruments of torture: the familiar thud of a tool bag slung to the ground, the rattle of metal against metal as hammer and nails were unwrapped from within its folds. Almost curious to watch this administration of death, he nonetheless resisted the temptation, and continued to gaze heavenwards, though now forced to shut his eyes against the sun's intrusive brightness. He felt, with curiosity, the cold point of a square nail positioned carefully over the soft flesh of his wrist, where the arteries carried to his wounded, healing hands the life-giving blood. He felt the nail twisted between the workman's thumb and forefinger, then held still to await the driving blow. Let him strike firm and sure, without hesitation. Let him strike with a carpenter's precision, the skill of his father's hands.

The weight of the iron hammer clanged against the nail's flattened head, and its squared shaft ripped easily through skin and sinew, tissue and vein, driving cleanly into the cleft between ulna and radius. At the second blow he felt iron bump and grate against bone, and heard the point bite deep into the wood of the crossbeam. Nerves cauterized by the friction, there was little pain, beyond a dull ache of discomfort as the metal twisted and grazed against his exposed bones. He could feel his hands growing wet, as the arteries began to release his blood, the blood of Christ, to the open air.

The executioner's shadow fell across his face as he moved to the other side of the cross. Again he felt the squared bulk of a nail pressed down onto his flesh, but now the man's hands were trembling, and the nail's point slid unevenly around the wrist-bones. Jesus twisted his neck to look round at him, and saw an overmastering fear clouding the man's eyes, as if he had begun to realize what it was that he was doing. Poor instrument of greater powers, from Herod's petty tyranny to the will of God!

—I forgive you, whispered Jesus. Strike now.

The executioner's hands steadied, and with a single blow he drove down the second nail, slicing swiftly through the wrist, and splintering into the wood below.

Jesus heard, rather than felt, the jar of the last nail banged through the bones of his feet. Already his sight was beginning to darken as the black blood ebbed easily into the thirsty ground.

—I have trodden the winepress alone, he thought. May the labourer be worthy of his hire.

But it was when they raised the cross, pulled upright by ropes caught around the crossbeams, the shaft shouldered clumsily up from behind; and when he heard its foot slide and drop into the buried wooden socket; and when he felt the whole weight of his body dragged down against the nails, and the full force of the Judaean sun blister downwards onto his bruised and broken forehead, then he knew: that though his being enfolded the entire love of the universe, one ragged little human body could contain all the pain that the world may feel.

XII

Consummatum est. It is finished.

Resurrection

Christ is not the end. He is the beginning.

NIKOS KAZANTZAKIS

It was as if a hand had touched his shoulder, gently but firmly shaking him awake. His own hand, but felt as coming from outside, extending across immensities of space, reaching through the mysteries of life and death, stretching even into the tomb to stir him from his sleep. O tender hand! O gentle touch![12] A hand that could annihilate the world, and melt the poles; make the earth tremble, and the mountains shatter into fragments. But laid on him now, softly, lovingly, in tenderness of spiritual touch.

His own hand, but not the hands of his body, which lay tightly trussed and sheathed inside his shroud. These hands of blood and bone now began to twitch and grasp, exploring their captivity, seeking their freedom. Cramped fingers pushed away encircling cloth, unwrapping his body from its winding sheet; then fumbled upwards to unwind the bandages that bound his face. Freed from the integument of death, he lay still for a while, feeling the icy cold of the rock-hewn tomb strike with an animating chill on his naked flesh. The black air was perfumed with strange scents: oils of embalming, ointments of death.

Did the body possess its own memory? For as he lay there, in absolute darkness, the wounds at his wrists were aching, and the holes in his feet were intolerably sore, and the great incision where the spear-thrust had penetrated his side smarted and clamoured with pain. Yet he knew his wounds to be healed, and the flesh in which he had awoken to be restored. It was no longer the ruined body of his Passion, but a clean white body, grown from the soil of his death, a seed germinating in the darkness, putting forth tentative Easter buds. Pain had transmuted from sensation to knowledge, but its record was burned into his memory, its deeply etched signature would never be obliterated from his flesh.

The enveloping darkness, complete and impermeable, recalled his time in the womb, that other sealed vessel of shadows. Although the comforting, remembered warmth of the uterus was utterly unlike the inhospitable cold of this stony mausoleum, yet it was here, from this hollow in the rocks, that he was to be reborn; in the flesh still, yet not of it; released from the earth, as he had been expelled from the womb in that previous incarnation. In my end is my beginning.

A chink of light pierced the darkness, showing the aperture where the cave's mouth had been sealed. The rising sun was calling him to revisit earth for the last time. He rose, following the light, and laid his hand on the stone. It yielded easily, and rumbled aside at a touch of his fingers. At first, as the light came crashing in, he winced from its intensity, and crouched blindly on the threshold, recoiling from light's laceration, shrinking from the touch of daybreak's sharp breath on his naked skin.

But morning beckoned him outside. The sun was beginning to touch with silver the grey leaves of the olive trees, and the blue sky was as bright as glass. Clustering anemones purpled the garden's tumbling rocks, and bright green leaves were spurting from the tips of the fig trees. A trickle of water sounded from the runnels of an irrigation trench, and from the thickets a nightingale winsomely whistled a reveille, a melodious final farewell to the dark. God so loved the world. In my beginning is my end.

Leaning against the rock-face was an abandoned gardener's hoe that had been used to seal the tomb. He picked it up, and resting his weight on it strolled through the garden, in no particular hurry, as one who had travelled so far, and had another journey shortly to go. His newborn body was clean and white, solid in its muscularity, yet glimmering with the life of the spirit. His flesh absorbed delightfully the stirring warmth of the sun. All the pleasures of sensation were still available to him in the body – a soft breeze stirring against his skin; the dew of the grass cool against his naked feet – and the imaginary aching of his wounds began to be soothed into a great healing peace.

Under the shade of a myrtle bush, bright taches of blue and red against the garden's green, he saw a glimmering of figures, the women who had come to attend on him. Among them he recognized his mother, though on a mission of mourning still dressed in blue, in Mary's colour. He could see, even at that distance, that his mother's old eyes did not recognize him, or could not believe what her eyes perceived.

But Mary Magdalene, still dressed in her magenta robe, came hesitantly, but quickly towards him, the strength of her hope quelling all disquietude of fear. In her hand she bore a jar of precious spices, brought there to anoint his corpse. Seeming unsure now of what she saw – a gardener taking the sun in the privacy of the early morning, or a pale ghost fleeing the glimpses of the light – she held the jar out towards him as if in gift or propitiation. Then suddenly, seeing, against all hope, that it was he, restored and whole, she fell to her knees, her lovely features luminous with grace. The unwanted urn she placed on the grass, and leaned a hand on it to stop herself from trembling. In a craving for the reassurance of touch, she stretched out her hand towards him.

With fastidious delicacy, he curled about him the diaphanous folds of his winding-sheet, and swayed his body gently away from her questing hand.[13]

*   *   *

Not the end. The beginning.

NOTES

Introduction

1 *The Da Vinci Code*, directed by Ron Howard (Columbia Pictures, 2006).
2 Darren J. Middleton and S. Brent Plate, '"Who Do You See That I Am?": *Son of Man* and Global Perspectives on Jesus Films', in *Son of Man: An African Jesus Film*, edited by Richard Walsh, Jeffery L. Staley and Adele Reinharz (Sheffield: Sheffield Phoenix Press, 2013), p. 133.
3 Anne Rice, *Christ the Lord: Out of Egypt* (London: Chatto and Windus, 2005) and *Christ the Lord: The Road to Cana* (London: Chatto and Windus, 2008); Philip Pullman, *The Good Man Jesus and the Scoundrel Christ* (London: Canongate, 2010); Jeffrey Archer, *The Gospel According to Judas, by Benjamin Iscariot* (London: Macmillan, 2007); Colm Toibin, *The Testament of Mary* (London: Penguin, 2013).
4 See John Erskine, *The Human Life of Jesus* (New York: William Morrow, 1945); F. W. Dilliston, *The Novelist and the Passion Story* (New York: Sheed and Ward, 1960); Alice L. Birney, *The Literary Lives of Jesus: An International Bibliography of Poetry Drama Fiction and Criticism* (New York: Garland Publishing, 1989); Warren S. Kissinger, *The Lives of Jesus: A History and Bibliography* (New York: Garland Publishing, 1985).
5 Nikos Kazantzakis, *The Last Temptation*, translated by P. A. Bien (1961; London: Faber and Faber, 1975); Anthony Burgess, *Man of Nazareth* (New York: McGraw-Hill, 1979); Jim Crace, *Quarantine* (London: Viking, 1997); Ernest Renan, *La Vie de Jésus* (Paris: Michel Levy Frères, 1863); George Moore, *The Brook Kerith* (London: T. Werner Laurie, Ltd., 1916); D. H. Lawrence, *The Man Who Died* (Paris: Black Sun Press, 1929); Robert Graves, *King Jesus* (London: Cassell, 1946).
6 Among the novels I would regard as significant contributors to the form are Iwan Naschiwin, *A Certain Jesus: The Gospel According to Thomas*, translated by Emil Burns (London: Victor Gollancz, 1930); Toyohiko Kagawa, *Behold the Man* (London: Lutterworth Press, 1941); Bo Giertz, *With My Own Eyes: A Life of Jesus*, translated by Maurice Michael (London: George Allen and Unwin, 1960); Michael Moorcock, *Behold the Man* (London: Millennium, 1969); Michele Roberts, *The Wild Girl* (London: Methuen, 1984); Jose Saramago, *The Gospel According to Jesus Christ*, translated by Giovanni Pontiero (1993; London: Harvill Press, 1996); Norman Mailer, *The Gospel According to the Son* (New York: Random House, 1997).

7   *The Life of Jesus* is quoted from *Renan's Life of Jesus, Translated with an Introduction*, by William G. Hutchinson (London: Walter Scott, 1898). Renan's 'Author's Introduction' is quoted from Ernest Renan, *Life of Jesus* (Wattpad, 2007). Available at [http://www.wattpad.com/19052-the-life-of-jesus]. Accessed 1 May 2014.

8   David Strauss *Das Leben Jesu, kritisch bearbeitet* (Tubingen: C. F. Osiander, 1836).

9   Peter Bien suggests that Kazantzakis may even have derived the idea of the 'last temptation' from this passage of Renan, which he copied into his notebook while doing research preparatory to writing his novel *The Last Temptation [of Christ]*. 'Renan's speculations include the entire kernel of Kazantzakis' novel'. See Peter Bien, 'Renan's *Vie de Jesus* as a primary source for *The Last Temptation*', in *Scandalizing Jesus: The Last Temptation of Christ Fifty Years On*, edited by Darren J. N. Middleton (London: Continuum, 2005), p. 4.

10 *The Escaped Cock* (Paris: Black Sun Press, 1929); quotations from *The Man Who Died* (New York: Harper Collins, 2002).

11 A full account of Lawrence's Christian upbringing is given in Graham Holderness, *D. H. Lawrence: History, Ideology and Fiction* (Dublin: Gill and Macmillan, 1982).

12 A fuller account of the story in relation to Lawrence's religious thought and modern Christology can be found in Graham Holderness, '"The Resurrection and the Life": D. H. Lawrence's *The Man who Died*', in *Resurrection*, edited by Stanley Porter, Michael A. Hayes and David Tombs (Sheffield: Sheffield Academic Press, 1999).

13 Bibhu Padhi, *D. H. Lawrence: Modes of Fictional Style* (New York: Whitston Publishing, 1988), p. 207.

14 See also Robert Graves and Joshua Podro, *The Nazarene Gospel* (London: Cassell, 1955), and *Jesus in Rome: A Historical Conjecture* (London: Cassell and Co., 1957).

15 See Robert Graves, *The White Goddess* (1949; Faber and Faber, 1999).

16 'I undertake to my readers that every important element in my story is based on some tradition, however tenuous, and that I have taken more than ordinary pains to verify my historical background'. Robert Graves, *King Jesus*, 2nd edition (London: Cassell, 1947), p. 353.

17 See W. H. Cadman, *The Open Heaven: The Revelation of God in the Johannine Sayings of Jesus*, edited by G. B. Caird (Oxford: Blackwell, 1969).

18 If considered human but not divine, 'Jesus Christ might remain an inspiring moral teacher, to be set alongside Socrates and Confucius, but he could not be a Saviour or Redeemer'. John Macquarrie, *Christology Revisited* (London: SCM Press, 1998), p. 17.

19 Kahlil Gibran, *Jesus the Son of Man* (1928; London: Penguin, 1993). In another book *Sand and Foam: A Book of Aphorisms* (New York: Knopf, 1926), Gibran has Jesus of Nazareth and Jesus the Christian meeting, talking and never agreeing with one another.

20 A widely admired promulgation of this approach was Dennis Potter's TV play *Son of Man* (London: Andre Deutsch, 1969).

21 Rowan A. Greer, 'The Leaven and the Lamb: Christ and Gregory of Nyssa's Vision of Human Destiny,' in *Jesus in History and Myth*, edited by R. Joseph Hoffmann and Gerald A. Larue (Buffalo, NY: Prometheus Books, 1986), pp. 135–42.

22 Hans Küng, 'The Christ of Literature', in *On Being a Christian*, translated by Edward Quinn (London: Collins, 1978), p. 138.

23 Lew Wallace, *Ben Hur: A Tale of the Christ* (New York: Harper, 1880). A similarly tangential approach characterizes the very popular books by Lloyd C. Douglas, *The Big Fisherman* (London: Peter Davies, 1949) and *The Robe* (London: Peter Davies, 1953), set in 30 and 37 AD respectively. See also Dostoevsky: 'he appears . . . he does not say anything, only makes his appearance and goes on his way'. *The Brothers Karamazov*, 1880, translated by David McDuff (London: Penguin 1993), p. 285. Also in this category see Ernest Hemingway's brilliant story 'To-day is Friday', in *Men without Women* (1928; London: Penguin, 1955); and Gerd Theissen, *The Shadow of the Galilean: The Quest of the Historical Jesus in Narrative Form*, translated by John Bowden (Minneapolis, MN: Fortress Press, 1987).

24 Charles Dickens wrote, but did not publish, such a work in *The Life of Our Lord, Written for His Children during the Years 1846 to 1849* (published posthumously 1934, New York: Simon and Shuster, 2000). See also Giovanni Papini, *The Story of Christ* (*Storia di Cristo*, 1921); Jan Dobraczynski, *Give me Your Cares* (1952); Par Lagerkvist, *Barabbas*, 1950, translated by Alan Blair (New York: Vintage Books, 1989); Brian Hession, *More Than a Prophet* (London: Peter Davies, 1959). For all their shortcomings, such books seem to have played a role in the Jesus-novel tradition. Nikos Kazantzakis read both Papini and Lagerkvist before writing *The Last Temptation*.

25 Albert Schweizer, *The Quest for the Historical Jesus*, translated by W. Montgomery (London: A. and C. Black, 1910).

26 Charlotte Allen, *The Human Christ: The Search for the Historical Jesus* (Oxford: Lion Publishing, 1998), p. 69.

27 Martin Kähler, *The So-Called Historical Jesus and the Historic Biblical Christ*, translated and edited by Carl E. Braaten (1964; Philadelphia: Fortress Press, 1988), pp. 46 and 80.

28 Schweitzer, *Quest*, p. 396.

29 Theodore Ziolkowski, *Fictional Transfigurations of Jesus* (Princeton, NJ: Princeton University Press, 1972) pp. 13 and37.

30 Macquarrie, *Christology*, pp. 17 and19.

31 See for example Macquarrie, *Christology*, p. 5.

32 For a survey see Barnes Tatum, *Jesus at the Movies: A Guide to the First Hundred Years* (Polebridge Press, 1998), and for a more detailed study of nine films see Richard C. Stern, Clayton Jefford and Guerric Debona, *Savior on the Silver Screen* (Paulist Press, 1999).

33 Jeffrey L. Staley, 'What Hath New York City to Do with Khayelitsha? An Intertextual Reading of Two Jesus Films', in Walsh, Staley and Reinharz, *Son of Man*, p. 96.

34 *Screening the Sacred: Religion, Myth and Ideology in Popular American Film*, edited by Joel W. Martin and Conrad E. Ostwalt Jr. (Boulder, CO: Westview Press, 1995), p. 2.

35 Lloyd Baugh, S. J., *Imaging Jesus in Film: Sources and Influences, Limits and Possibilities* (Saskatchewan: Campion College, 2007), p. 5. This Canadian essay alternates between English and French, and I have respected its transcultural language. The English translation reads: 'Furthermore the filmic word is never divinely inspired or guaranteed, regardless of how approved or praised it might be by ecclesiastical authorities', p. 34, n. 9.

36 David Jasper, *The Sacred Desert: Religion, Literature, Art and Culture* (Oxford: Blackwell, 2004), p. 5.

37 For instance Mel Gibson claimed this for *The Passion of the Christ*, though the film is based more immediately on a nineteenth-century text, *The Dolorous Passion of Our Lord Jesus Christ*, and incorporates traditional non-scriptural elements such as the Stations of the Cross. See Mel Gibson, 'Foreword', in Ken Duncan and Philippe Antonello, *The Passion: Photography from the Movie 'The Passion of the Christ'* (USA: Icon Distribution, 2004).

38 'We have not only competing images of Jesus in the New Testament itself, but also additional images from non-canonical material'. Douglas K. Mikkelson and Amy C. Gregg, '*King of Kings': A Silver Screen Gospel* (Lanham, NY: University Press of America, 2001), p. 6.

39 See Burgess, *Man of Nazareth*, p. 79.

40 'In many of the Jesus films, the source material for the portrait of Jesus is not the canonical gospels but rather the non-canonical, apocryphal gospels or popular-devotional biographies of Jesus'. Baugh, *Imaging Jesus*, p. 4.

41 A more textually purist approach is evident in Pasolini's *Gospel According to St Matthew*, which makes it for that very reason something of a *cause celebre* for theological scholars of the Jesus-film. Richard Walsh in *Reading the Gospels in the Dark: Portrayals of Jesus in Film* (Harrisburg, PA: Trinity Press International, 2003) attempts to pair up Jesus-films with specific gospels.

42 Allen, *Human Christ*, p. 225.

43 Letter of 13 Nov 1951. Helen Kazantzakis, *Nikos Kazantzakis: A Biography Based on His Letters*, translated by Amy Mims (Oxford: Bruno Cassirer, 1968), pp. 505–6.

44 Peter Bien, *Tempted by Happiness: Kazantzakis' Post-Christian Christ* (Wallingford, PA: Pendle Hill, 1984), p. 20. See also Bien's *Kazantzakis: Politics of the Spirit*, vol. 2 (Princeton and Oxford: Princeton University Press, 2007).

45 Helen Kazantzakis, *Biography*, pp. 505–6.

46 Colin Wilson, 'Kazantzakis' (1962), in Colin Wilson and Howard F. Dossor, *Nikos Kazantzakis* (Nottingham, UK: Pauper's Press, 1999), p. 30.

47 Bien, *Tempted*, p. 18.

48 Nikos Kazantzakis, 'Prologue,' *The Last Temptation*, translated by Peter Bien (Oxford: Bruno Cassirer, 1961; reprinted, London: Faber & Faber, 1975), p. 7. This passage appears in much the same form in Kazantzakis's autobiographical work *Report to Greco* (Oxford: Bruno Cassirer, 1965; reprinted, London: Faber & Faber, 1973), pp. 290–2.

49 *Scorsese on Scorsese*, edited by David Thompson and Ian Christie (London: Faber & Faber, 1989), pp. 116–17, discussing *The Last Temptation of Christ*, directed by Martin Scorsese (Universal Pictures, 1988).

50 'The First Ecumenical Council: The First Council of Nicaea, 325. *The Creed of Nicaea*' and 'The Fourth Ecumenical Council: The Council of Chalcedon, 451: *The Definition of Faith*,' in *Creeds and Confessions of Faith in the Christian Tradition*, vol. 1, edited by Jaroslav Pelikan and Valerie Hotchkiss (London: Yale University Press, 2003), pp. 158–9 and 174–81. Quotations p. 159 and p. 181.

51 'The Athanasian Creed: *Quicunque vult*, 5th–6th c.,' in *Creeds and Confessions*, pp. 675–7. Quotation p. 677.

52 Critics sometimes appear unsure about the sequence. See for example Frank Kermode: 'His new novel is based on the scripts that he wrote for the television production' ('Love and Do as You Please', *New York Review of Books*, 16 August 1979, p. 44); and an anonymous reviewer in *Booklist*: 'Burgess developed this impressive novel from his screenplay' (quoted in Paul Boytinck, *Anthony Burgess: An Annotated Bibliography and Reference Guide* [New York: Garland Publishing, 1985], p. 82). Boytinck is correct: 'On this novel, first published in France, Burgess based his filmscript for Zeffirelli's *Jesus of Nazareth*' (*Annotated Bibliography*, p. 82). The novel was published first in French translation as *L'Homme de Nazareth*, translated by Georges Belmont and Hortense Chabrier (Paris: Laffont, 1976), and in Italian as *L'Uomo di Nazareth*, translated by Liana Burgess (Milano: Editoriale Nuovo, 1978) before publication in English as *Man of Nazareth* (New York: McGraw-Hill, 1979).

53 William Barclay, *Jesus of Nazareth* (London: Collins, 1977), p. 8. The 'novelisation' clearly had some official status beyond the producer's commissioning of it: Lew Grade signed copies and distributed them to cast members (I have seen a copy inscribed to Rod Stieger, who played Pilate). Barclay's theological writing is not without value, but his novelization of the TV film has no literary merit, and often reads like lesson-plans for Sunday school instruction.

54 Anthony Burgess, 'Lord Grade's Will', *Observer Review*, 20 May 1977, p. 28.

55 Jim Crace, 'Preface to Quarantine' (1998). [Available at http://www.jim-crace.com/] [Accessed 6 December 2013].

56 Philip Tew, *Jim Crace* (Manchester: Manchester University Press, 2006), p. 29.

57 Crace, *Quarantine*, p. 242.

58 Tew, *Crace*, p. 13.

59 Philip Pullman and Rowan Williams, 'The Dark Materials Debate: God, Life, the Universe', *Arts.Telegraph* (17 March 2004).

60 See Karen Armstrong, *The Battle for God* (New York: Alfred A. Knopf, 2001).

61 Joseph Cunneen, 'Film and the Sacred', *Cross Currents*, 10: 1 (1993), p. 93.

62 Timothy K. Beal and Tod Linafelt, 'Introduction' to their edition, *Mel Gibson's Bible: Religion, Popular Culture and 'The Passion of the Christ'* (Chicago, IL: University of Chicago Press, 2006), p. 4.

63 Reinhold Zwick, 'Between Chester and Capetown: Transformations of the Gospel in *Son of Man*', in Walsh, Staley and Reinharz, *Son of Man*, pp. 110–19.

64 Lloyd Baugh, 'The African Face of Jesus in Film: Two Texts, a New Tradition', in Walsh, Staley and Reinharz, *Son of Man*, p. 120. See also Richard Walsh, 'A Beautiful Corpse: Fiction and Hagiography in *Son of Man*', in the same volume, p. 192.
65 *Jesus of Montreal*, directed by Denys Arcand (CNC, 1989).

Chapter 1

1 Gibran, *Sand and Foam*, p. 85.
2 Kazantzakis, *Last Temptation*, 287.
3 See Michael Antonakes, 'Christ, Kazantzakis and Controversy in Greece,' in *God's Struggler: Religion in the Writings of Nikos Kazantzakis*, edited by Darren J. Middleton and Peter Bien (Macon, GA: Mercer University Press, 1996), pp. 23–35.
4 Alister E. McGrath, *Christian Theology: An Introduction* (Cambridge, MA: Blackwell, 1997), p. 251.
5 Rowan Williams, *The Wound of Knowledge: Christian Spirituality from the New Testament to St. John of the Cross* (London: Darton, Longman & Todd, 1979), p. 14.
6 Dietrich Bonhoeffer, *Letters and Papers from Prison*, translated by Eberhard Bethge (London: SCM Press, 1971); Jürgen Moltmann, *The Crucified God: The Cross of Christ as the Foundation and Criticism of Christian Theology*, translated by R. A. Wilson and John Bowden (New York: Harper & Row, 1974); Kazoh Kitamori, *Theology of the Pain of God*, translated by M. E. Bratcher (London: SCM Press, 1966), p. 160.
7 Moltmann, *Crucified God*, p. 249.
8 Brian Hebblethwaite, *The Incarnation: Collected Essays in Christology* (Cambridge, MA: Cambridge University Press, 1987), p. 22.
9 Ibid., p. 66.
10 Williams, *Wound*, p. 14.
11 Kitamori, *Pain*, p. 161.
12 Quoted in Darren J. N. Middleton, 'Literary Lord, Screen Saviour' in his edition *Scandalizing Jesus* (2005), p. xvi.
13 Kazantzakis, *Last Temptation*, p. 287.
14 Ibid.
15 No attempt was made by his teachers to explain how these contradictions could co-exist. See Kazantzakis, *Greco*, pp. 116–17.
16 Ibid., p. 115.
17 Ibid., pp. 118–19.
18 Ibid., p. 120.
19 Ibid.
20 Kazantzakis, *Last Temptation*, p. 7. For a different view of Kazantzakis's understanding of the dual nature see David A. Dombrowski, 'Kazantzakis, Chalcedonian Orthodoxy and Monophysitism', in Middleton, *Scandalizing Jesus* (2005), pp. 47–60.

21 'Athanasian Creed', *Creeds and Confessions*, p. 676.
22 Thomas Aquinas, 'The Passion of the Christ', *Summa Theologica*, translated by Fathers of the English Dominican Provinces; 5 vols. (Allen, TX: Christian Classics, 1911; revised, 1948; reprinted 1981) vol. 4, pt. 3, Q. 46, art. 12, p. 2271.
23 Marie Katheryn Connelly, *Martin Scorsese: An Analysis of His Feature Films, with a Filmography of His Entire Directorial Career* (Jefferson, NC: McFarland, 1993), p. 128.
24 Kazantzakis, *Last Temptation*, p. 56.
25 Ibid., p. 47.
26 Ibid., p. 34.
27 Ibid., p. 156.
28 Leo I, 'The Tome of Leo, 449,' in *Creeds and Confessions*, pp. 114–21. Quotation p. 116.
29 Kazantzakis, *Last Temptation*, pp. 205–7.
30 Ibid., pp. 222–3.
31 Ibid., p. 207.
32 Ibid., p. 230. See also *Greco*, p. 511.
33 Kazantzakis, *Last Temptation*, p. 28.
34 Ibid., pp. 23–4.
35 Ibid., p. 87.
36 For a fuller account of the notebooks see Bien, *Politics of the Spirit*, vol. 2 (2007). See also Bien, *Tempted*, pp. 4–5; and 'Primary Source' in Middleton, *Scandalizing Jesus* (2005). Kazantzakis uses 'son of man' as a human descriptor, while in biblical usage the phrase usually denotes the apocalyptic figure of Daniel 7.13 and Revelation 1.13, 14.14. See I. Howard Marshall's fine discussion in *The Origins of New Testament Christology* (Leicester: Apollos, 1976, 1990), pp. 63–82.
37 Kazantzakis, *Last Temptation*, p. 155.
38 Ibid., p. 156.
39 Ibid., p. 163.
40 Ibid.
41 Ibid., p. 190.
42 Ibid., pp. 188–92.
43 Ibid., pp. 181–2.
44 Ibid., p. 230.
45 Ibid., p. 223.
46 Ibid., p. 198.
47 Ibid.
48 Ibid., p. 247.
49 Ibid., p. 267.
50 'Buddha, Christ and Dionysus Are One – the Eternal Suffering Man'. Morton P. Levitt, in *The Cretan Glance* (Columbus, OH: Ohio State University Press, 1980), p. 75.
51 As Kazantzakis wrote in a letter: 'I've raised and sanctified Judas Iscariot right alongside Jesus in this book I'm writing now,' Helen Kazantzakis, *Biography*, p. 477.
52 Kazantzakis, *Last Temptation*, p. 209.

53 Ibid., p. 163.
54 Ibid., p. 309.
55 Ibid., p. 377–8.
56 Ibid., p. 379.
57 Ibid., p. 396.
58 Ibid.
59 Ibid., p. 397.
60 Ibid., p. 438.
61 Ibid., p. 507.
62 Kazantzakis, *Greco*, p. 290. 'Christ Is Not the End. He Is the Beginning'. Notebook of Kazantzakis, cited in Middleton, 'Introduction', in *Scandalizing Jesus* (2005), p. xvii.
63 Kazantzakis, *Last Temptation*, pp. 8–9.
64 Letter of 1 May 1954, in Helen Kazantzakis, *Biography*, p. 523.
65 Letter of 27 November 1952, in Helen Kazantzakis, *Biography*, pp. 515–16.
66 Kiolkowski, *Transfigurations*, 16, referring to Robert Graves, *King Jesus*. Georg Langenhorst partially endorses this view in 'The Rediscovery of Jesus as a Literary Figure,' *Literature and Theology* 9: 1 (March 1995), pp. 85–98.
67 'Virtually every incident originates in the New Testament, but all are filtered through the screen of comparative myth and enhanced by the author's imaginative vision'. Levitt, *Cretan*, p. 63.
68 Levitt, *Cretan*, p. 73.
69 *Scorsese on Scorsese*, pp. 116–17. Thomas R. Lindlof provides a very full and detailed account of the film's production history with particular emphasis on the controversies it generated in *Hollywood under Siege: Martin Scorsese, the Religious Right and the Culture Wars* (Lexington: University Press of Kentucky, 2008).
70 Les Keyser emphasizes Scorsese's researches into biblical criticism, history, and archaeology, in *Martin Scorsese* (London: Twayne, 1992), pp. 170–1. Scorsese also admits to having been inspired by seeing Pasolini's *The Gospel According to St Matthew*: see Martin Scorsese, 'On Reappreciating Kazantzakis', in Middleton, *Scandalizing Jesus* (2005), p. 229.
71 *Scorsese on Scorsese*, p. 124.
72 Macquarrie, *Christology*, p. 21.
73 *Scorsese on Scorsese*, p. 120.
74 Ibid., p. 124.
75 Paul Schrader, *Schrader on Schrader*, edited by Kevin Jackson (London: Faber & Faber, 1990), p. 139.
76 An odd definition of Arius's 'subordinationism'. See his 'Statement of Belief to Alexander of Alexandria, c. 320,' in *Creeds and Confessions*, pp. 77–8.
77 Küng, *On Being*, p. 138.
78 Robin Riley, *Faith and Cultural Conflict: The Case of Martin Scorsese's 'The Last Temptation of Christ'* (Westport, CT: Praeger, 2003), p. 37. Vrasidas Karalis writes at length on the 'self-perception' of Kazantzakis's Jesus in 'The Unreality of Repressed Desires in *The Last Temptation*', in Middleton, *Scandalizing Jesus* (2005), pp. 73–84.
79 Riley, *Faith*, p. 37.
80 *Scorsese on Scorsese*, p. 139.

81 Riley, *Faith*, p. 48.
82 Ibid., p. 47.
83 Ibid., p. 38.
84 Letter of 4 March 1988, quoted in Ibid., p. 65.
85 Quoted in Mary Pat Kelly, *Martin Scorsese: A Journey* (New York: Thunder's Mouth, 1991), p. 6.
86 Lloyd Baugh, 'Martin Scorsese's *The Last Temptation of Christ*: A Critical Reassessment of Its Sources, Its Theological Problems, and Its Impact on the Public', in Middleton, *Scandalizing Jesus* (2005), p. 174.
87 Schrader, *Schrader on Schrader*, p. 135.
88 Kazantzakis, *Last Temptation*, p. 8.
89 Ibid.
90 Macquarrie, *Christology*, p. 52.
91 Gregory of Nazianzus, 'Gregory of Nazianzus on Apollinarinism', in Alister E. McGrath, *The Christian Theology Reader* (Cambridge, MA: Blackwell, 1995, 2nd edition 2001), pp. 258–9. Quotation p. 259.
92 Michael Bliss, *The Word Made Flesh: Catholicism and Conflict in the Films of Martin Scorsese* (London: Scarecrow Press, 1995), p. 92.
93 See Richard A. Blake, 'Redeemed in Blood: The Sacramental Universe of Martin Scorsese,' *Journal of Popular Film and Television* 24: 1 (1996), pp. 1–20.
94 Leo Braudy, 'The Sacraments of Genre: Coppola, De Palma, Scorsese,' in *Film Quarterly*, 39: 3 (1986), pp. 17–28. Quotation p. 18.
95 Christine Hoff Kraemer, 'Wrestling with Flesh, Wrestling with Spirit: The Painful Consequences of Dualism in *The Last Temptation of Christ*,' *Journal of Religion and Popular Culture* 8 (Fall 2004).
96 Macquarrie, *Christology*, p. 21.
97 Williams, *Wound*, p. 2.
98 Darren J. N. Middleton, 'Kazantzakis and Christian Doctrine: Some Bridges of Understanding,' *Journal of Modern Greek Studies* [*JMGS*] 16: 2 (1998), pp. 285–306. Quotation p. 285.
99 *Zorba the Greek*, translated by Carl Wildman (London: John Lehmann, 1952; repr. Oxford: Bruno Cassirer, 1959), p. 142.
100 Kazantzakis, *Greco*, p. 364.
101 Carnegie Samuel Calians, 'Kazantzakis: Prophet of Non-Hope,' *Theology Today* 28: 1 (1971), pp. 37–48. Quotation p. 40. The epitaph on Kazantzakis's grave in Heraklion reads 'Δεν ελπίζω τίποτε. Δεν φοβούμαι τίποτε. Είμαι λεύτερος' ('I hope for nothing. I fear nothing. I am free'.).
102 Lewis Owens, '"Does This One Exist?": The Unveiled Abyss of Nikos Kazantzakis,' *JMGS* 16: 2 (1998), pp. 331–43. Quotation pp. 336–7.
103 Charalampos-Dēmētrēs Gounelas, 'The Concept of Resemblance in Kazantzakis's Tragedies *Christ* and *Buddha*,' *JMGS* 16: 2 (1998), pp. 313–30. Quotation p. 316.
104 John Climacus, *The Ladder of Divine Ascent*, translated by Colm Luibheid and Norman Russell (Mahwah, NJ: Paulist Press, 1982).
105 Kazantzakis, *Greco*, p. 223.
106 Vladimir Lossky, *The Mystical Theology of the Eastern Church*, translated by the Fellowship of St Alban and St Sergius (London: J. Clarke, 1957; reprinted, Crestwood, NY: St Vladimir's Seminary Press, 2002), p. 17.

107 Paul Evdokimov, *L'Orthodoxie* (Paris: Neuchâtel, Delachaux et Niestlé, 1959), quoted in Timothy Ware, *The Orthodox Church* (London: Penguin, New Edition, 1993), p. 36.

108 Alar Laats, *Doctrines of the Trinity in Eastern and Western Theologies: A Study with Special Reference to K. Barth and V. Lossky* (Frankfurt-am-Main: Peter Lang, 1999), p. 11.

109 Bishop Kallistos Ware, *The Orthodox Way* (Crestwood, NY: St. Vladimir's Seminary Press, 1995), p. 11.

110 Ware, *Orthodox Church*, p. 209.

111 Lossky, *Mystical*, p. 28.

112 Vladimir Lossky, *The Vision of God*, translated by Asheleigh Moorhouse (Crestwood, NY: St. Vladimir's Seminary Press, 1963), p. 168.

113 Laats, *Doctrines*, p. 82.

114 Ibid.

115 Lossky, *Mystical*, p. 9.

116 Ibid., p. 25.

117 Ibid.

118 Allen, *Human*, p. 68.

119 Vladimir Lossky, *Orthodox Theology: An Introduction* (Crestwood, NY: St. Vladimir's Seminary Press, 1978), p. 34.

120 Vladimir Lossky, *In the Image and Likeness of God*, edited by John H. Erickson and Thomas E. Bird (Crestwood, NY: St. Vladimir's Seminary Press, 1974; reprinted, London and Oxford: Mowbray, 1975), p. 150.

121 Williams, *Wound*, p. 23.

122 Ware, *Orthodox Church*, pp. 208–9.

123 Ibid., p. 210. 'This interpolation . . . must have seemed to the theological layman mere hair-splitting,' Vivian Green, *A New History of Christianity* (New York: Continuum, 1996), p. 70.

124 In reality the shared Christian heritage reveals far more commonality than difference. Docetic variants of Christology have been frequent in the West. The path of spiritual ascent is a shared concept familiar from mediaeval and early modern Western mysticism, from *The Ladder of Perfection* and *The Cloud of Unknowing* to St John of the Cross and beyond. Ascetic Christianity has flourished in different times and places across the schismatic divide, often drawing on common roots from the first millennium.

125 Kazantzakis, *Last Temptation*, p. 7.

126 Ibid., p. 8.

127 Alfred North Whitehead, *Process and Reality: An Essay in Cosmology* (New York: Macmillan, 1929; New edition), edited by David Ray Griffin and Donald W. Sherburne (New York: The Free Press, 1978), p. 348.

128 Hebblethwaite, *Incarnation*, p. 23.

129 Letter of 27 November 1952, Helen Kazantzakis, *Biography*, p. 515.

130 Hebblethwaite, *Incarnation*, p. 43.

131 Kazantzakis, *Last Temptation*, p. 7.

132 'The Traditional Armenian Cross Sprouts Blossoming Branches,' Elizabeth Theokritoff, in 'Embodied Word and New Creation: Some Modern Orthodox Insights Concerning the Material World,' in *Abba: The Tradition of Orthodoxy in the West*, edited by John Behr, Andrew Lough, Dimitri

Conomos (Crestwood, NY: St Vladimir's Seminary Press, 2003), pp. 221–38. Quotation p. 226.

133 Kazantzakis, *Last Temptation*, p. 454.
134 Ibid.
135 Ibid., p. 455.
136 Ibid., p. 456.
137 Ibid.
138 Ibid., p. 457.
139 Ibid., p. 458.
140 Ibid.
141 Ibid., p. 459.
142 Ibid., p. 460.
143 Ibid.
144 Ibid., p. 464.
145 Ibid.
146 Ibid., p. 465.
147 Ibid., pp. 336–7.
148 Ibid.
149 Ibid., p. 466.
150 Ibid.
151 Ibid., p. 469.
152 Ibid., p. 479.
153 Ibid., p. 488.
154 Ibid.
155 Fyodor Dostoevsky, *The Brothers Karamazov*, translated by Constance Garnett (London: William Heinemann, 1912), p. 271.
156 Keyser, *Scorsese*, p. 179.
157 See Paul Schrader, *The Last Temptation of Christ*, draft script, *American Film Scripts Online* (Chicago, IL: Alexander Street Press, 2002), scene 73. The draft script retains the angelic/demonic 'old man'.
158 *Scorsese on Scorsese*, p. 143.
159 Schrader, Draft Script, scene 87.
160 Williams, *Wound*, p. 165.
161 Schrader, Draft Script, scene 73.
162 Ibid.
163 Søren Kierkegaard, *Fear and Trembling*, translated by Alistair Hannay (London: Penguin, 1985; reprinted 2003), p. 65. 'Abraham for the second time received a son against every expectation,' p. 44.
164 Hebblethwaite, *Incarnation*, p. 37.
165 Schrader, Draft Script, scene 73. My italics.
166 Ibid., scene 77.
167 Kazantzakis, *Last Temptation*, p. 466.
168 Peter Bien, 'Scorsese's Spiritual Jesus' (1988), Society of Cretan Historical Studies, *Nikos Kazantzakis Homepage*.
169 'Freedom was my first great desire. The second, which remains hidden within me to this day, tormenting me, was the desire for sanctity. Hero together with saint: such is mankind's supreme model,' Kazantzakis, *Greco*, p. 71.

170   A resurrected Kazantzakis would find the contemporary Orthodox Church
        much more hospitable than that of the 1950s. In a discussion of iconoclasm
        Timothy [Bishop Kallistos] Ware rejects iconoclasm for assuming that
        'the spiritual must be non-material': 'This is to betray the Incarnation, by
        allowing no place to Christ's humanity, to His body; it is to forget that
        our body as well as our soul must be saved and transfigured,' *Orthodox
        Church*, p. 33. And in a recent article Elizabeth Theokritoff cites a substantial
        Orthodox consensus to the effect that 'the material world' is 'integral to the
        divine purpose. It is not disposable packaging for the spiritual,' Theokritoff,
        'Embodied,' p. 226.
171   *Scorsese on Scorsese*, p. 135.
172   Ibid., pp. 118 and 143.
173   Bien, 'Spiritual Jesus', p. 2.
174   Calians, 'Prophet', p. 48.
175   Middleton, 'Christian Doctrine', p. 286.
176   Keyser, *Scorsese*, pp. 176–7.
177   Middleton, 'Christian Doctrine', p. 285.

Chapter 2

1   Anthony Burgess, 'Author's Note', *The Kingdom of the Wicked* (London:
        Hutchinson, 1985), p. 379.
2   Anthony Burgess, *You've Had Your Time: Being the Second Part of the
        Confessions of Anthony Burgess* (London: Heinemann, 1999), p. 303.
3   'I am an unbeliever'. Anthony Burgess, 'On Being a Lapsed Catholic',
        Triumph, February 1967, p. 31.
4   Burgess, *You've Had Your Time*, p. 304.
5   The film implements this detail, Episode 4, chapter 10 (4.10). References in
        this format to *Jesus of Nazareth*, produced by Vincenzo Labella, directed by
        Franco Zeffirelli (ITC Entertainment/Television Italia, 1977; DVD, Granada
        Ventures Ltd, 2006). This recording represents the 374-minute version,
        initially broadcast in two parts on Palm and Easter Sundays of 1977 by
        NBC Television. The film is divided into four episodes, each sub-divided
        into 12 or 13 'chapters'.
6   Burgess, *You've Had Your Time*, p. 304.
7   Ibid.
8   To claim this as psychological development is frankly embarrassing. Burgess'
        disciples are far more one-dimensional than those of the Gospels.
9   Burgess, *You've Had Your Time*, p. 305. Burgess also refers to T. S. Eliot's
        phrase 'Christ the tiger'. Jesus's size and physical strength are clearly an
        unsuccessful attempt to give physical form to supernatural power.
10   Burgess's own word. *You've Had Your Time*, p. 306.
11   Ibid.
12   Franco Zeffirelli, *Il Mio Gesu* (Milan: Sperling and Kupfur, Editori-Campi
        and C., 1977); *Franco Zeffirelli's Jesus: A Spiritual Diary*, translated by Willis
        J. Egan (San Francisco: Harper and Rowe, 1984).

13 According to Boytinck the novel was rejected by American and British
    publishers (*Annotated Bibliography*, p. 82).
14 'I admired the total absence of intellectuality', Burgess, *You've Had Your Time*,
    p. 302.
15 Zeffirelli, *Jesus: A Spiritual Diary*, p. 39.
16 Ibid.
17 Ibid.
18 Ibid., p. 44.
19 Ibid., p. 43.
20 Ibid., p. 44. The account given in Zeffirelli's *Autobiography* is basically the
    same in content with slightly different inflections. Here Burgess is said to have
    'disappeared to get on with the writing', and to have produced by mid-1975
    a 'tour de force' of a script. The discrepancies between Burgess's dialogue and
    the gospels are here reduced to 'minor matters'. The quest to find 'speakable
    words' for Christ continued: on set the actors would be given 'a set of
    paraphrases of the Gospel sayings' from which to select. See Franco Zeffirelli,
    An Autobiography (New York: Weidenfeld and Nicolson, 1986), pp. 275 and
    277.
21 Barclay's chapters 1–6 cover virtually the same ground as Burgess's Books 1–6,
    except that Barclay's chapter 2 includes the Temptation in the Wilderness
    which opens Burgess's Book 3. In the 347-minute broadcast version of the film
    we can see the chapters or 'scenes' distributed evenly across the divisions of
    Burgess's six books, especially the sequence from Book 3 to Book 6. Part Two
    of the film is shorter (and Part One longer), not surprisingly as most of
    Burgess's Book Two is concerned with Jesus's married life.
22 Zerah is Burgess's most obvious and isolable contribution to the screenplay.
    Baugh strangely refers to the Zerah of the film as an 'invention of Zeffirelli'.
    Although he acknowledges in a note that Zerah is there in Burgess's novel, this
    seems to be an afterthought, as his whole discussion presupposes that Zeffirelli
    invented Zerah '*ex novo*' (Baugh's phrase) or 'original with Zeffirelli'. See
    Lloyd Baugh, *Imaging the Divine: Jesus and Christ-figures in film* (Lanham,
    MD: Sheed and Ward, 1997), p. 76.
23 Bruce Babington and Peter William Evans, *Biblical Epics: Sacred Narrative in
    the Hollywood Cinema* (Manchester, UK: Manchester University Press, 1993),
    p. 98.
24 Anthony Burgess, *Man of Nazareth* (New York: McGraw-Hill, 1979), p. 5.
25 Benjamin deMott describes the novel as opening 'with a cool Foucaultian
    account of a crucifixion'. 'According to Burgess', *New York Times Book
    Review*, 15 April 1979, p. 1.
26 Burgess, *Man of Nazareth*, p. 5.
27 Ibid., p. 6. Azor is supposed to be writing in the first-century CE before the
    composition of the gospels, so he anticipates Manicheism by two centuries.
28 Burgess, *Man of Nazareth*, p. 6.
29 Ibid., p. 354.
30 Ibid., p. 355.
31 Ibid.
32 Ibid., p. 356.
33 Burgess quoted in John Cullinan, 'Interview with Anthony Burgess', *Paris
    Review*, 56 (1973), reprinted in Geoffrey Aggeler, *Critical Essays on Anthony*

Burgess (London: G. K. Hall and Co., 1986), p. 44. See also Burgess, 'The Manicheans', *Times Literary Supplement*, 3 March 1966; and John J. Stinson, 'The Manichee World of Anthony Burgess', in *Anthony Burgess: Modern Critical Views*, edited by Harold Bloom (New York: Chelsea House Publishers, 1987), pp. 51–62.

34 Harold Bloom, 'Introduction' to his edition *Anthony Burgess: Modern Critical Views*, pp. 4–5.

35 Zeffirelli, *Autobiography*, p. 275.

36 Ibid., p. 274.

37 Kiolkowski, *Fictional Transfigurations of Jesus*, p. 13.

38 Burgess quoted in Martina Ghosh-Schellhorn, *Anthony Burgess: A Study in Character* (Frankfurt-Am-Main: Peter Lang, 1981), p. 156.

39 'The true grotesque vision sees the position of man in the universe as radically incongruous. Given hints and longings of immortality, man must live in an organism that he realizes all too painfully is finite'. Burgess, 'The Manicheans', quoted Stinson, 'The Manichee World', p. 55.

40 deMott, 'According to Burgess', p. 20.

41 Anon., *Kirkus Reviews*, 47: 4 (15 February 1979), p. 206.

42 Gerald Twomey, 'Life Taken Whole', *America*, 140: 23–5 (23 June 1979), p. 517.

43 Burgess, *Man of Nazareth*, p. 15.

44 Ibid., p. 16.

45 Ibid., pp. 25–6.

46 Ibid., p. 17.

47 Ibid., p. 121.

48 Ibid., p. 122.

49 Burgess, *You've Had Your Time*, p. 304.

50 Burgess, *Man of Nazareth*, p. 237.

51 Ibid., p. 238.

52 Ibid., p. 237.

53 Ibid., p. 281.

54 Ibid., p. 282.

55 Ibid., p. 283.

56 Kermode, 'Love', p. 45. This rather depends on how important you think the doctrine is.

57 Burgess, *Man of Nazareth*, pp. 325–6.

58 Ibid., p. 352.

59 Burgess, *You've Had Your Time*, p. 303.

60 Zeffirelli, *Autobiography*, p. 274.

61 Zeffirelli, *Spiritual Diary*, p. viii.

62 Zeffirelli, *Autobiography*, pp. 273 and 274.

63 Ibid., p. 274. In *Spiritual Diary* Zeffirelli describes how he went to the Vatican library to read the original. He quotes almost the whole of paragraph 4 of *Nostra Aetate* in his text, pp. 5–6.

64 Burgess makes his Jesus ordinary, but not common. He is much bigger than everyone else.

65 Zeffirelli, *Autobiography*, p. 284.

66 Ibid.

67 Baugh, *Imaging Jesus*, p. 78. Baugh draws heavily on prior opinion: here he is quoting from Roy Kinnard and Tim Davis, *Divine Images: A History of Jesus on the Screen* (New York: Citadel Press, 1992), p. 189.

68 Baugh, *Imaging Jesus*, p. 78.

69 Ibid., p. 79.

70 Ibid.

71 Ibid., p. 77.

72 Pasolini's film, Baugh says, 'in the minds of most serious critics' is 'still the greatest, the most authentic, the most religious film on Jesus ever made' (Baugh, *Imaging Jesus*, p. 94). 'Zeffirelli created a very free adaptation of all four gospels, in the end producing a work more of fiction than Gospel . . . Pasolini, inspired by the raw power of Matthew's text, was determined to be utterly faithful to it' (p. 95).

73 Zeffirelli, *Autobiography*, p. 280. The annunciation is chapter 1.2 of the film. Barclay restores the angel, who speaks like a scoutmaster: 'God has chosen you for a very precious privilege' (Barclay, *Jesus*, p. 11).

74 Baugh, *Imaging Jesus*, p. 75.

75 Zeffirelli, *Autobiography*, p. 380. See also *Spiritual Diary*, pp. 80–1.

76 Baugh, *Imaging Jesus*, p. 8. The English translation reads: Film 'renders visible the invisible, renders material the spiritual, and it does not pause in front of Mystery, but rather makes it material, invades it, reveals and even explains it' (p. 34, n. 9).

77 Chapter 2.1 of the film.

78 'A voice is heard, which I imagine as resounding in John's inmost conscience and becoming the inner voice of the Baptist . . .'. Zeffirelli, *Spiritual Diary*, p. 76. Barclay again restores the gospel reading: 'and then came a voice from heaven'. Before that John 'had a sudden flash of recognition' (Barclay, *Jesus*, p. 24). He knows the name but just can't remember the face.

79 Chapter 3.6 of the film.

80 *Jonah*, from *The Jerusalem Bible* (London: Darton, Longman and Todd, 1966), p. 1495, ll. 8–10. *Jonah* is the only book in this edition to have been translated by J. R. R. Tolkien, who is named as one of the 'principal collaborators' (p. ii). 'Naming me among the "principal collaborators" was an undeserved courtesy on the part of the editor of the Jerusalem Bible. I was consulted on one or two points of style, and criticized some contributions of others. I was originally assigned a large amount of text to translate, but after doing some necessary preliminary work I was obliged to resign owing to pressure of other work, and only completed "Jonah", one of the shortest books.' *The Letters of J. R. R. Tolkien*, edited by Humphrey Carpenter (London: George Allen and Unwin, 1981), p. 378.

81 Barclay deviates from both novel and film by restoring gospel details, showing Jesus delaying his journey, promising glorification and weeping over Lazarus's death. When revived, Lazarus is uncovered by the sisters, and his gaze falls on Jesus. 'The incident' Barclay comments, 'was awesome' (Barclay, *Jesus*, p. 72).

82 Chapter 4.2 of the film.

83 Zeffirelli is unashamedly supersessionist: '"The Last Supper" . . . marked the moment when Jesus superseded the ancient rite and gave his disciples and all humanity the Eucharistic mystery' (Zeffirelli, *Spiritual Diary*, p. 116).

84   Chapter 4.10 of the film.
85   Dismissed by Baugh as 'utter theatricality' (Baugh, *Imaging Jesus*, p. 78) this moment is a supremely beautiful liturgical composition that takes film beyond the limits of its secular paradigms.
86   'Zeffirelli was not quite orthodox in wishing to end the series with a great *Pietà* . . . he had to be reminded, gently, that the Resurrection was the whole point of the death.' Burgess, *You've Had Your Time*, p. 307.
87   Zeffirelli, *Spiritual Diary*, pp. 115–16.
88   Burgess, *Man of Nazareth*, p. 67.

Chapter 3

1   Quoted in Tew, *Crace*, p. 116.
2   Jim Crace, 'Preface to Quarantine' (1998).
3   Tew, *Crace*, p. 118.
4   Sally Vincent, 'Death and the Optimist', *The Guardian*, 25 August 2001. [Available at Guardian Unlimited].
5   Tew, *Crace*, p. 118.
6   Vincent, 'Death'.
7   Ibid.
8   Tew, *Crace*, p. 135.
9   Richard Dawkins, *The God Delusion* (London: Bantam Books, 2006), p. 15.
10   Frank Kermode, 'Into the Wilderness', *New York Times*, 12 April 1998. [Available at *New York Times*] http://www.nytimes.com/books/98/04/12/reviews/980412.12kermodt.html [Accessed 6 December 2013].
11   John Updike, *More Matter: Essays and Criticism* (New York: Knopf, 1999), p. 53.
12   Tew, *Crace*, p. 135.
13   Crace, 'Preface'.
14   Ibid.
15   Tew, *Crace*, p. 132.
16   Crace, 'Preface'.
17   Caroline Walker Bynum, *The Resurrection of the Body in Western Christianity* (New York: Columbia University Press, 1995), p. 35.
18   Wolfhart Pannenberg, 'History and the Reality of the Resurrection', in *Resurrection Reconsidered*, edited by Gavin da'Costa (Oxford: One World, 1996), p. 68.
19   John Macquarrie, *Jesus Christ in Modern Thought* (London: SCM Press, 1990), p. 406.
20   Karl Barth, quoted in Macquarrie, *Jesus Christ*, p. 406.
21   M. E. Dahl, 'The Resurrection of the Body', *Studies in Biblical Theology* 36 (1962), p. 7.
22   Paul Avis, 'The Resurrection of Jesus: Asking the Right Questions', in *The Resurrection of Jesus Christ*, edited by Paul Avis (London: Longman, Darton and Todd, 1993), p. 8.

23 Moltmann, *Crucified God*, p. 174.
24 Macquarrie, *Jesus Christ*, p. 406.
25 Jasper, *Sacred Desert*, p. 103.
26 Tew, *Crace*, p. 117.
27 Kermode, 'Wilderness'.
28 Irwin, quoted Tew, *Crace*, p. 122.
29 Graham Ward, 'The Displaced Body of Jesus Christ', in *Radical Orthodoxy: A New Theology*, edited by John Milbank, Catherine Pickstock and Graham Ward (London: Routledge, 1999), p. 163.
30 Tew, *Crace*, p. 131.

Chapter 4

1 Beal and Linafelt, 'Introduction', *Mel Gibson's Bible* (2006), p. 3.
2 Robert L. Webb and Kathleen E. Corley, 'Introduction: *The Passion*, the Gospels and the Claims of History' in *Jesus and Mel Gibson's 'The Passion of the Christ': The Film, the Gospels and the Claims of History*, edited by Kathleen E. Corley and Robert L. Webb (New York and London: Continuum, 2004), p. 1.
3 See Gary North, *The War on Mel Gibson: The Media vs. The Passion* (New York: American Vision, 2004).
4 Mark Silk, 'Gibson's Passion: A Case Study in Media Manipulation?', *Journal of Religion and Film*, 8: 1 (2004).
5 Rene Girard, 'On Mel Gibson's *The Passion of the Christ*', *Anthropoetics*, 10: 1 (2005), n.p. Available at [http://www.anthropoetics.ucla.edu/ap1001/RGGibson.htm] [Accessed 6 December 2013].
6 *Re-viewing The Passion: Mel Gibson's Film and Its Critics*, edited by Brent S. Plate (London: Palgrave Macmillan, 2004), and Rabbi Klein, *Jewish Answer to Mel Gibson's 'The Passion of the Christ'*, CD-ROM (New York: BN, 2004).
7 An attempt at ecumenical balance can be found in Jorge J. E. Gracia, *Mel Gibson's Passion and Philosophy: The Cross, the Questions, the Controversy* (New York: Open Court, 2004).
8 Obvious examples are Martin Scorsese's *The Last Temptation* and the Monty Python parody *The Life of Brian*.
9 Paula Frederickson, 'History, Hollywood and the Bible: Some Thoughts on Gibson's *Passion*', *Journal of Religion and Film*, 8: 1 (2004).
10 Nicola Denzey, 'Biblical Allusions, Biblical Illusions: Hollywood Blockbuster and Scripture', *Journal of Religion and Film*, 8: 1 (2004). Mark C. Taylor was also struck by the 'theological naivetee, or perhaps ignorance' displayed in responses to the film. See his 'The Offense of Flesh', in Beal and Linafelt, *Mel Gibson's Bible* (2006), pp. 141–2.
11 Jakob Lother, *Narrative in Fiction and Film: An Introduction* (Oxford: Oxford University Press, 2000), p. 1.

12 See *The Image of Christ: The Catalogue of the Exhibition 'Seeing Salvation'*, edited by Gabriele Finaldi (London: National Gallery Company, 2000); Neil McGregor and Erika Langmuir, *Seeing Salvation: Images of Christ in Art* (New Haven, CT: Yale University Press, 2000); Helen de Borchgrave, *A Journey into Christian Art* (Minneapolis, MN: Fortress Press, 2000); John Drury, *Painting the Word* (New Haven, CT: Yale University Press, 1999); Jaroslav Pelikan, *The Illustrated Jesus through the Centuries* (New Haven, CT: Yale University Press, 1997); Nancy Grubb, *The Life of Christ in Art* (New York and London: Artabras, 1996). For discussions of this topic see David Morgan, 'Catholic Visual Piety and *The Passion of the Christ*', in Plate, *Re-viewing* (2004), pp. 85–96; and Diane Apostolos-Cappadona, 'On Seeing *The Passion*: Is There a Painting in This Film? Or is This Film a Painting?' in Plate, *Re-viewing* (2004), pp. 97–108.

13 '*Kerygma*', that is, gospel proclamation as distinct from '*didache*' or doctrinal instruction. Theodore Ziolkowski argues that modern fictional representations of Christ normally eschew 'kerygmatic' events such as the Resurrection in favour of 'transfigurative' events that can be portrayed naturalistically. Ziolkowski, *Fictional Transfigurations*, p. 11.

14 Romans, 1 and 2 Corinthians, Galatians, Philippians, 1 Thessalonians and Philemon.

15 St Paul, 1 Corinthians 11.23–26, quoted from *The Bible: Authorized King James Version*, edited by Robert Carroll and Stephen Prickett (Oxford: Oxford University Press, 1997), NT, p. 216.

16 T. S. Eliot, 'The Dry Salvages', *Four Quartets* (London: Faber and Faber, 1944), p. 32.

17 1 Corinthians 15.3–8, Caroll and Prickett, NT, p. 219.

18 Mel Gibson, 'Foreword' in Duncan and Antonello, *The Passion: Photography* (2004).

19 See John Dominic Crossan, 'Hymn to a Savage God', in Corley and Webb, *The Passion*, p. 12.

20 *Daily Missal* (Birmingham, UK: C. Goodliffe Neale, 1956), p. 507.

21 Terry Mattingley, quoted in Berit Kjos, 'Mel Gibson's Passion', *Kjos Ministries* (February 2004), p. 2.

22 Gerald Mast, *Film/Cinema/Movie: A Theory of Experience* (Chicago, IL: University of Chicago Press, 1983), p. 113.

23 Anna Catherine Emmerich, *The Dolorous Passion of Our Lord Jesus Christ, from the Meditations of Anna Catherine Emmerich*, with a preface by the Abbe de Cazales (London: Burns and Lambert, 1862).

24 John Strohmeier, 'Introduction' to Anna Catherine Emmerich, *The Dolorous Passion of Our Lord Jesus Christ, According to the Meditations of Anna Catherine Emmerich*, translated and edited by Klemens Maria Brentano (El Sobrante, CA: North Bay Books, 2003), p. 9.

25 Emmerich, *Dolorous Passion* (1862), pp. 204–7.

26 Strohmeier in Emmerich, *Dolorous Passion* (2003), p. 10.

27 Pullman and Williams, 'Dark Materials Debate'.

28 Philip Horne, '*The Passion of the Christ*', *Arts.Telegraph*, 30 August 2004.

29 Emmerich, *Dolorous Passion* (1862), p. 61.

30 Emmerich, *Dolorous Passion* (1862), pp. 1–2.

31 'Foreword' to Duncan and Antonello, *The Passion: Photography* (2004).

32 Gibson quoted in Peter J. Boyer, 'The Jesus War: Mel Gibson's Obsession', *New Yorker*, 15 September 2004.

33 Vincent J. Miller relates *The Passion of the Christ* to the Stations of the Cross, and also to the Mysteries of the Rosary, in 'Contexts: Theology, Devotion and Culture', in Beal and Linafelt, *Mel Gibson's Bible* (2005), pp. 39–50.

34 See Robert L. Webb, 'The Flashbacks in *The Passion*: Story and Discourse as a Means of Explanation', in Corley and Webb, *The Passion* (2004).

35 Mark Goodacre, 'The Power of *The Passion*: Reacting and Over-reacting to Gibson's Artistic Vision', in Corley and Webb, *The Passion* (2004).

36 Mark Kermode, 'The Passion of the Christ', *Sight and Sound* (London: BFI, 2004).

37 Emmerich, *Dolorous Passion* (1862), pp. 209–10.

38 Both in Finaldi, *Image of Christ* (2000), p. 65.

39 Grubb, *Life of Christ* (1996), p. 55.

40 See *Daily Missal* (1956), p. 528.

41 Emmerich, *Dolorous Passion* (1862), p. 294.

42 Article XXXI, *Book of Common Prayer* (1662) (Cambridge, MA: John Baskerville, 1762).

43 Duncan and Antonello, *The Passion: Photography* (2004), p. 115.

44 *Daily Missal* (1956), p. 565.

45 Ibid., p. 3.

46 Thomas J. J. Altizer suggests that by insisting on the absolute violence of the Passion as endured by a dual-natured Christ, the film dramatizes 'the death of God'. In fact, by effecting a parallel between the Passion and the Mass, the film celebrates the daily death and Resurrection of a living Christ. See Altizer, 'The Passion and the Death of God', in Beal and Linafelt, *Mel Gibson's Bible* (2006), p. 256.

47 Vittorio Messori, 'A Passion of Violence and Love', *Zenit* (18 February 2004).

48 Robert K. Johnston, 'The Passion as Dynamic Icon', in Plate, *Re-viewing* (2004), p. 66. See also Peter T. Chattaway, 'Come and See: How Movies Encourage Us to Look at (and with) Jesus', in Plate, *Re-viewing* (2004), pp. 121–36.

49 *Rocky* is in any case a Christian allegory, minus the bit about the other cheek.

50 Mark D. Jordan and Kent L. Brintnall, 'Mel Gibson: Bride of Christ', in Beal and Lanafelt, *Mel Gibson's Bible* (2006), p. 82.

51 Quoted in Kjos, 'Mel Gibson's Passion' (2004), pp. 2–3.

52 Goodacre, 'Power' (2004), p. 35.

53 'I wanted to bring you there'. Gibson quoted in Horne, '*The Passion of the Christ*' (2004).

54 Emmerich, *Dolorous Passion* (1862), pp. 165–6.

55 'Foreword' to Duncan and Antonello, *The Passion: Photography* (2004).

56 Mast, *Film/Cinema/Movie* (1983), p. 113.

57 John Dean quoted in Kjos, 'Mel Gibson's Passion' (2004), p. 2.

58 Andrew J. Webb and Kurt Feich, quoted in Kjos, 'Mel Gibson's Passion' (2004), p. 3.

59 Melvyn Bragg, *The Seventh Seal* (London: BFI, 1993).

60 John Legare, 'Why I Will Not See *The Passion of the Christ*', InformedChristians.com (2004).

61 David Bordwell, *Narration in the Fiction Film* (Madison, WI: Wisconsin University Press, 1985).

62 Frances Flannery-Dailey, 'Biblical Scholarship and the Passion Surrounding *ThePassion of the Christ*', *Journal of Religion and Film*, 8: 1 (2004).

63 Boris Eikhenbaum, 'Literature and Cinema' [1926], in *Russian Formalism: A Collection of Articles and Texts in Translation*, edited by Stephen Bann and John Bolt (Edinburgh, UK: Edinburgh University Press, 1973), pp. 122–7.

64 T. S. Eliot, 'The Dry Salvages', *Four Quartets* (London: Faber and Faber, 1945), p. 48.

65 Morris Beja, *Film and Literature* (NY and London: Longman, 1979), p. 21.

66 Seymour Chatman, *Coming to Terms: The Rhetoric of Narrative in Fiction and Film* (Ithaca and London: Cornell University Press, 1990), p. 7.

67 Beja, *Film and Literature* (1979), p. 22.

Chapter 5

1 Richard Whightman Fox, *Jesus in America: Personal Savior, Cultural Hero, National Obsession* (San Francisco, CA: HarperSanFrancisco, 2004), p. 11.

2 Lloyd Baugh, 'The African Face of Jesus in Film: Two Texts, a New Tradition', in Walsh, Staley and Reinharz, *Son of Man* (2013), pp. 121–32.

3 Middleton and Plate, 'Who Do You See That I Am?' in Walsh, Staley and Reinharz, *Son of Man* (2013), p. 137.

4 Richard Walsh, Jeffery L. Staley and Adele Reinharz, 'Introduction' to their edition, Walsh, Staley and Reinharz, *Son of Man* (2013), p. xvi.

5 The film 'merges the teachings of the Gospel Jesus and of Steve Biko to demonstrate that a "new humanity" can resist "the powers"'. W. Barnes Tatum, '*Son of Man's* "Son of Man": Becoming Human and Acting Humanely', in Walsh, Staley and Reinharz, *Son of Man* (2013), p. 90.

6 Staley, 'An Intertextual Reading', in Walsh, Staley and Reinharz, *Son of Man* (2013), p. 113.

7 Reinhold Zwick, 'Between Chester and Capetown: Transformations of the Gospel in *Son of Man* by Mark Dornford-May', in Walsh, Staley and Reinharz, *Son of Man* (2013), p. 114.

8 For instance in the film the child Jesus witnesses a 'massacre of the innocents', and is invited by the archangel Gabriel to return to heaven. He declines, saying 'This is my world'. This speech has no biblical source, but is entirely consistent with a theological exegesis of the incarnation story. 'Offered the chance to avoid its remorseless brutality and to secure himself to heaven, Jesus rebuffs his father's angels, and, instead, elects to walk among women, men and children, preaching a gospel of radical egalitarianism.' Middleton and Plate, 'Who Do You See That I Am?', in Walsh, Staley and Reinharz, *Son of Man* (2013), p. 136.

9 Baugh, 'African Face', in Walsh, Staley and Reinharz, *Son of Man* (2013), p. 126.

10 Zwick, 'Chester and Capetown', in Walsh, Staley and Reinharz, *Son of Man* (2013), pp. 113–14.
11 Tatum, 'Son of Man', in Walsh, Staley and Reinharz, *Son of Man* (2013), p. 94. This 'irony' of the Cross's mutation from instrument of torture to object of veneration has of course from the beginning lain at the heart of Christian soteriology.
12 Walsh, Staley and Reinharz, *Son of Man* (2013), p. xvi.
13 See Zwick, 'Chester and Capetown', in Walsh, Staley and Reinharz, *Son of Man* (2013), p. 111.
14 Middleton and Plate, 'Who Do You See That I Am?', in Walsh, Staley and Reinharz, *Son of Man* (2013), p. 137. For Tutu's theology see Michael Battle, *The Ubuntu Theology of Desmond Tutu* (Cleveland, OH: Pilgrim Press, 1997).

Ecce Homo: A life of Christ

1 Cp. Kurt Vonnegut, *Sun, Moon, Star* (London: Harper Collins, 1980).
2 Some of these images are collected in Gabriele Finaldi, *The Image of Christ*, Nancy Grubb, *Christ in Art*, and Neil McGregor and Erika Langmuir, *Seeing Salvation* (London: BBC Books, 2000).
3 See Simone Martini and Lippo Memmi, *Annunication* (1333). Reproduced in Finaldi, *The Image of Christ*.
4 These passages of description draw freely on Renan's topography in *Vie de Jesus*.
5 This section is indebted to Kurt Vonnegut and Ivan Chernieff, *Sun, Moon, Star* (1980).
6 See John Everett Millais, *Christ in the House of His Parents* (1849–50). Reproduced in Grubb, *Christ in Art*.
7 See *Our Lady of Perpetual Succour*, Byzantine Ikon, fifteenth century. Reproduced in Finaldi, *The Image of Christ*.
8 See Giotto, *The Kiss of Judas* (1304–6). Reproduced in Finaldi, *The Image of Christ*.
9 See Stanley Spencer, *Christ Carrying the Cross* (1920). Reproduced in Finaldi, *The Image of Christ*.
10 See Domenico Fetti, *The Veil of Veronica* (1618–22). Reproduced in Finaldi, *The Image of Christ*.
11 Bartolome Estaban Murillo, *The Infant Jesus Sleeping on the Cross* (1625). Reproduced in *Murillo at Dulwich Picture Gallery* (London: Dulwich Picture Gallery, 2013), p. 57.
12 St John of the Cross, *The Dark Night of the Soul* (1681). In *The Poems of St John of the Cross*, translated by Roy Campbell (London: Hague Gill and Davey, Ltd., 1951).
13 See Titian, *Noli Me Tangere* (1514). Reproduced in Finaldi, *The Image of Christ*.

INDEX